AF579224

CELEBRATING EL PASO

Photographs by Mark A. Paulda | Foreword by John F. Cook

TCU Press
Fort Worth, Texas

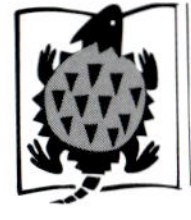

Library of Congress Cataloging-in-Publication Data
Paulda, Mark.
Celebrating El Paso / photographs by Mark Paulda ; foreword by John Cook, Mayor of El Paso. -- 1st ed.
p. cm.
ISBN 978-0-87565-402-7 (cloth : alk. paper)
1. El Paso (Tex.)--Pictorial works. 2. El Paso (Tex.)--Buildings, structures, etc.--Pictorial works.
3. El Paso (Tex.)--Social life and customs--Pictorial works. 4. Historic buildings--Texas--El Paso--Pictorial works. I. Title.
F394.E4P38 2009
976.4'96060222--dc22

2 0 0 9 0 1 3 6 8 9

TCU Press
P. O. Box 298300
Fort Worth, Texas 76129

817.257.7822
http://www.prs.tcu.edu

To order books: 800.826.8911

Designed by fusion29, inc.
Printed in China

Foreword

IF YOU LOOK OUT ACROSS THE VASTNESS OF TODAY'S EL PASO, you can be sure you'll see the more than obvious and other more subtle indicators and trademarks of this amazing city's epic history. El Paso is a city that has a myriad of cultural characteristics woven into the fabric of its unique and unmistakable being.

All of these influences are evident in the faces of its almost 700,000 people, the energy of its daily life, and the structures and landscape in which those lives are carried out.

The city began as a natural conduit for explorers and missionaries as their travels brought them through the *Paso del Norte* – or the Pass of the North. When people finally settled in the area, the historic sequence of major defining events that followed took El Paso on a path from an 1800s small town to a rapidly diversifying city with expansion in population and commerce. El Paso continued to grow out of its small town stature into a metropolitan area. All of the events, individuals, and geographical circumstances that have played a role in El Paso's development are numerous. Many they may be, but we have never stopped maintaining a deep appreciation for these contributions.

Not many cities can say they sit on the border of two countries, three states, a military installation, and an Indian reservation, and share the flavor of each while still maintaining a sense of uniqueness. Spanish, Mexican, Indian, Texan, and American – all of these are descriptors of the El Paso region.

This publication, beautifully shot and compiled by El Paso photographer Mark Paulda, offers any reader – or viewer – a poignant, visual take on the city's unforgettable land and cityscapes. People really have no idea that El Paso possesses the qualities and distinctions it does. You have to see this beautiful city for yourself in order to grasp the depth of its historical essence and profound soul. Once you do, El Paso becomes a familiar friend. We are, in short, a big city with a rich, small town feel.

The city continues even to this day to make its own way on the path to progress. We *are* growing, we *are* making history, and we *will* continue to remember and hold true to who we are as an international city and an international region.

– JOHN F. COOK, MAYOR OF EL PASO

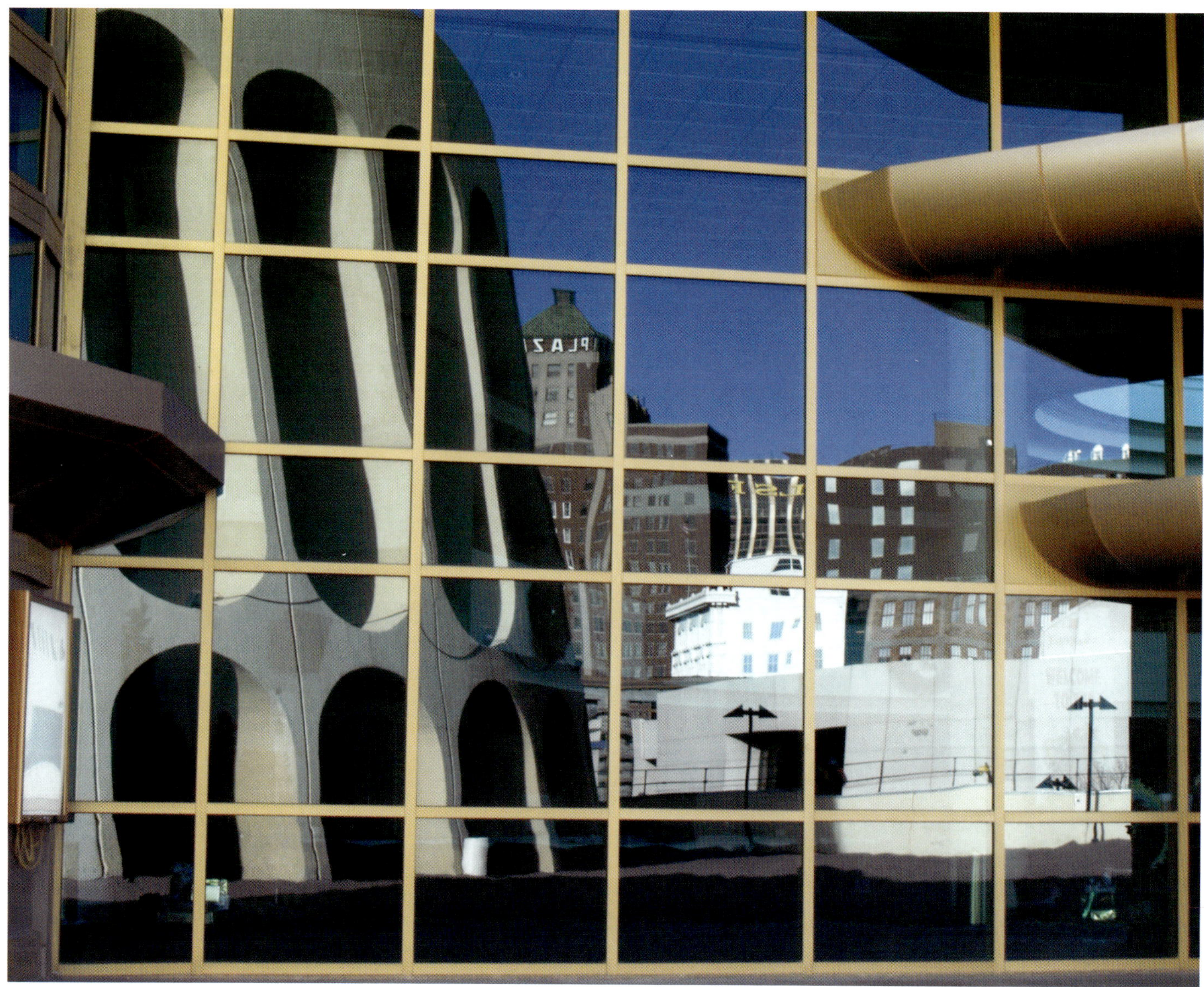

Downtown through the Looking Glass.
El Paso is the seat of El Paso County in the State of Texas and part of the American Southwest. The city has a population of 750,000. It is the sixth-largest city in Texas and the twenty-first-largest city in the United States, as well as the seventh fastest growing large city in the nation.

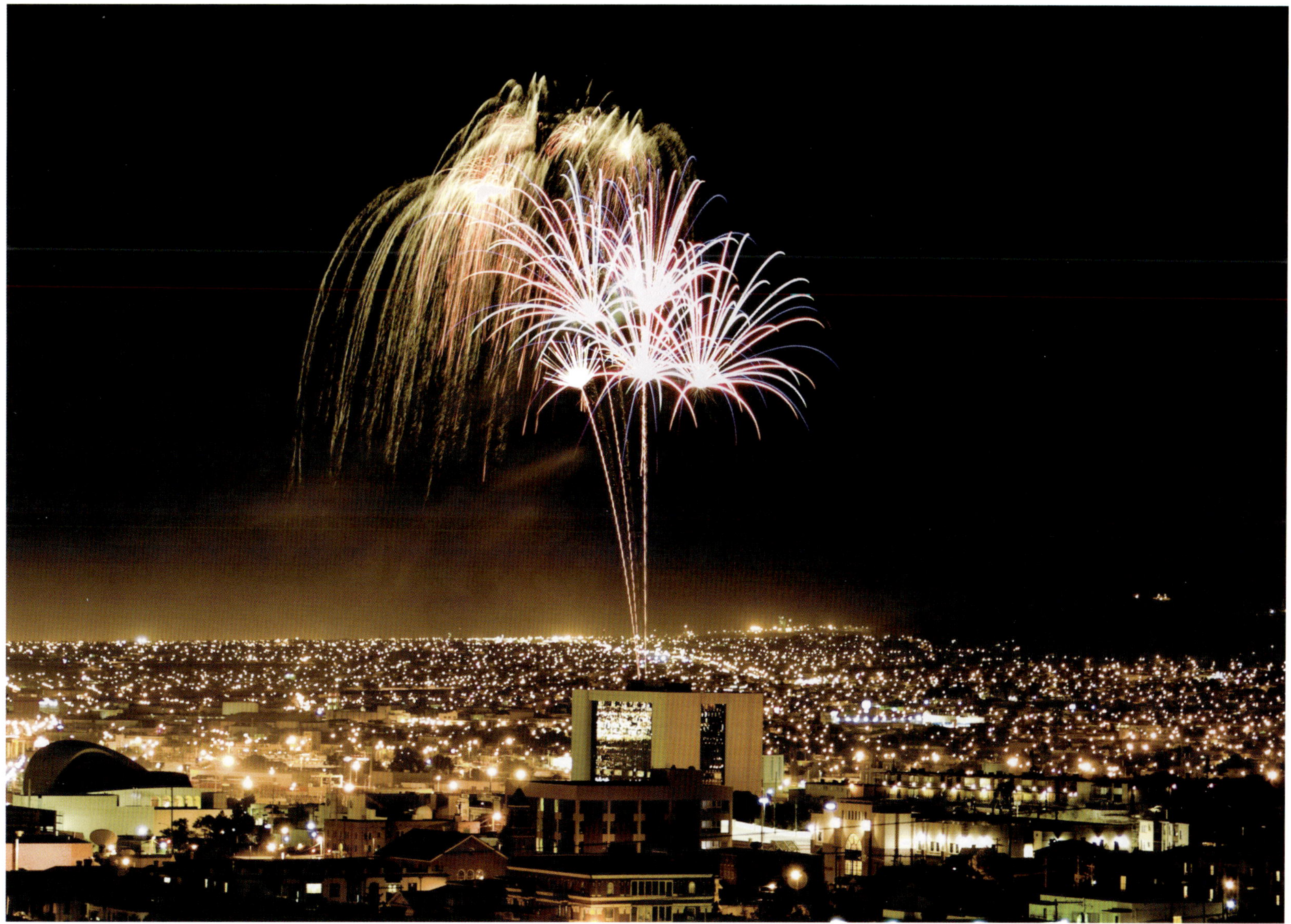

El Paso Celebrates.
To this day there is no bigger fireworks display than the one you will see at the Sun Bowl Fan Fiesta.

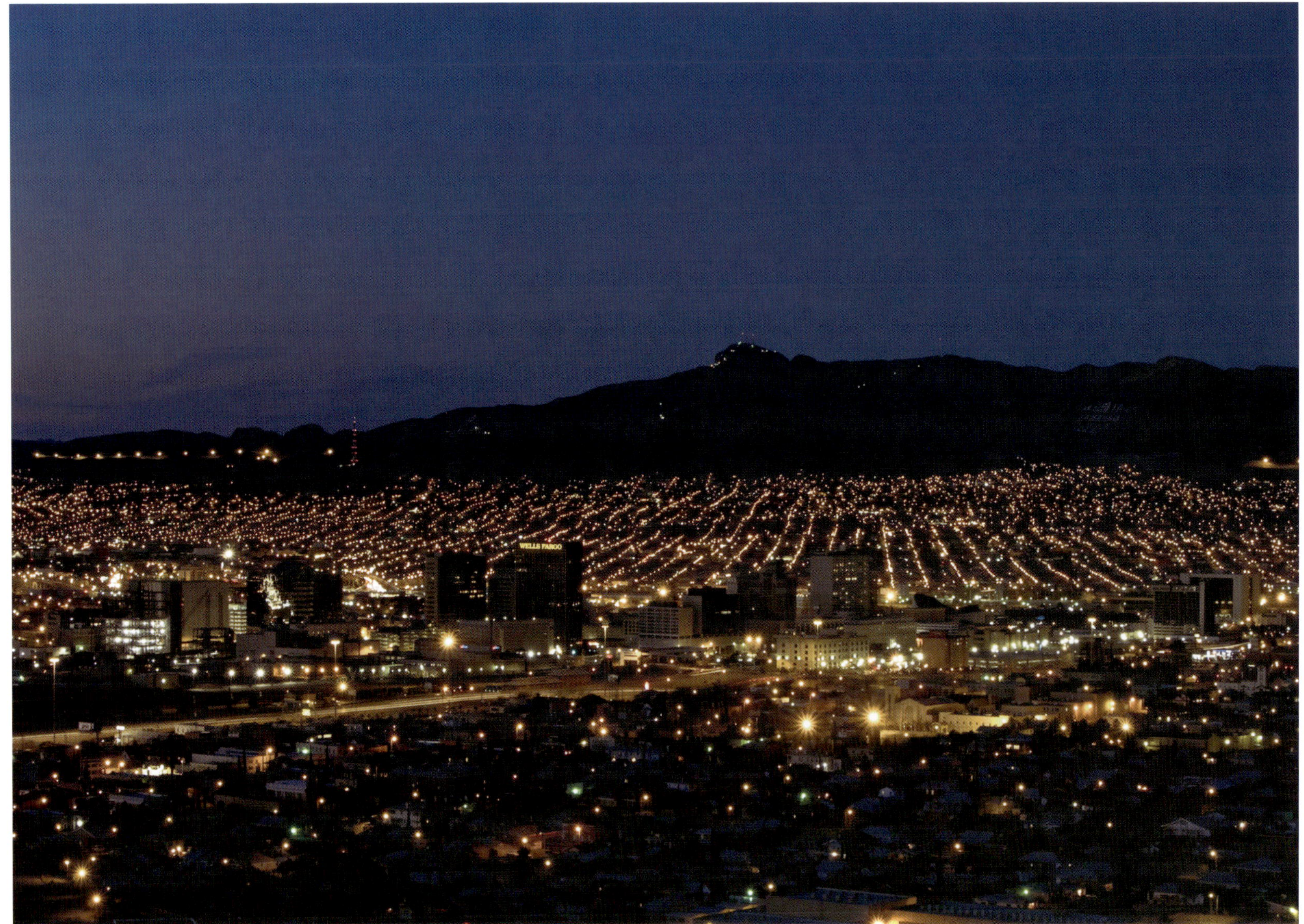

El Paso's Heart and Soul.
Much of the flavor of the history and culture of the Sun City can be experienced even by the tourist who has just a few hours to spend in downtown El Paso.

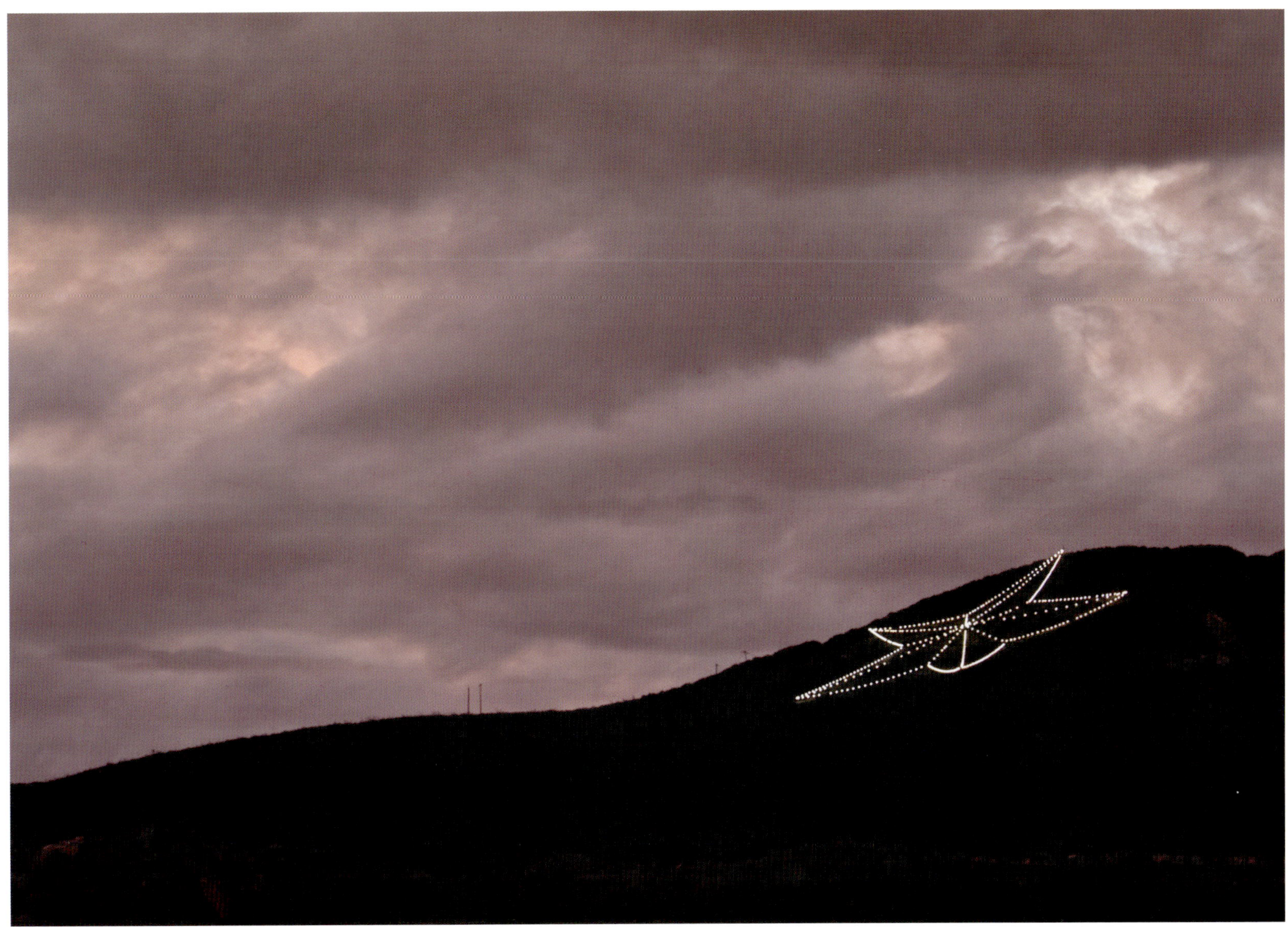

Presence.
The first star was built by El Paso Electric in 1940. It was only fifty feet wide and could barely be seen on the Carlsbad Highway. The star did not last long either – a storm blew out most of the bulbs on the first experimental star.

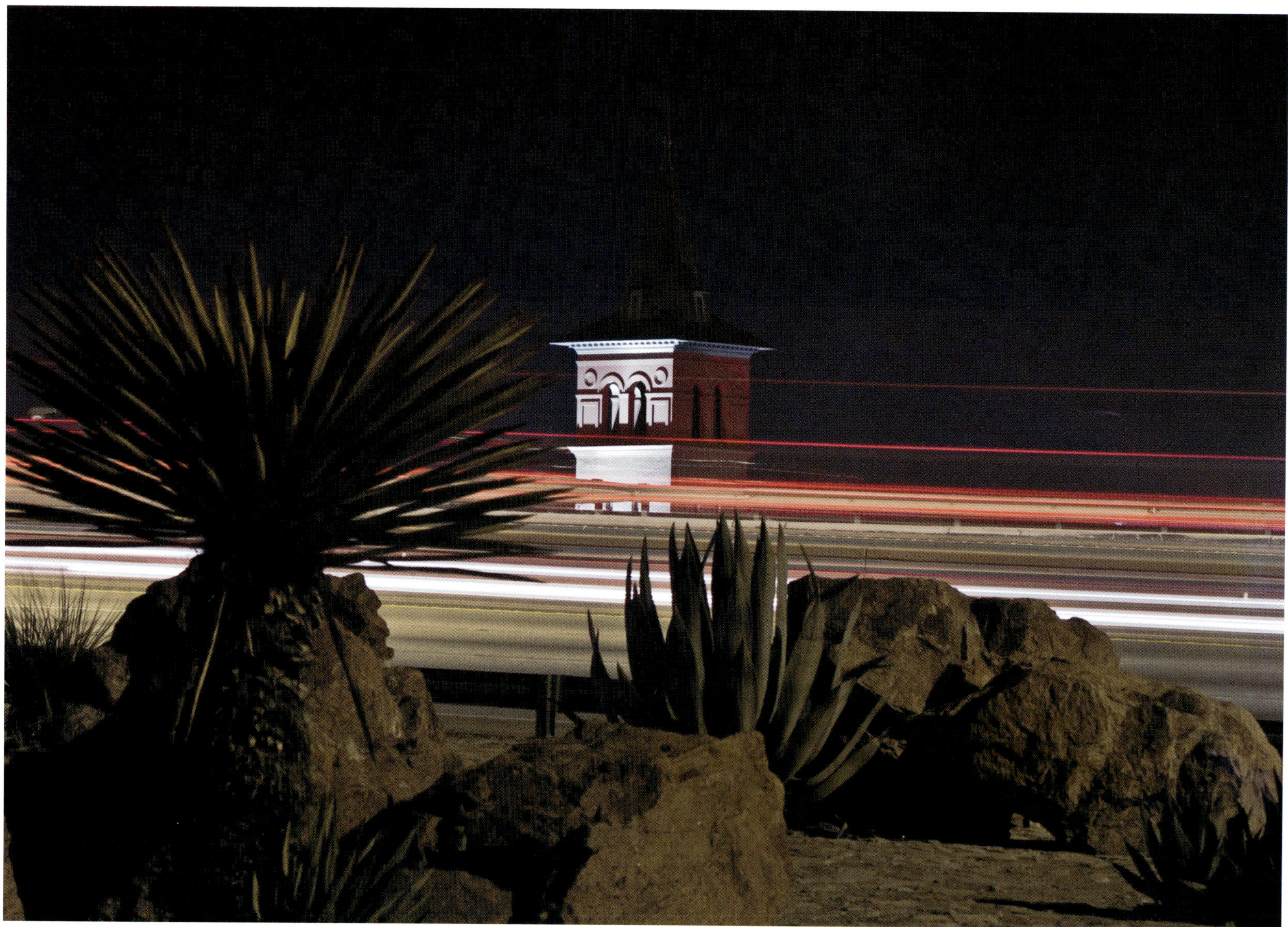

Peeking over Interstate 10.

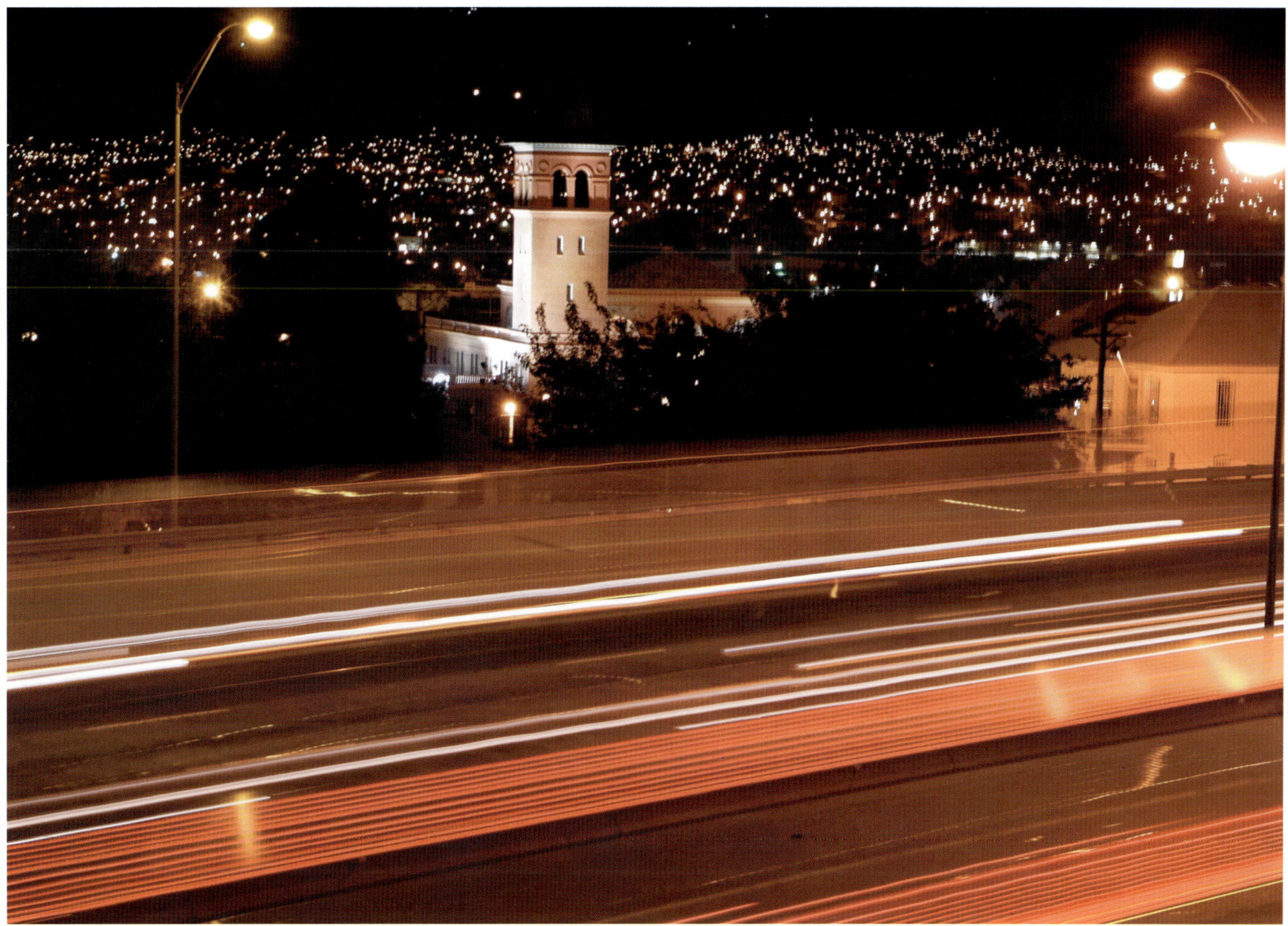

Union Depot Streaker.
Designed by architect Daniel Burnham, who also designed Washington, DC's Union Station, the El Paso Union Depot was built between 1905 and 1906 and was added to the National Register of Historical Places in 1971.

My El Paso is opportunity, wide-open spaces, and big possibilities with people of character.

— DEE MARGO, EL PASO BUSINESS LEADER

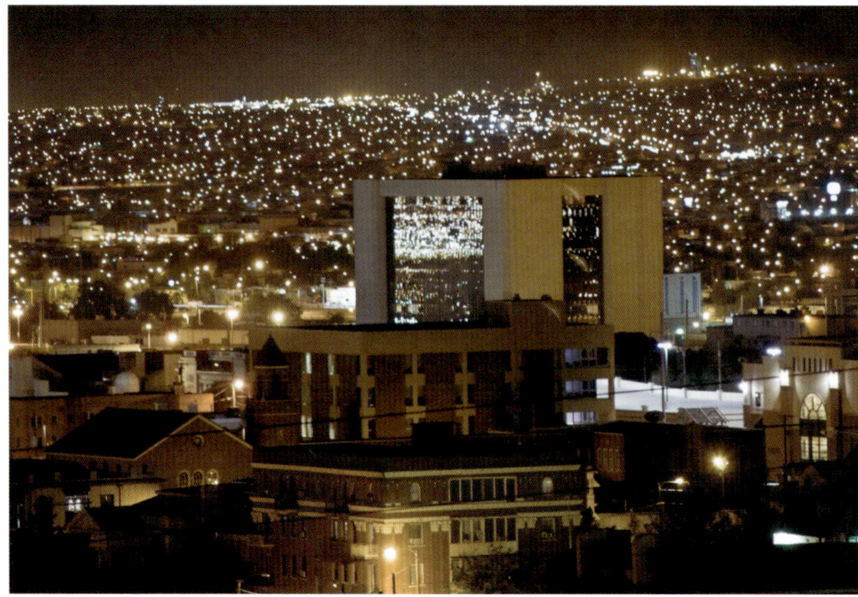

El Paso City Hall.

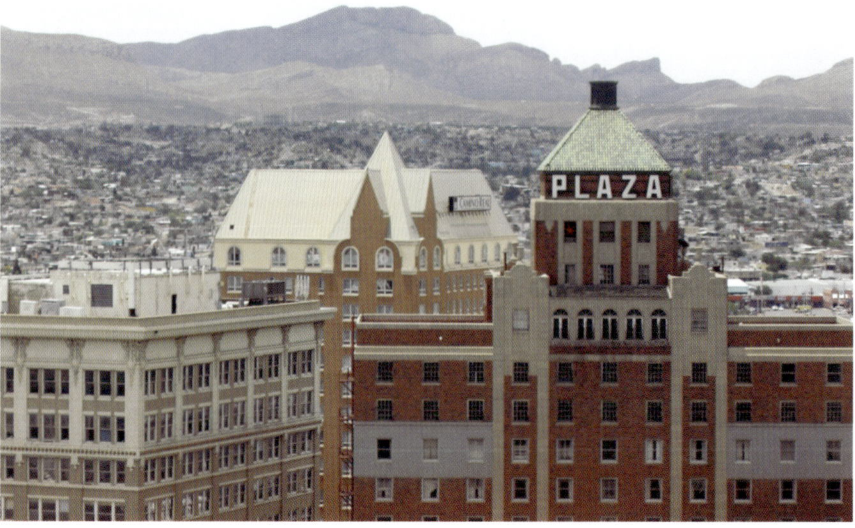

Historic Trio: Texas Tower, Camino Real Hotel, Plaza Hotel.

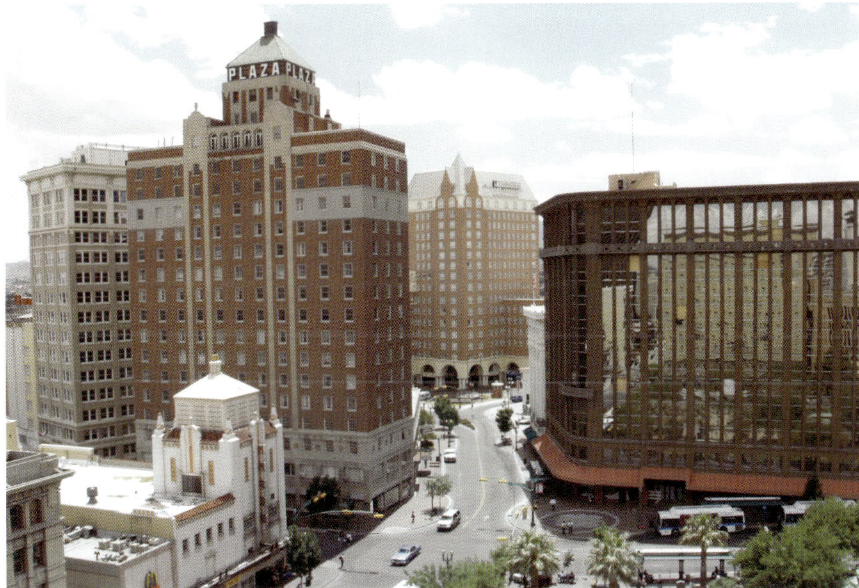

Historic Downtown El Paso and San Jacinto Plaza.

My El Paso is the home of not only my Hispanic culture but is nestled between two countries and three states and has been greatly influenced by the American and Native American cultures and cuisines.

— CARMEN NAVAR, EL PASO ARTIST

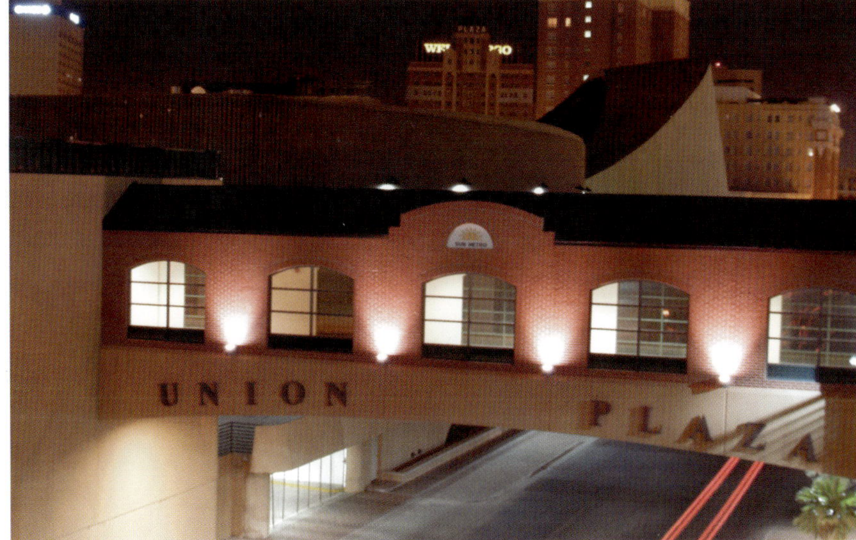

Union Plaza Complex.

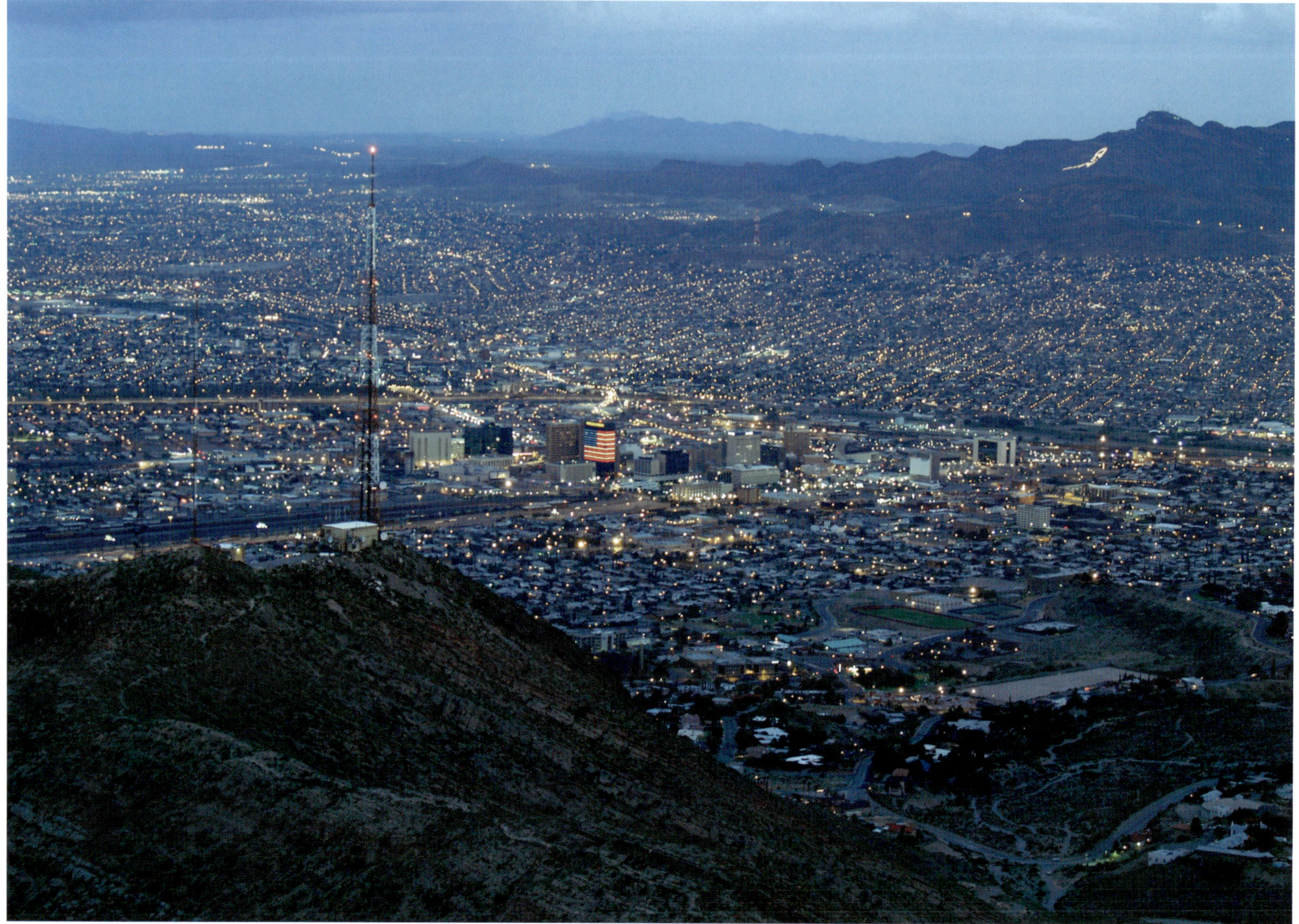

Tip of the Franklin Mountains.
The Franklin Mountains of Texas are a small range (twenty-three miles long, three miles wide) that extend from El Paso north into New Mexico. The Franklins were formed during the Laramide mountain-building period in late Cretaceous time, sixty to seventy million years ago.

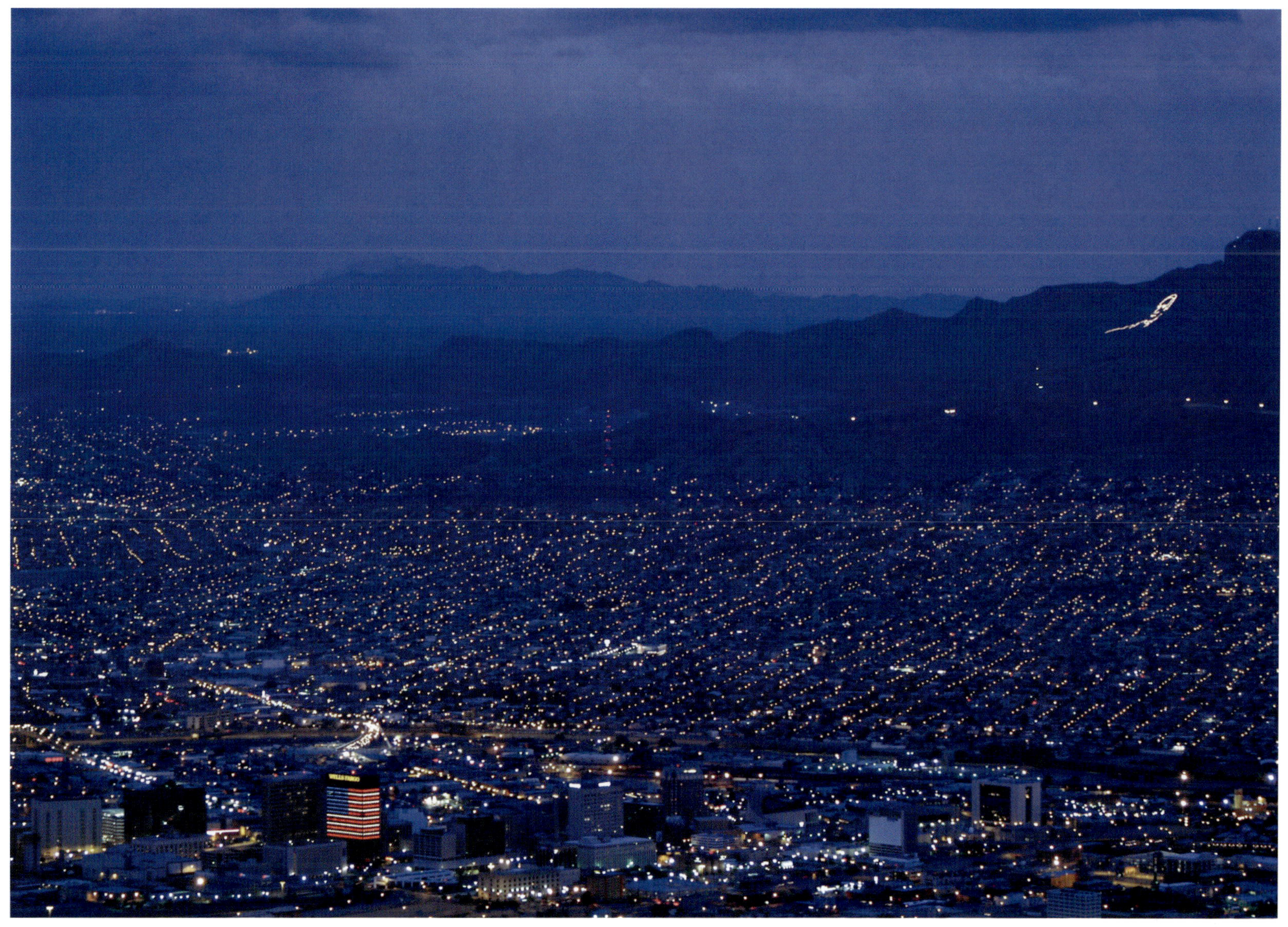

Sister Cities.
Downtown El Paso and Ciudad Juárez, Mexico.

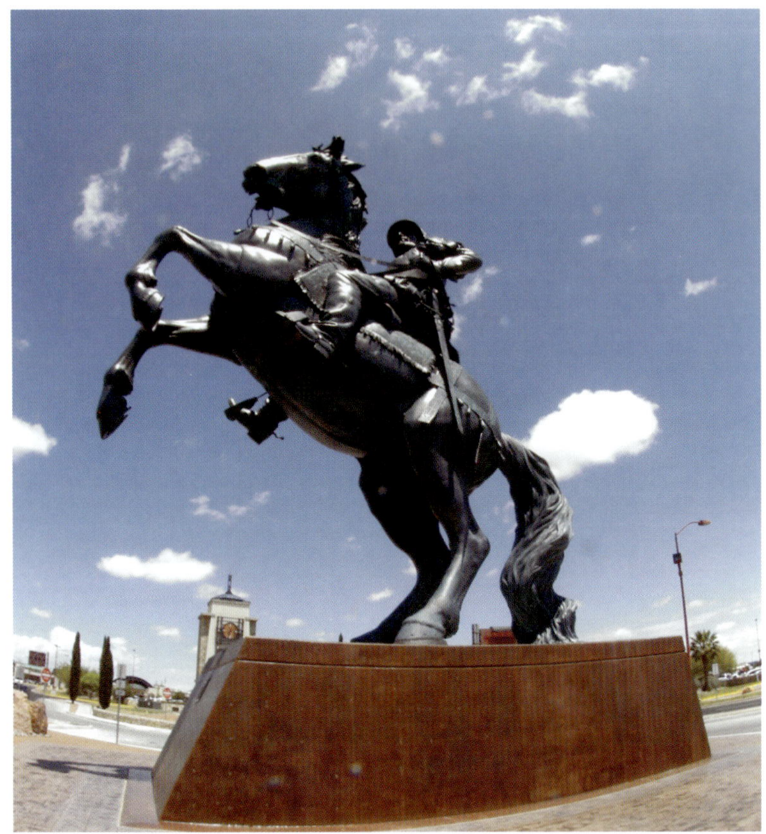

John Sherril Houser's Bronze Equestrian Statue of Don Juan Oñate.
The City of El Paso held a grand ceremony to unveil an eighteen-ton, thirty-six-foot tall statue of Don Juan Oñate on April 21, 2007. It was well received and welcomed by the majority of El Pasoans and the Spanish Ambassador to the United States, Carlos Westendorp. Oñate is mounted atop his Andalusian horse while holding the La Toma declaration in his right hand. On April 30, 1598, in present day San Elizario, Texas, Don Juan Oñate made a legal declaration that Spain was taking possession of all territory north of the Rio Grande for King Phillip II of Spain. According to sculptor John Houser, it is the largest and heaviest equestrian statue in the world.

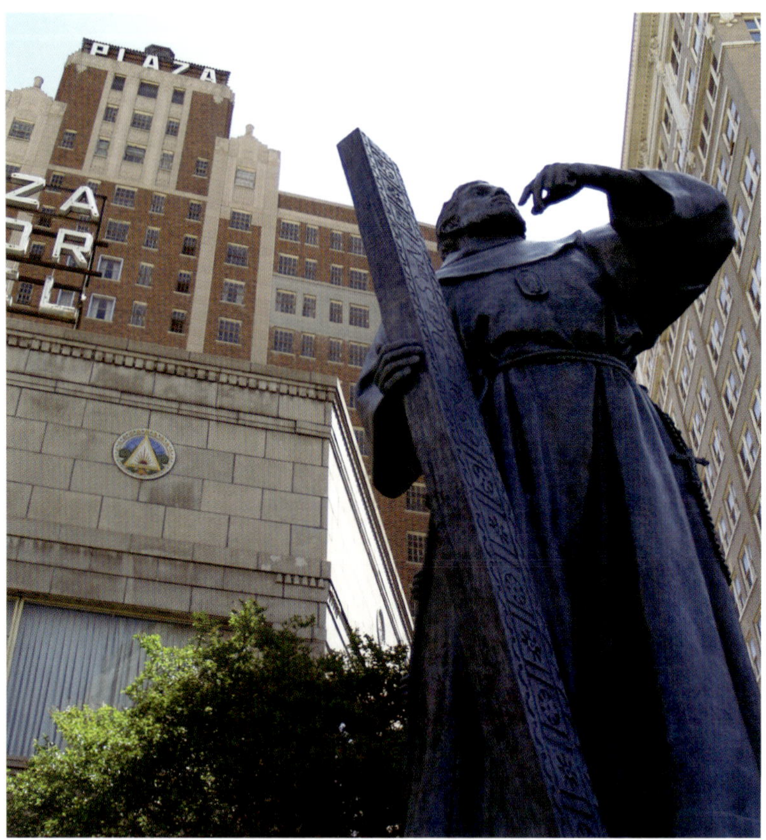

John Sherrill Houser's Fray Garcia Monument At the Horseshoe.
Fray Garcia Monument is a fourteen-foot bronze sculpture by John Houser honoring the priest who founded the area's first mission. It is located in Pioneer Plaza at the corner of El Paso and San Francisco streets downtown.

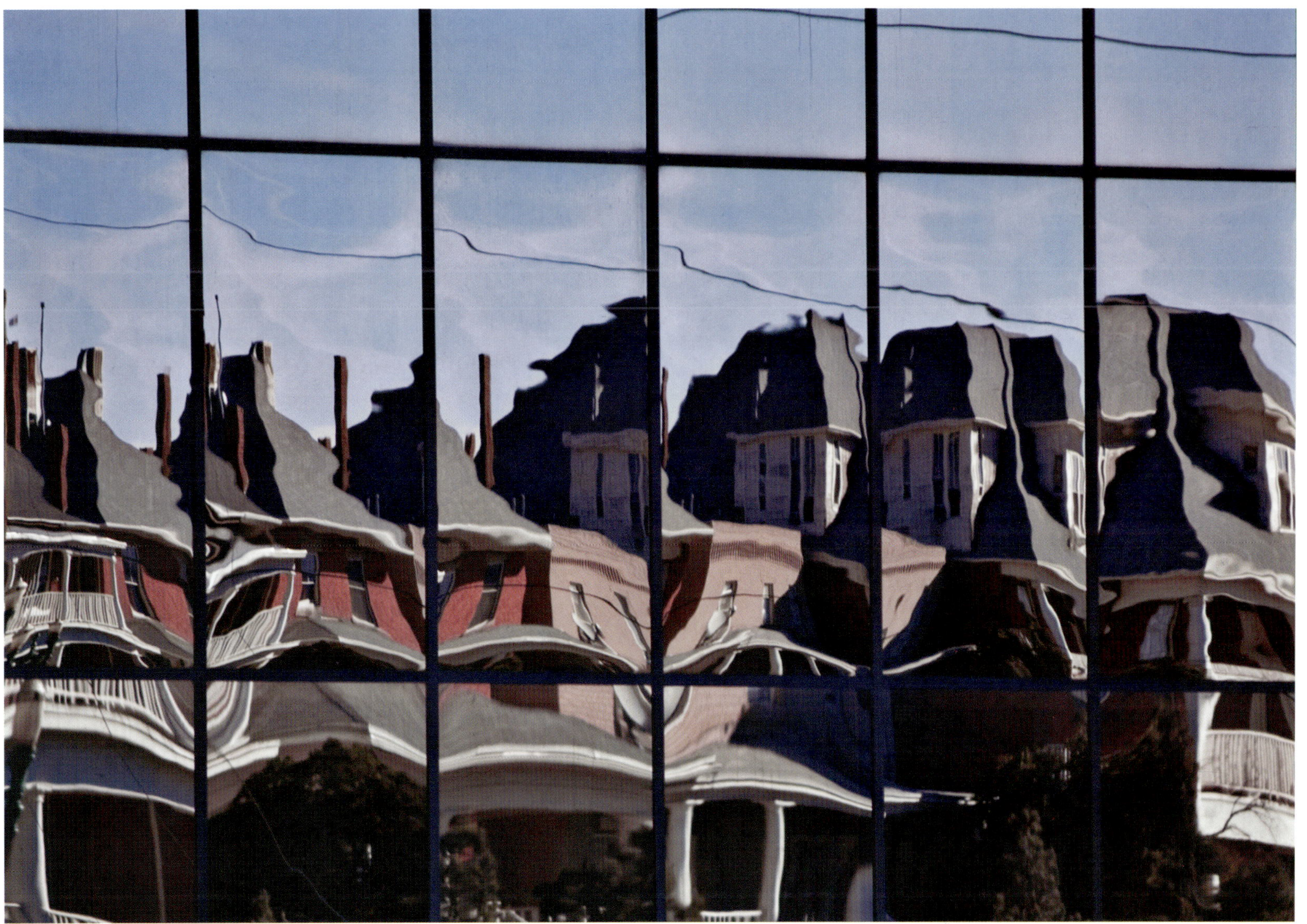

San Francisco Historic District Reflected in City Hall.
Originally built between 1900 and 1924, the Old San Francisco Historic District continues to thrive as a multi-family neighborhood. The area was added to the National Register of Historical Places in 1985 and is located directly across from El Paso's City Hall on Missouri Street. Noted for architectural style the district is reminiscent of the fine city of San Francisco.

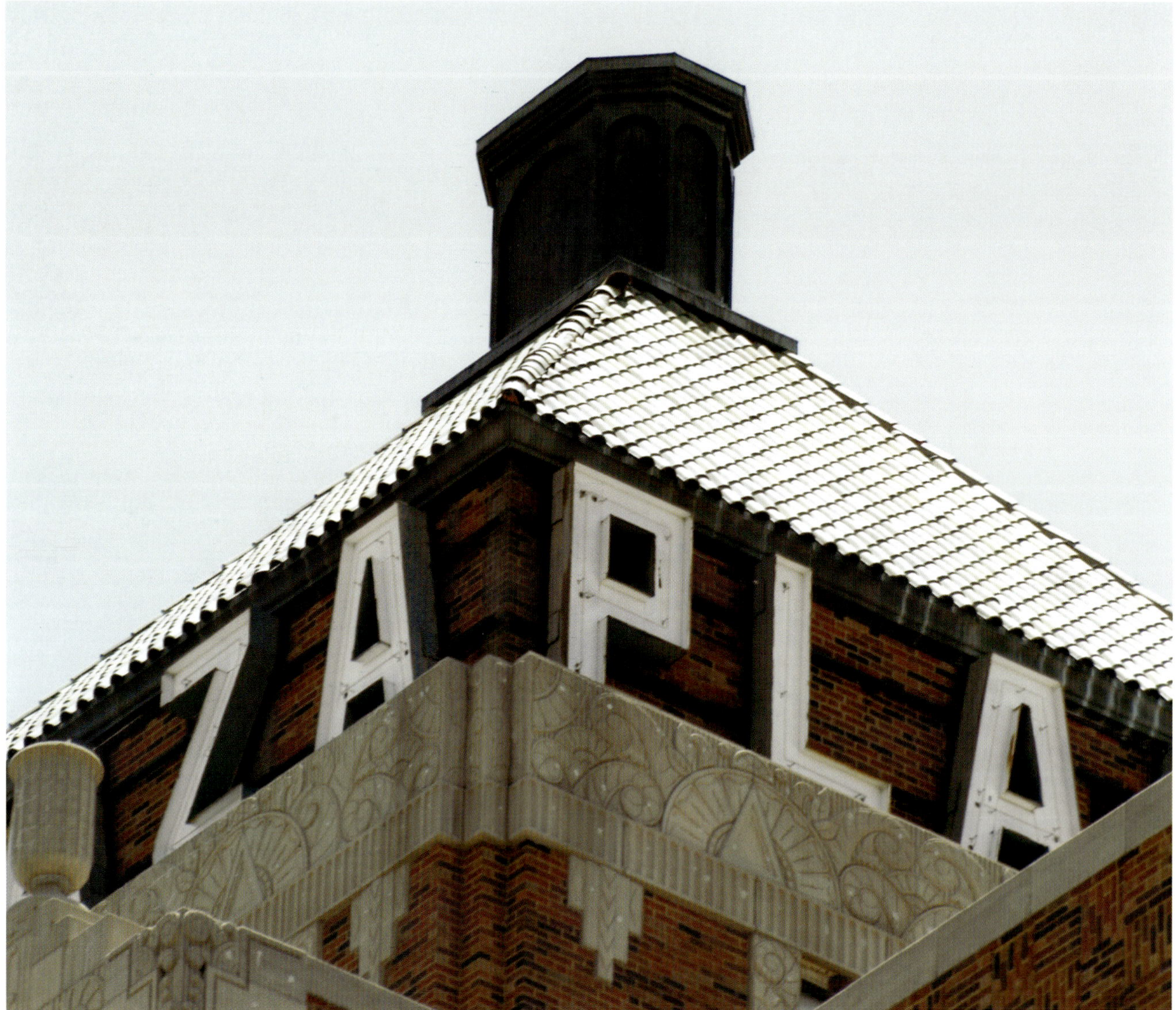

ZAPLA. Plaza Hotel.
Beginning in the 1920s and into the 1930s, El Paso became the birthplace of several locally and nationally well-known businesses and events. In 1930, Conrad Hilton opened his first high-rise hotel in El Paso, now the Plaza Hotel.

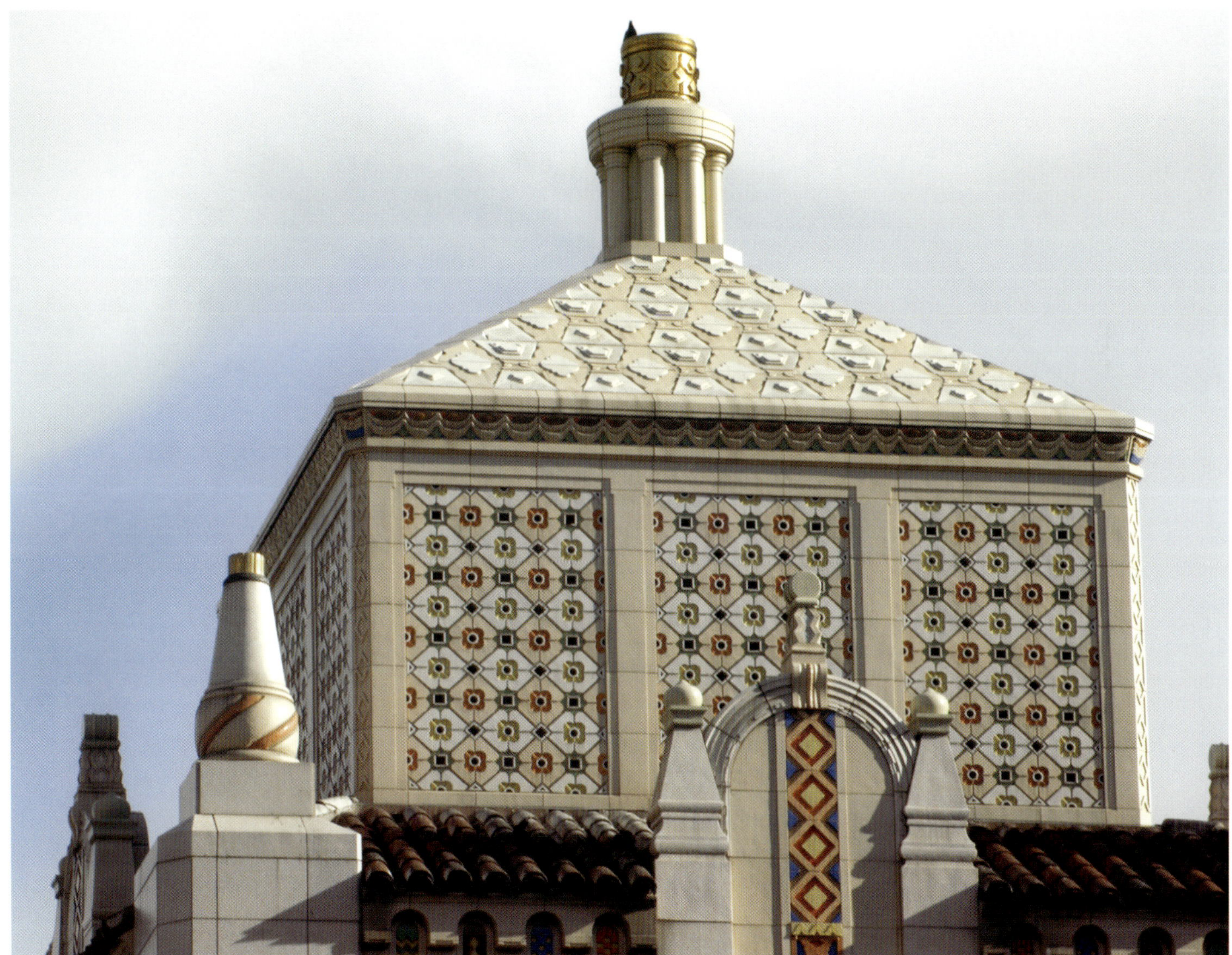

The Kress Store.
Designed by Edward F. Sibbert, the Kress store used terracotta extensively for the outside walls and the embellishments. Kress stores had been constructed in either brick or terracotta until 1934, when terracotta facades became standard. However, stores with more than one elevation were not made entirely with terracotta until the El Paso store, the only Kress in the country having entrances and exits on three different streets.

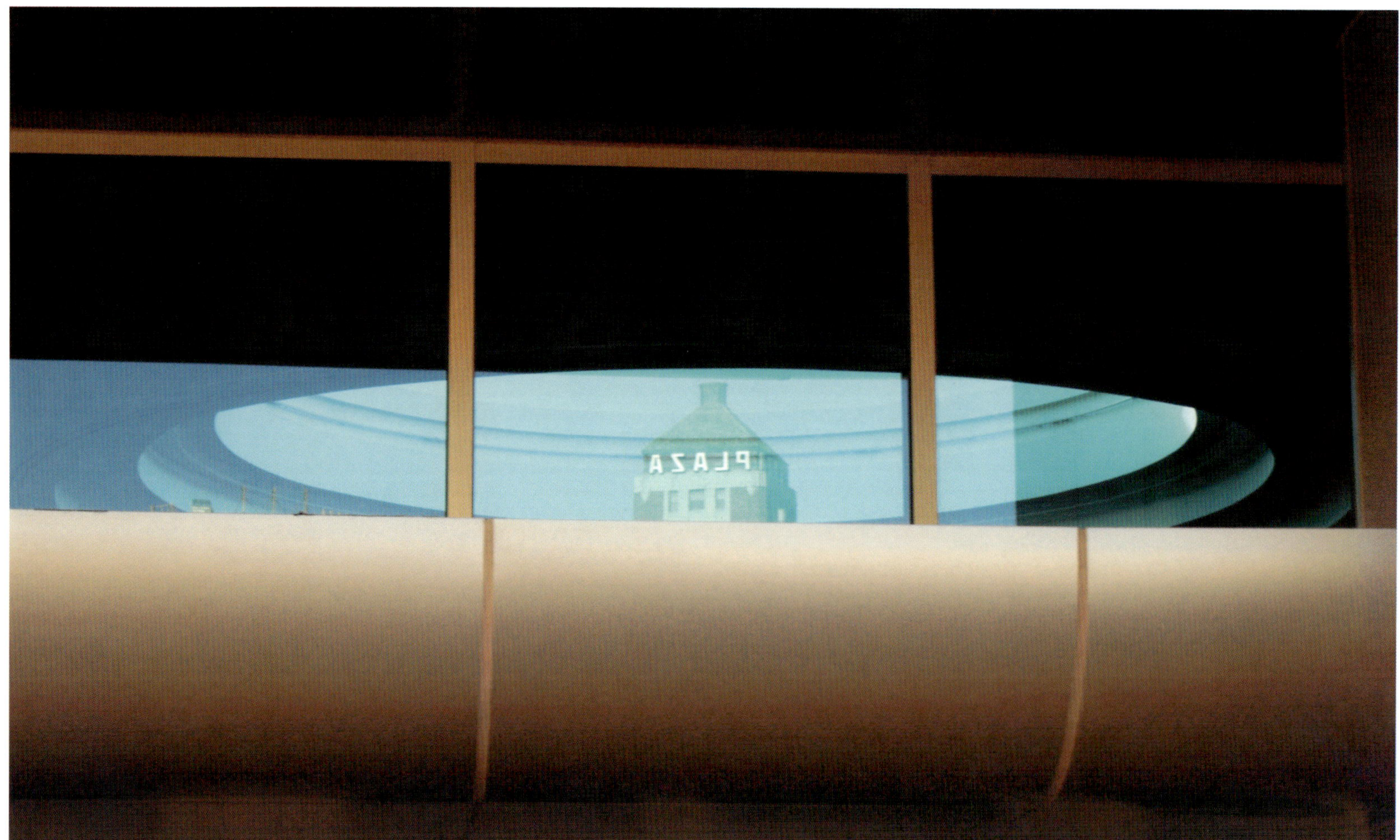

Plaza Reflection.
Reflection of the Plaza in the Judson F. Williams Convention Center.

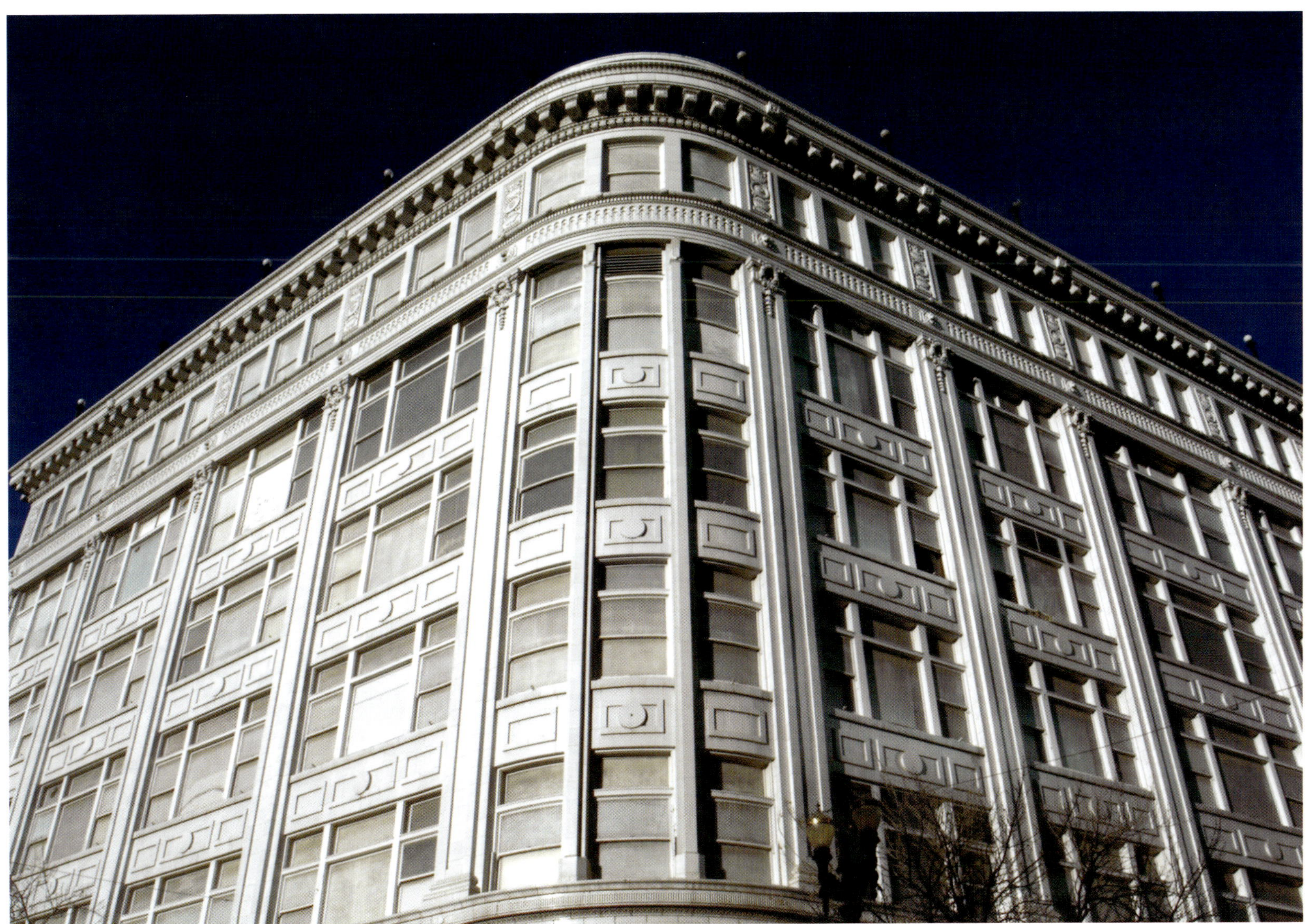

The Popular Dry Goods Company.
In 1902, Adolph Schwartz opened the Popular Dry Goods Company in El Paso after successfully establishing two other stores. The Popular would become the largest locally-owned department store, at one time having three branches in addition to the main store downtown. It would survive nearly one hundred years. Designed by Henry C. Trost.

My El Paso is an adventure into a culture which fills my art with inspiration. I am lucky it's also my home.

— HAL MARCUS, EL PASO ARTIST

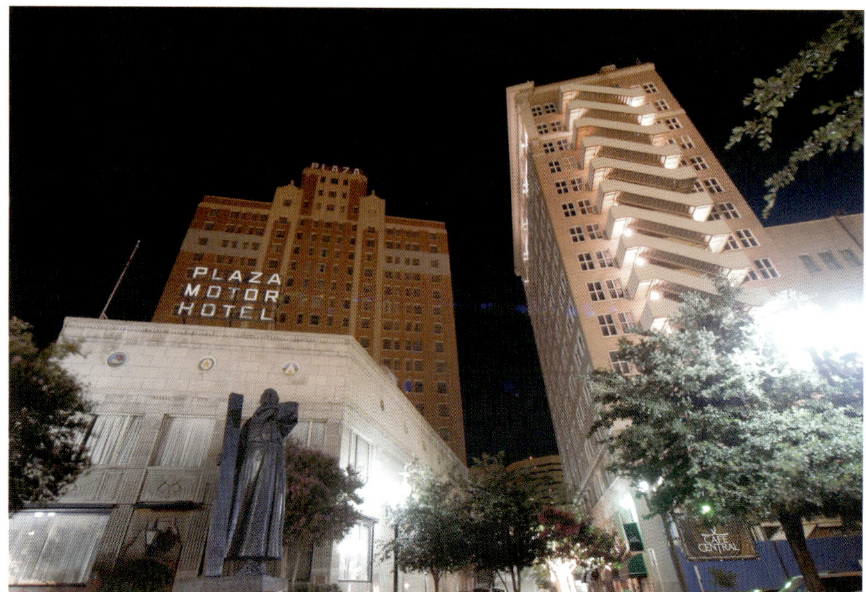

Pioneer Plaza. Downtown El Paso.

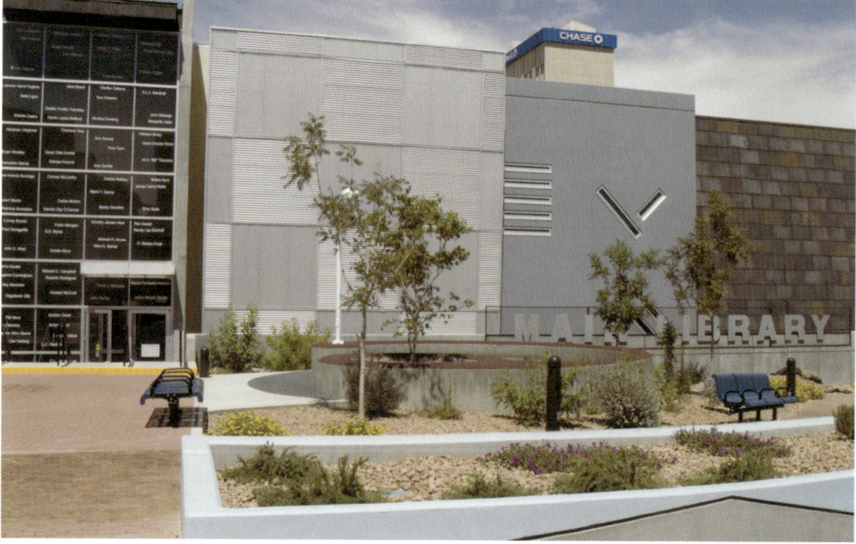

El Paso Public Library.

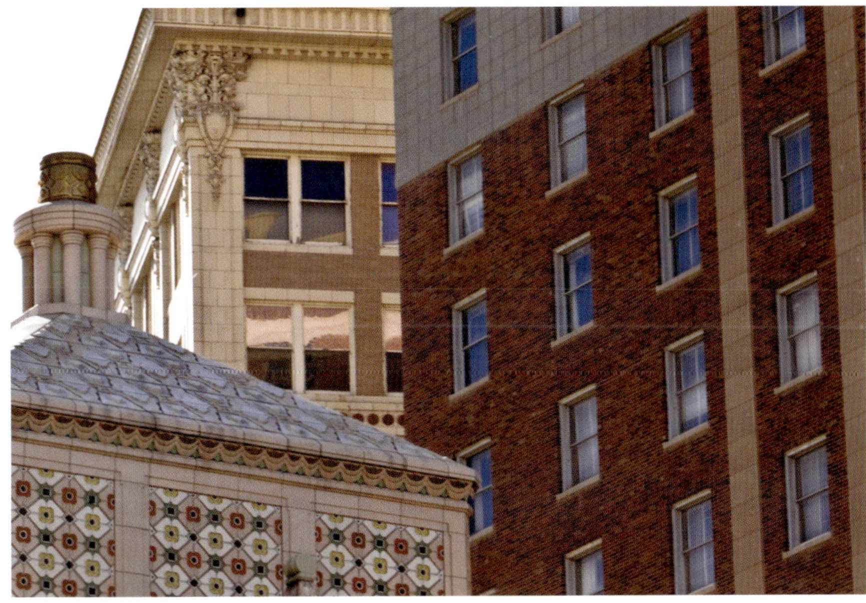

Downtown Character: Kress Building, Plaza Hotel, Texas Tower.

My El Paso is a unique historical, international metropolis ready to be discovered.

— PRES DEHRKOOP, PROUD EL PASOAN

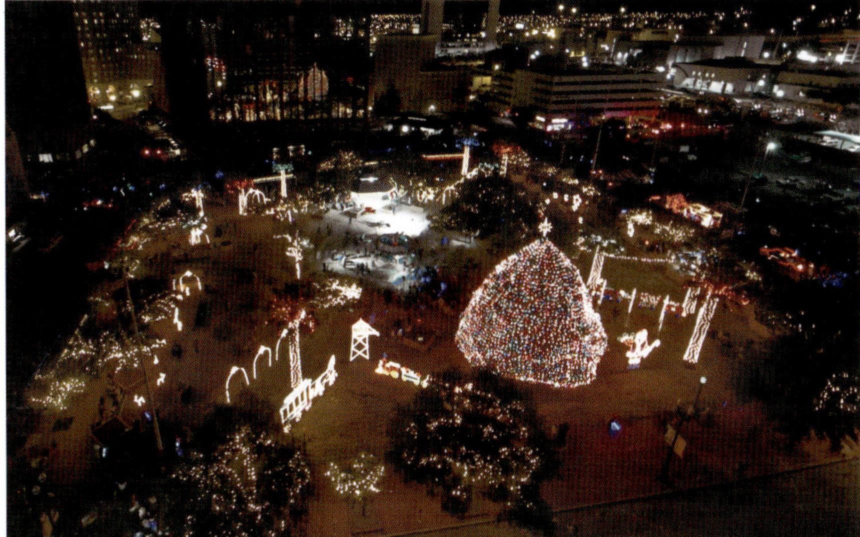

Celebrating the Holidays. Downtown's San Jacinto Plaza.

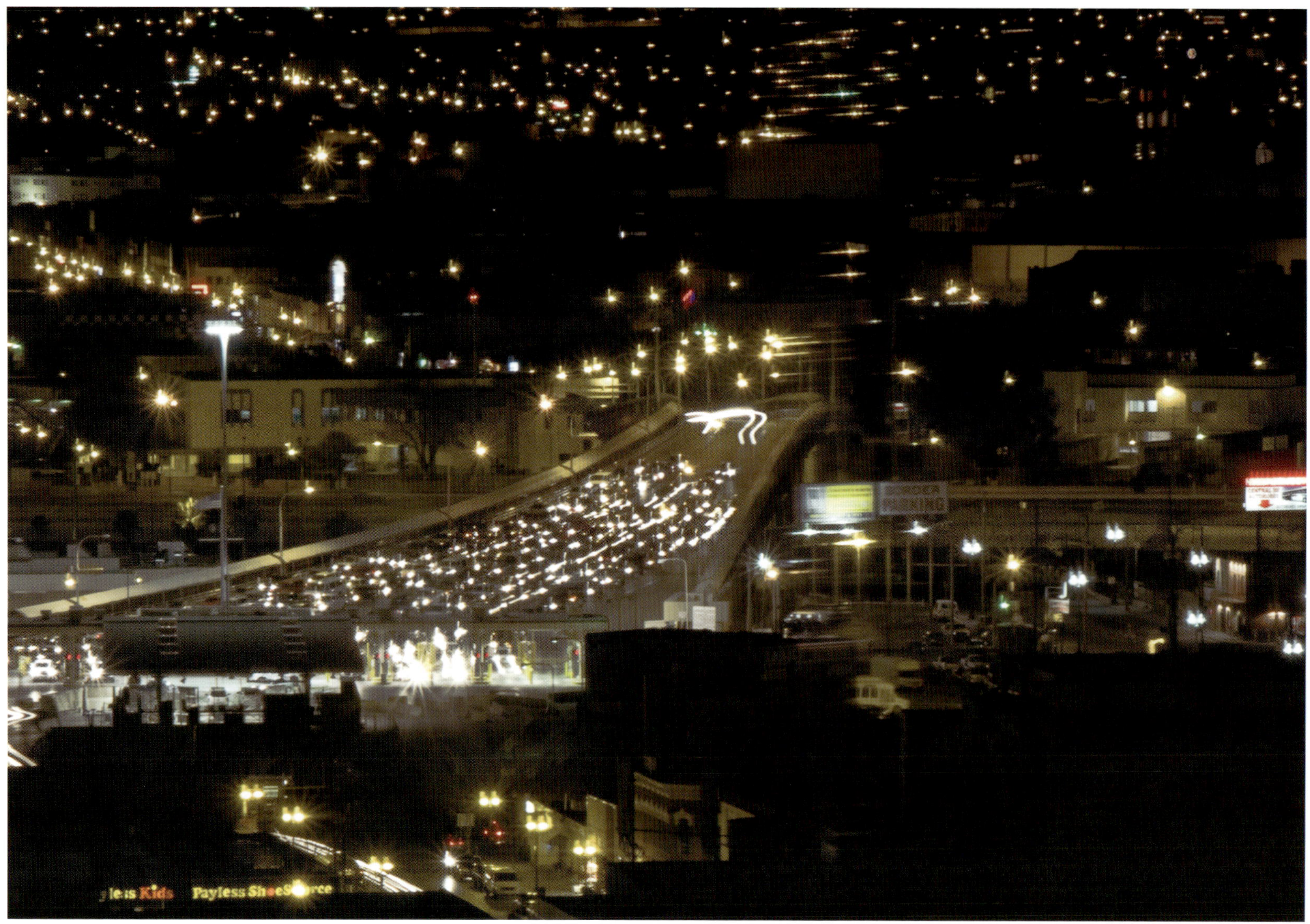

Santa Fe International Bridge.
What visitors will find is America's quintessential border city, a fascinating juxtaposition of First and Third Worlds where two metropolises come face to face; where you can walk across the bridge from the center of one city and directly into another. El Paso is more bilingual and bicultural than any other major city in the United States, with a history that stretches back 400 years.

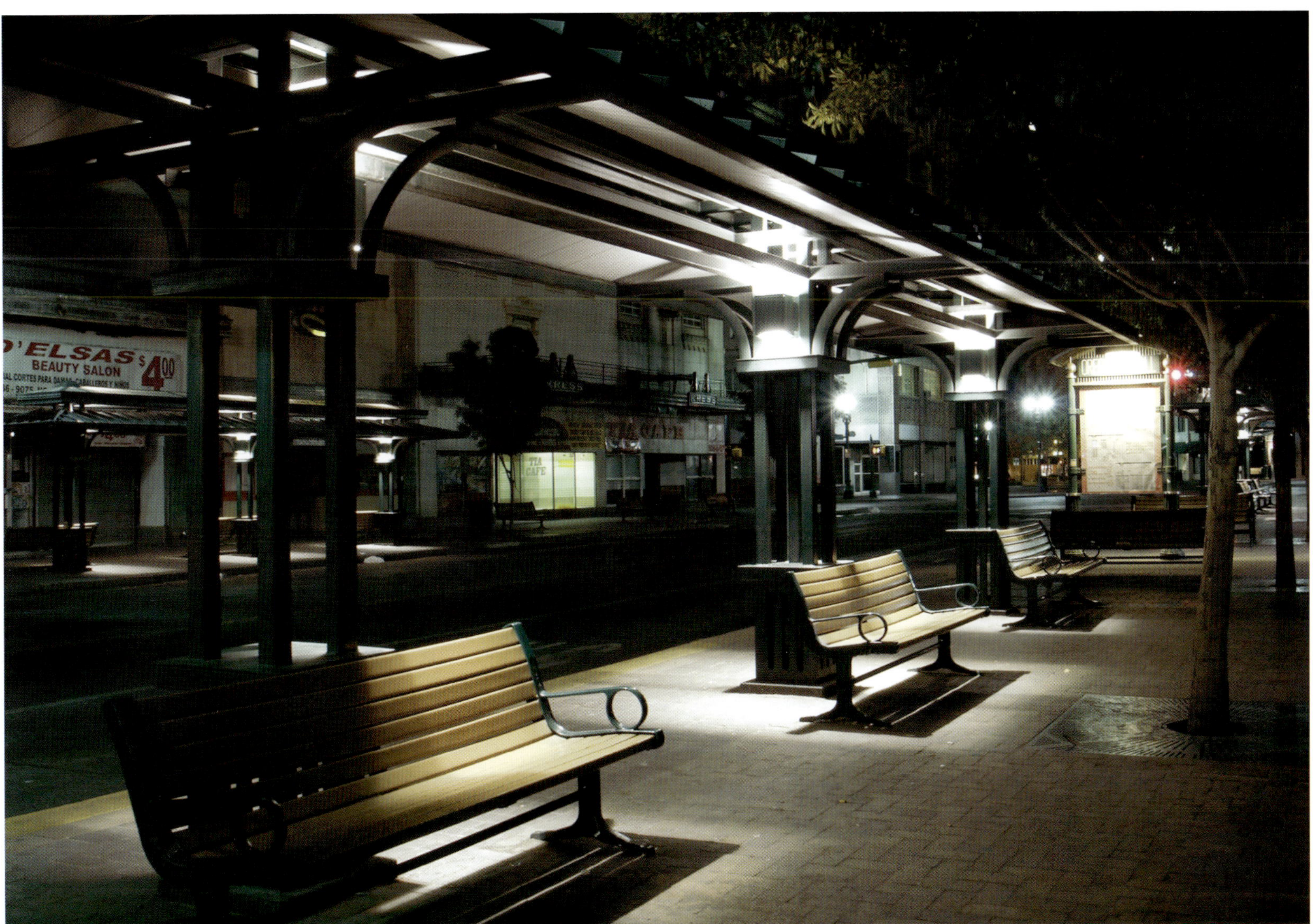

Hopperesque El Paso – The Plaza.
The Plaza has been the center of downtown El Paso for over 100 years – a source of entertainment, a center for public transportation, and a place to rest from the hustle and bustle of everyday life. Trost & Trost, Architects.

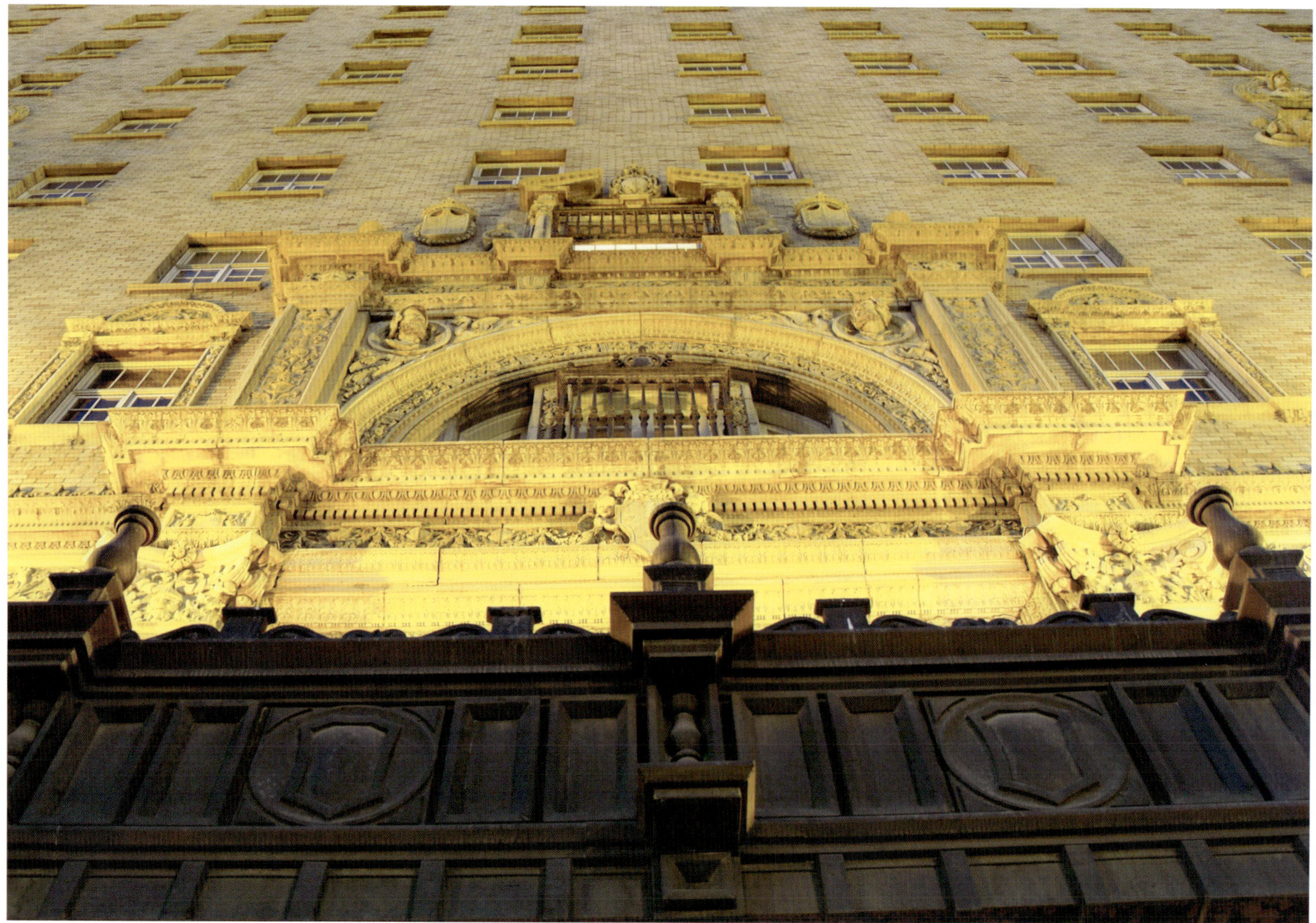

The Cortez.
Today, the Cortez Building remains a splendid castle overlooking San Jacinto Plaza in downtown El Paso. Architect Henry C. Trost altered El Paso's landscape with many different styles, designing unique buildings that today solidly stand and are considered classics. Trost was a man who affected the way El Paso would look into the twenty-first century.

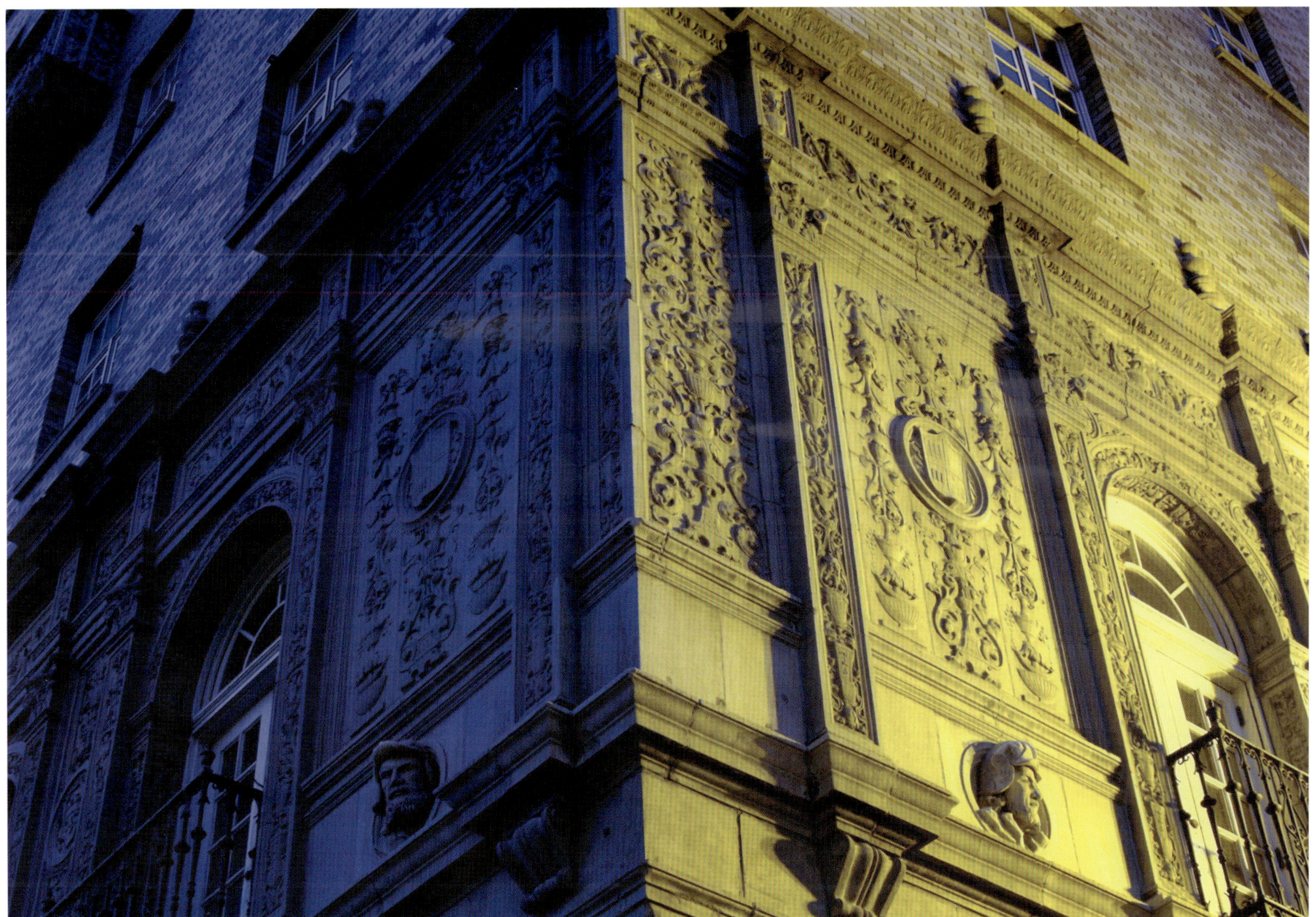

Cortez Corner.
The entrance on Mesa Street has a five-story cast relief portal and ornamented windows on the sixth and seventh levels. It is in the tradition of the Spanish Colonial Revival, which was popular in the 1920s. This revival included a blending of Renaissance, Moorish, and Baroque styles featuring many references to the Spanish and Spanish-American past. Trost & Trost, Architects.

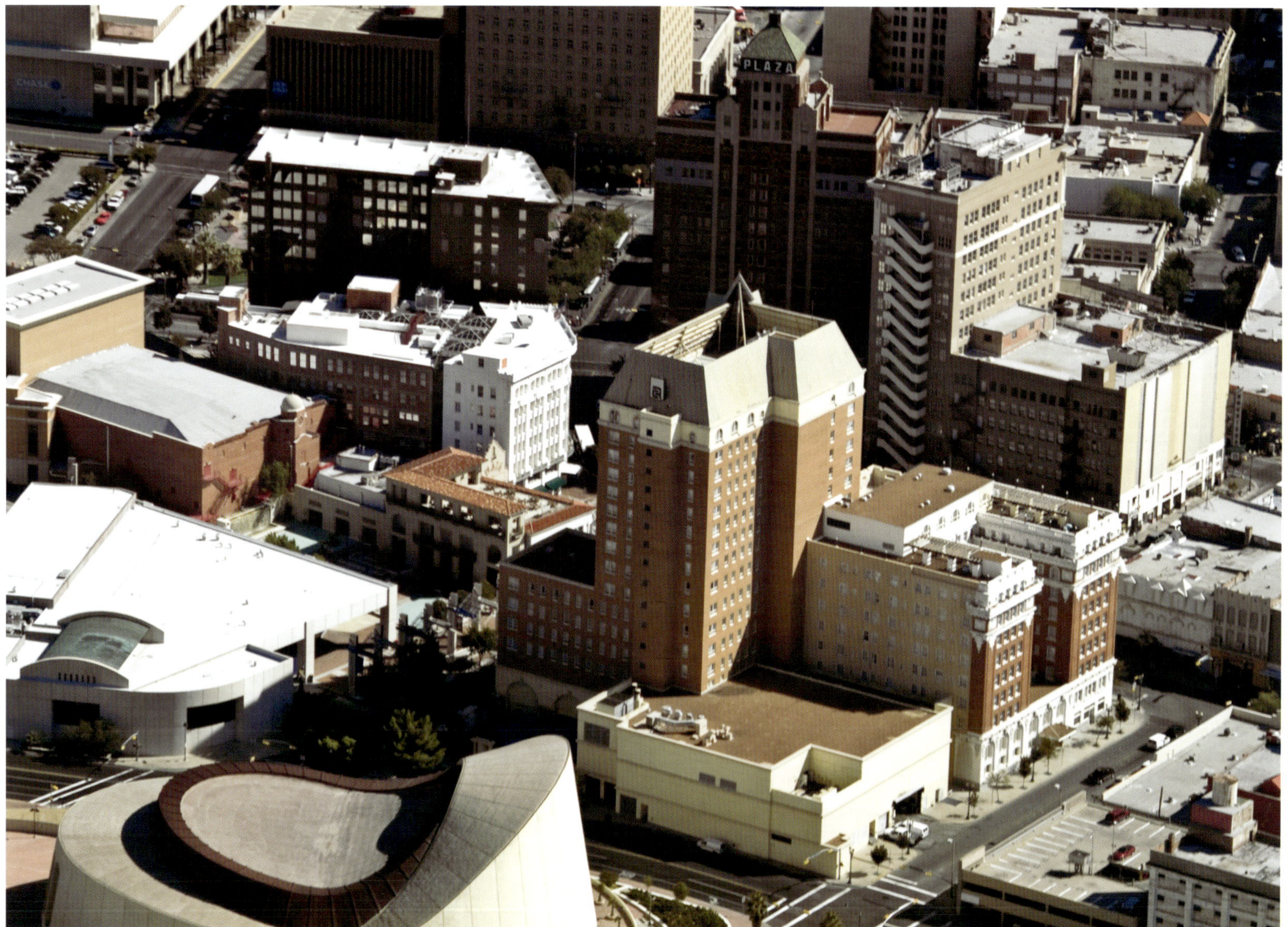

Downtown Old and New.
Since its founding in 1873, El Paso has been a gateway to the Western United States and Mexico. For over a century downtown El Paso was a vibrant center of industry, commerce, and social interaction for the region.

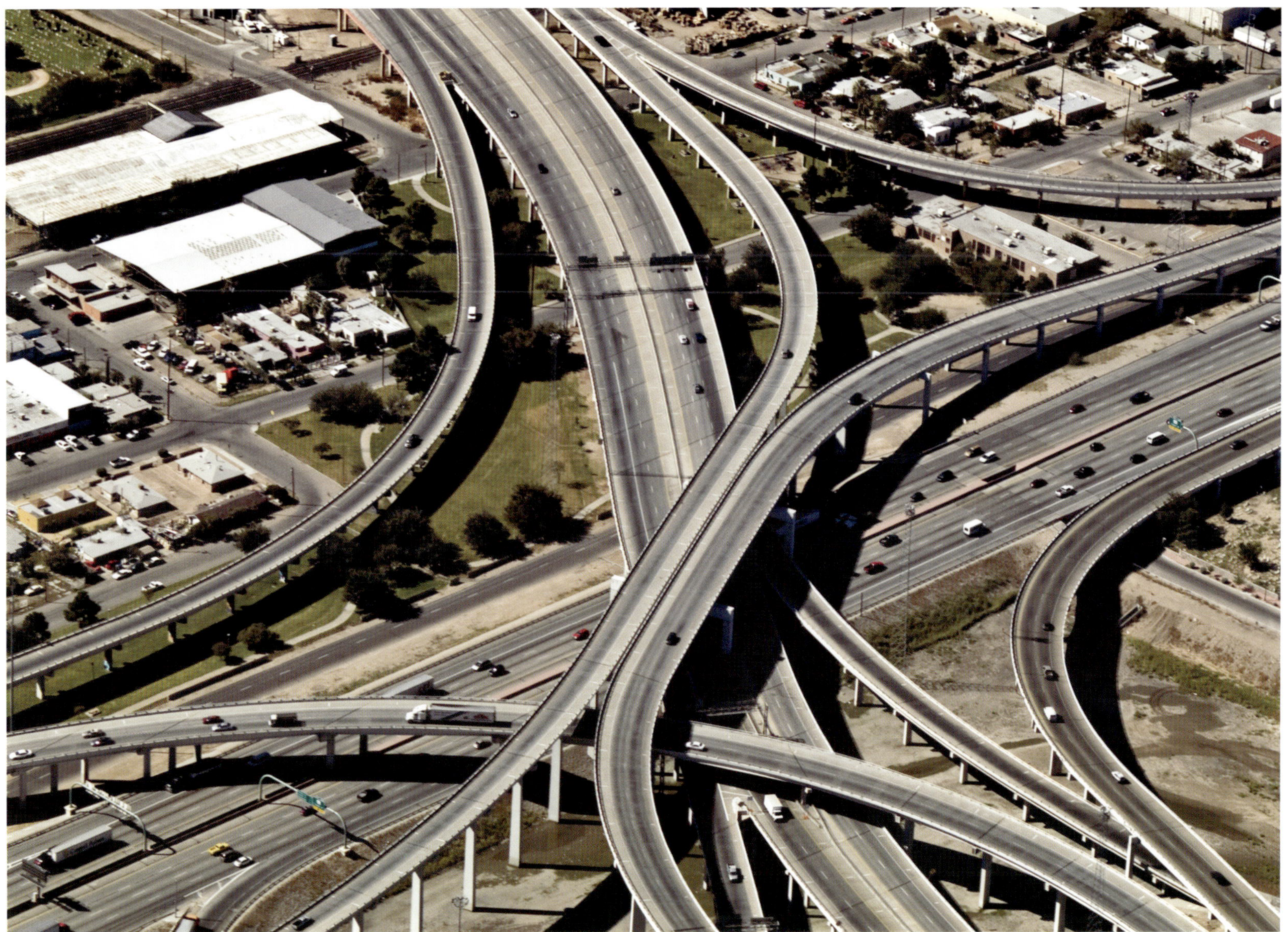

The Spaghetti Bowl.
The Spaghetti Bowl connects East, West, and Northeast El Paso with Ciudad Juárez, Mexico.

My El Paso is where my roots are, where it's easy to make a difference, where diversity is celebrated, and a strong sense of community thrives. It's home, in the most fulfilling sense of the word.

— REBECCA KRASNE, PROUD EL PASOAN AND COMMUNITY VOLUNTEER

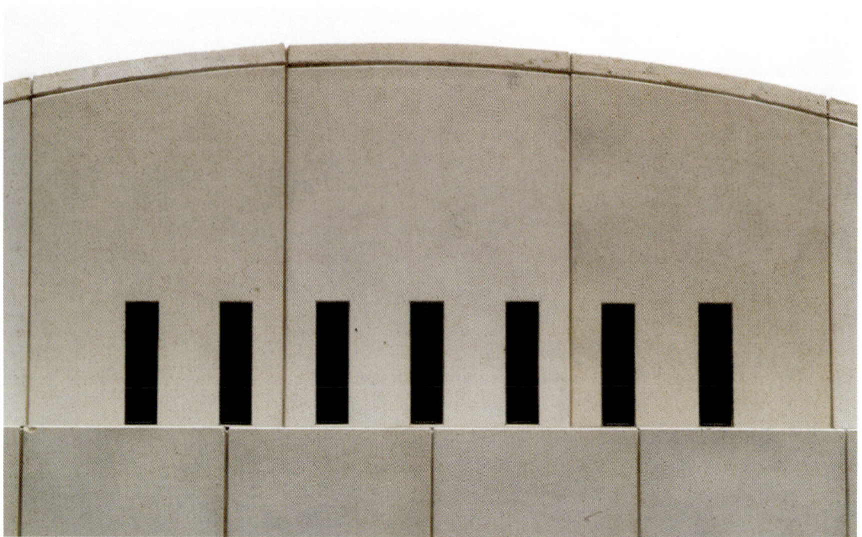

The El Paso Museum of Art houses a permanent collection of more than 5,000 works of art.

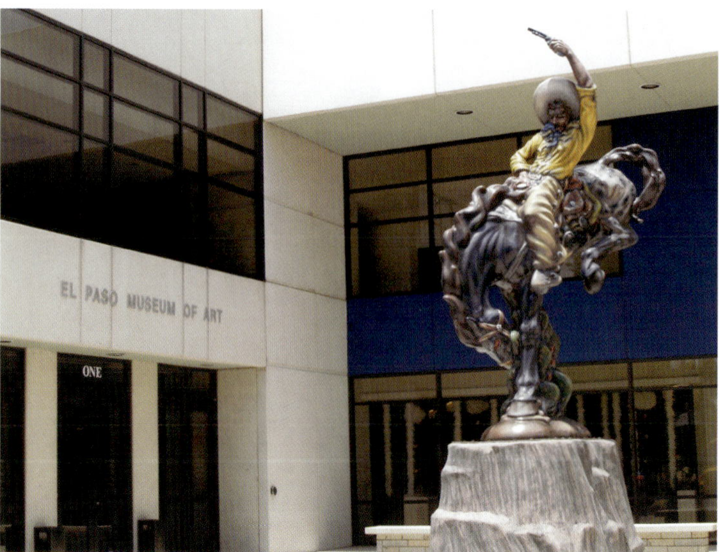

Vaquero **at One Arts Festival Plaza by Luis Jimenez.**

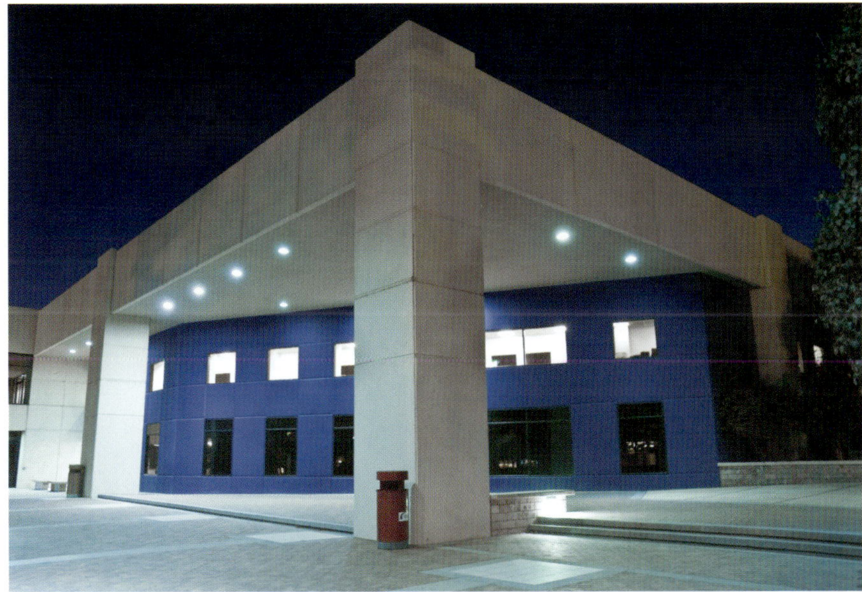

El Paso Museum of Art.

My El Paso is dynamic and vibrant and provides a canvas for all of us to be artistic and creative in how we live our lives.

— MICHAEL TOMOR, PHD, DIRECTOR,
EL PASO MUSEUM OF ART

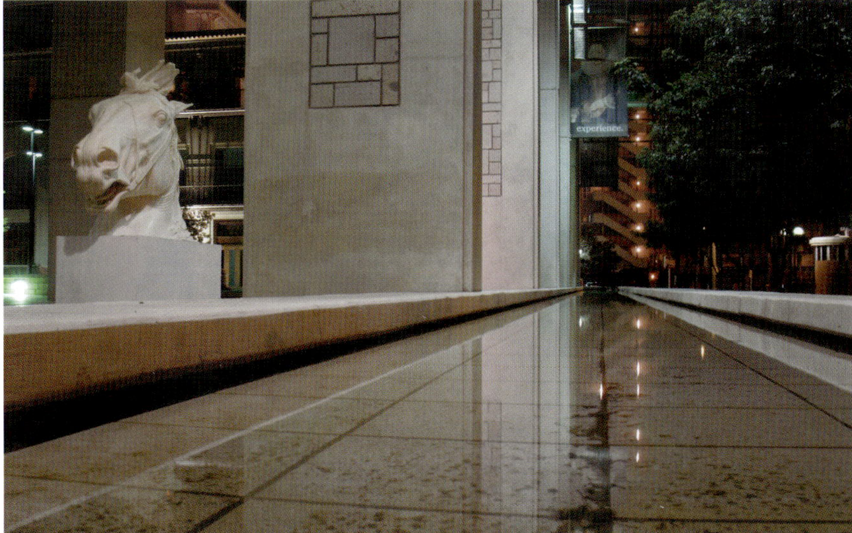

El Paso Museum of Art Fountain.

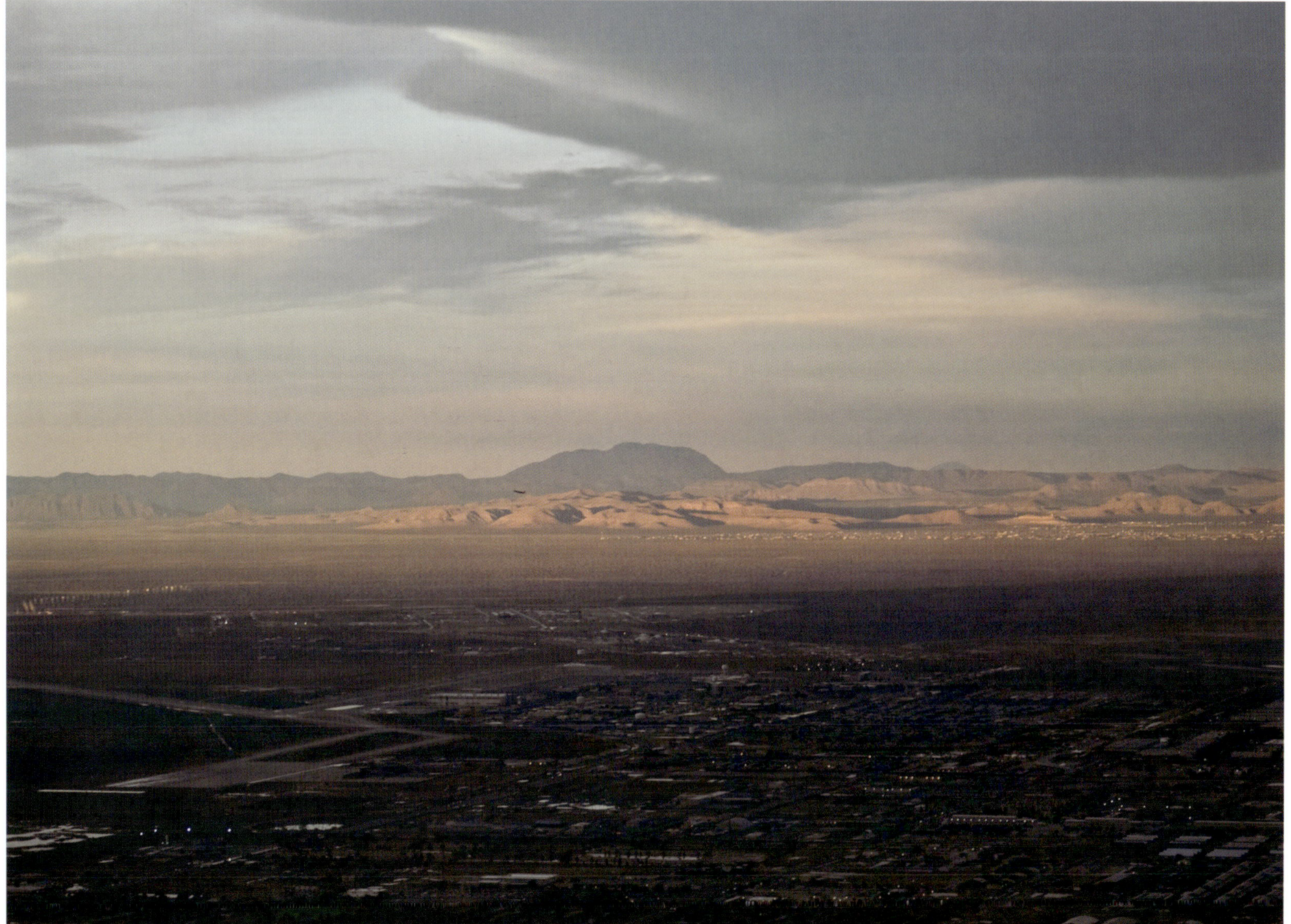

Transmountain View.
El Paso's Franklin Mountains provide a unique view that few other American cities can enjoy. Transmountain Road, which cuts through the Franklins, offers a view of two countries, USA and Mexico; three states, Texas, New Mexico and Chihuahua; and two cities, El Paso and Juárez.

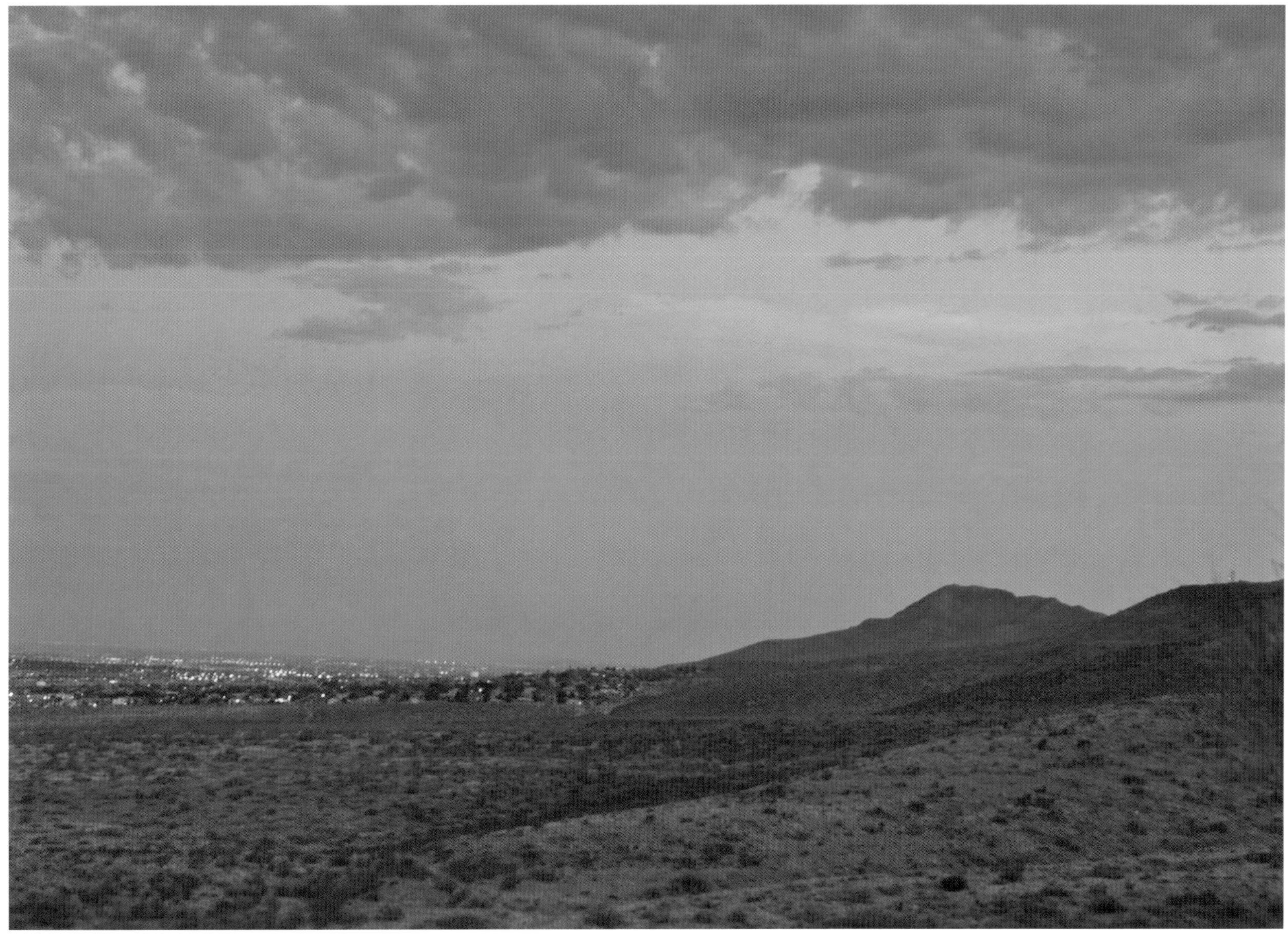

El Paso, Dusk.
There is no better place to watch the sun set in West Texas than from the Franklin Mountains. A drive through Transmountain Road or a hike up to the mountain top at the right time can also provide a fantastic experience of watching the sun rise and moon set at the same time.

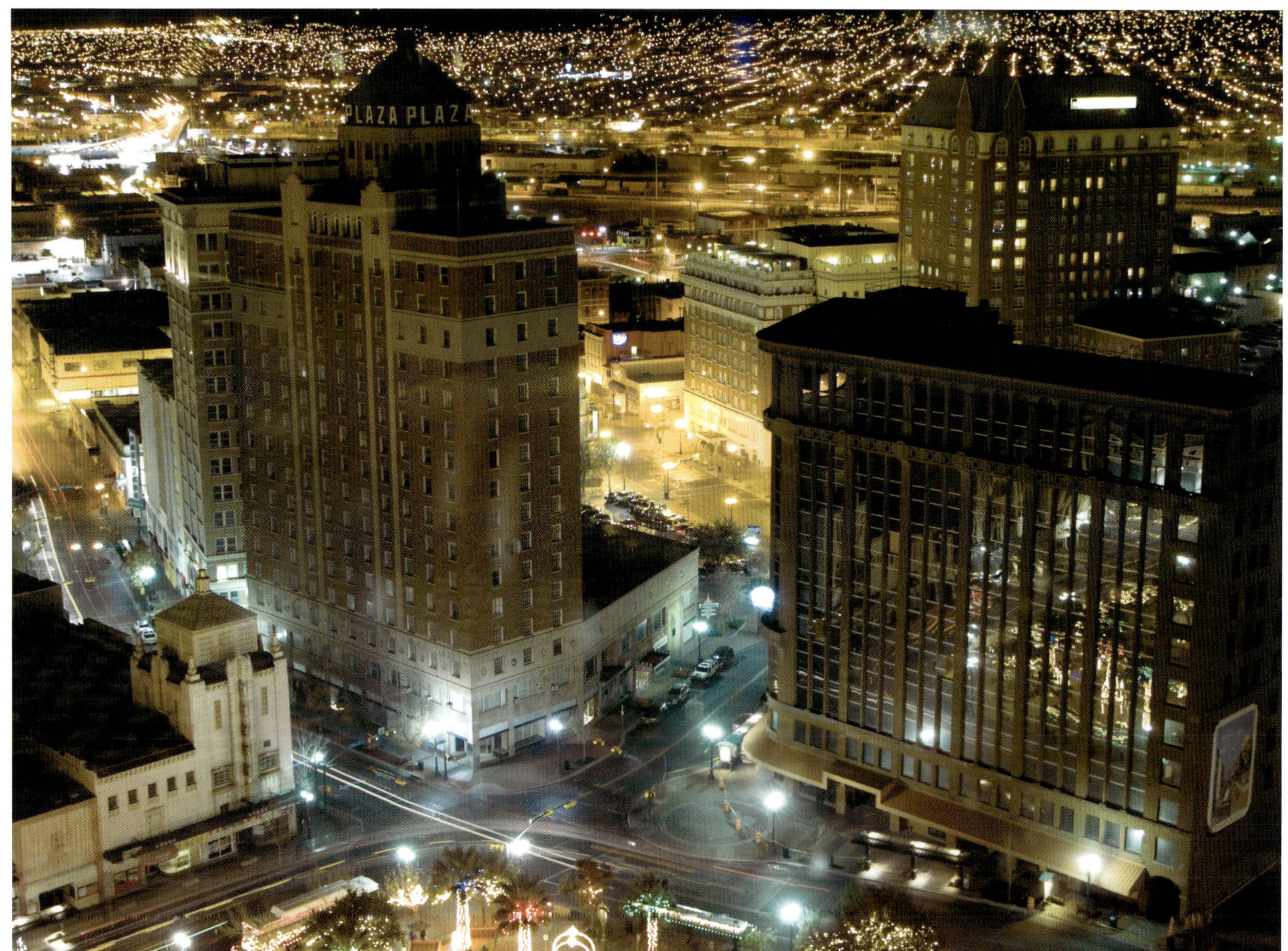

A Snapshot before Change in Downtown El Paso.
Re-development will reshape this area with revitalization in mind.

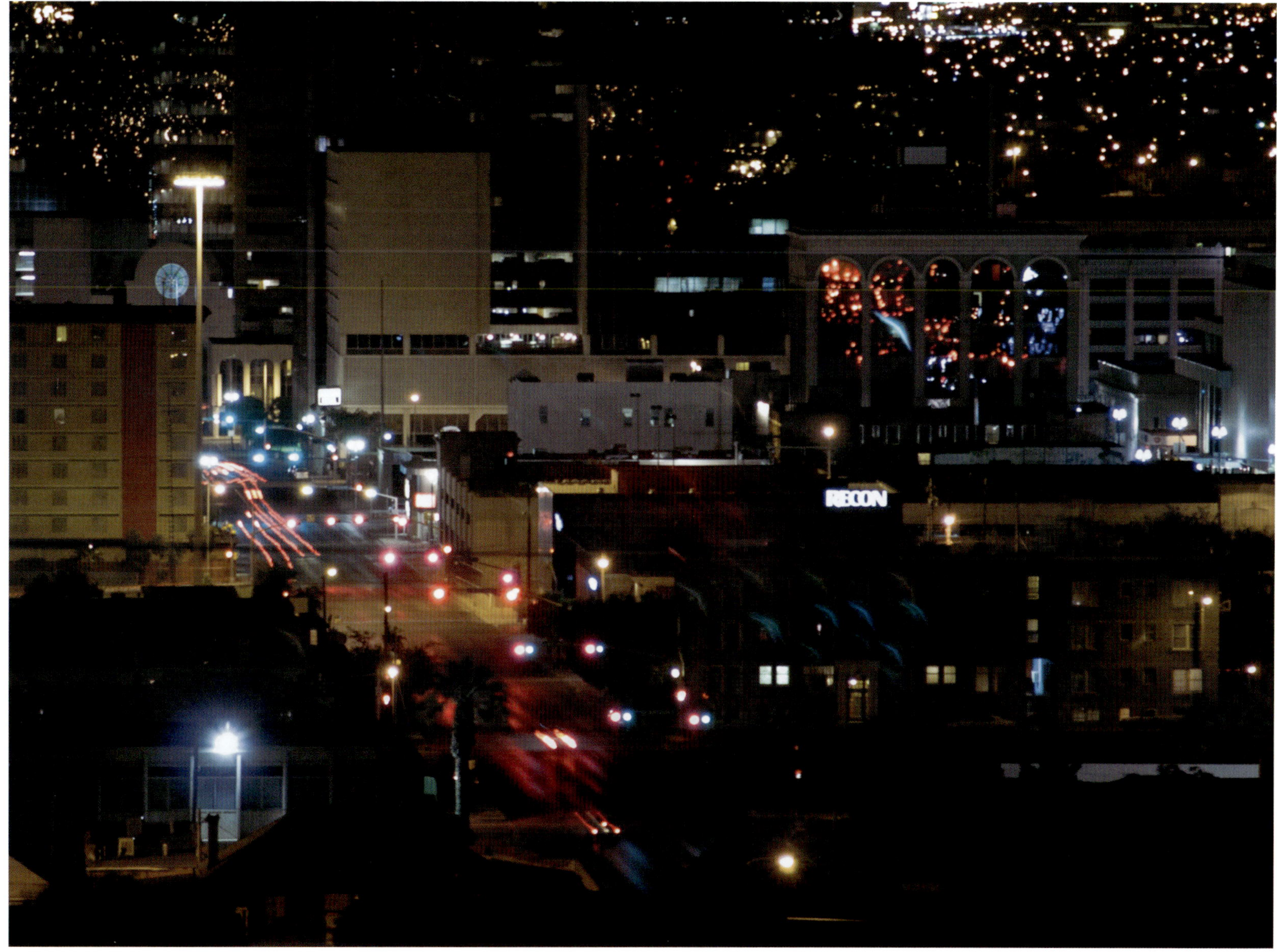

Downtown Reflections.
Perched above downtown El Paso on Rim Road one can catch the glowing lights of the city and watch the city come to life.

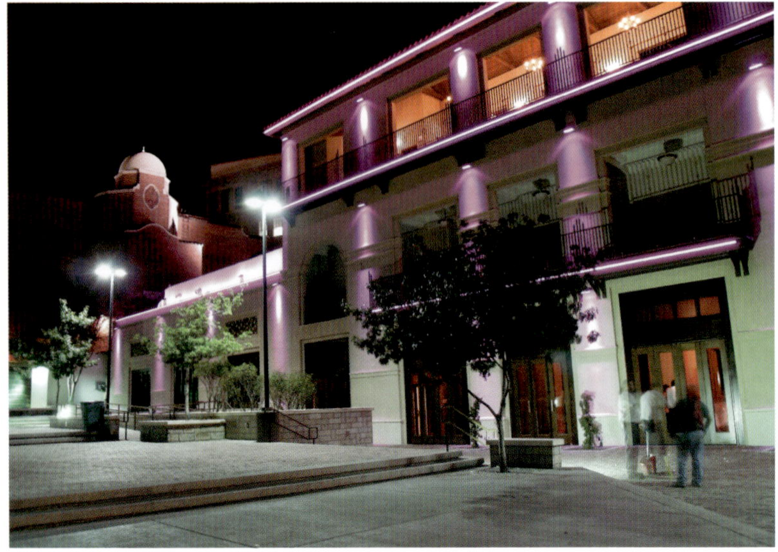

Plaza Theatre Annex.

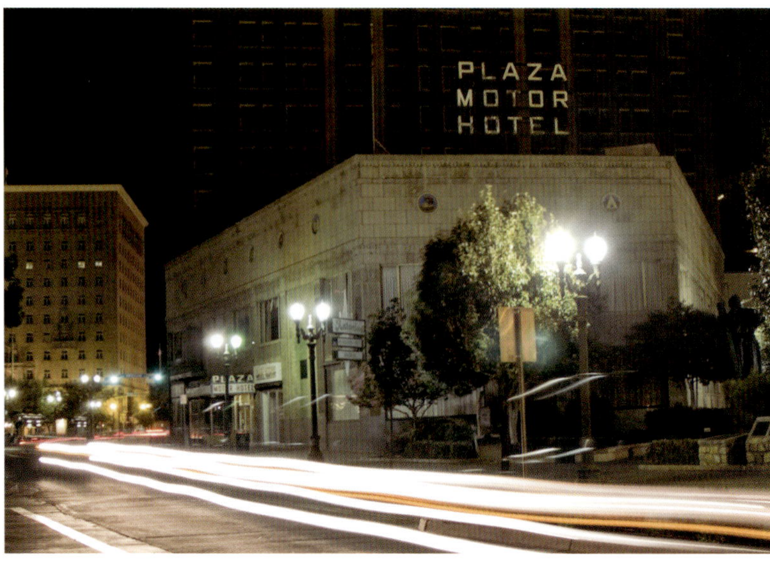

The Horseshoe. Downtown.

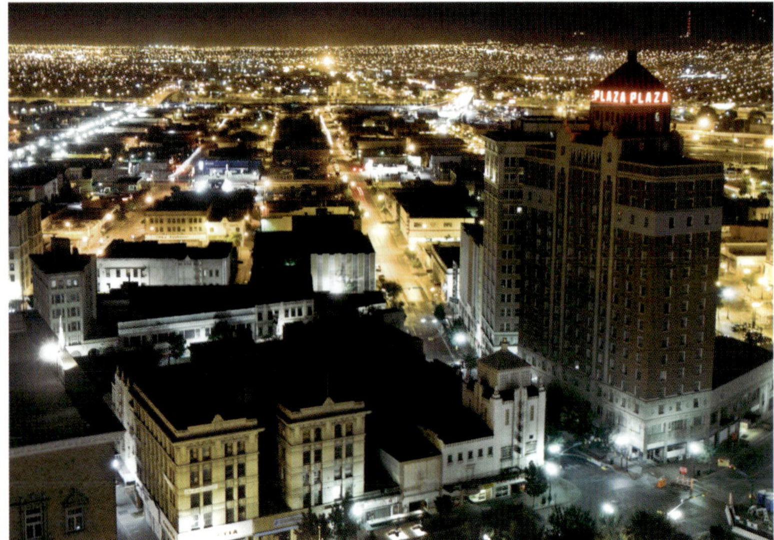

South El Paso and Juárez, Mexico.

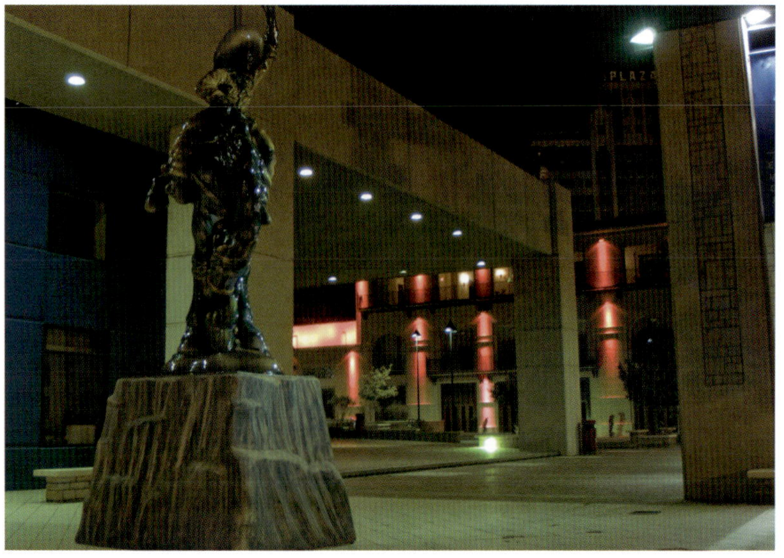

One Arts Festival Plaza.

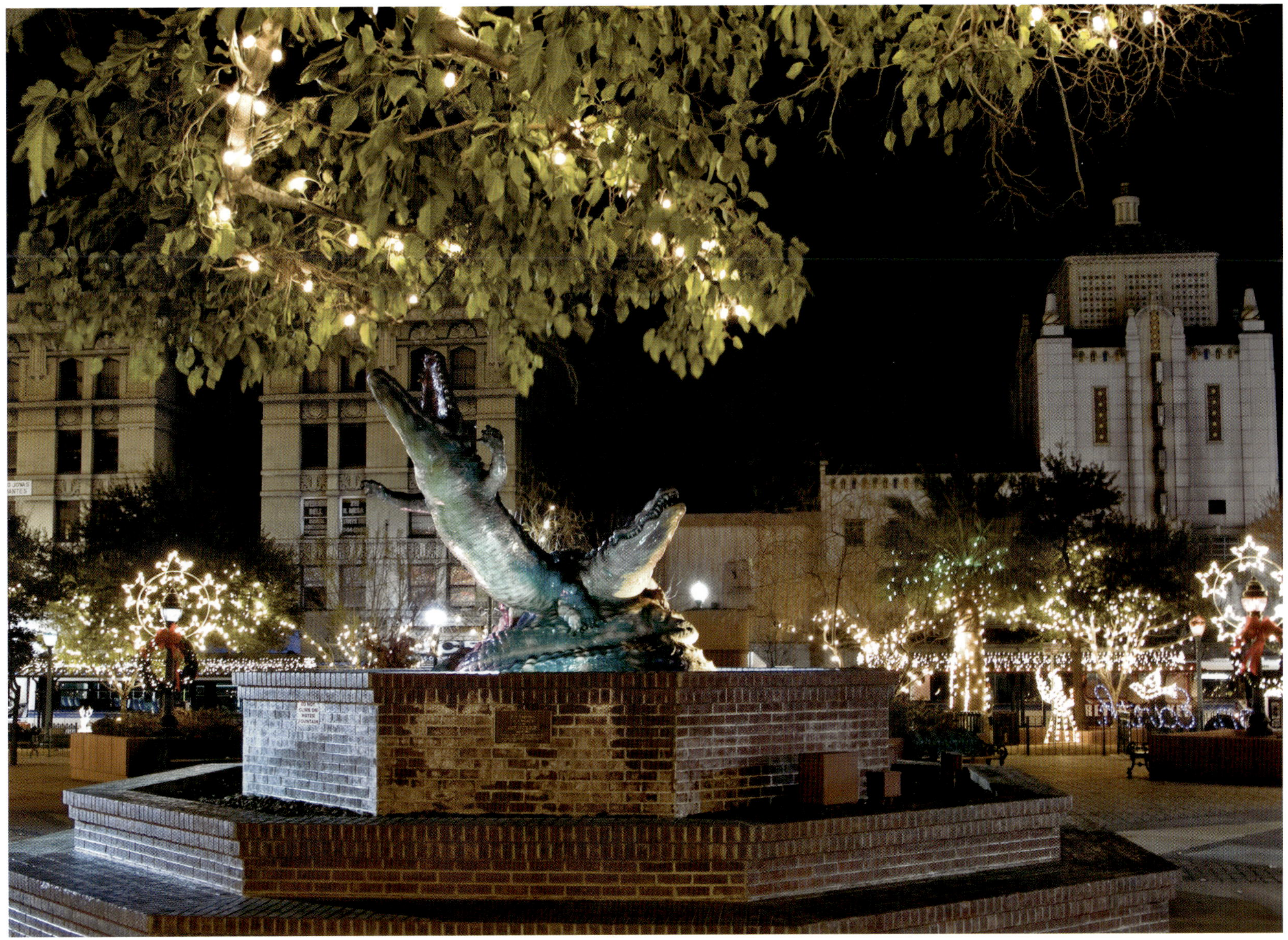

San Jacinto Plaza.
Many people still fondly refer to the plaza as "La Plaza de los Lagartos." Today, a fiberglass sculpture by nationally acclaimed local artist Luis Jimenez honors the original live alligators.

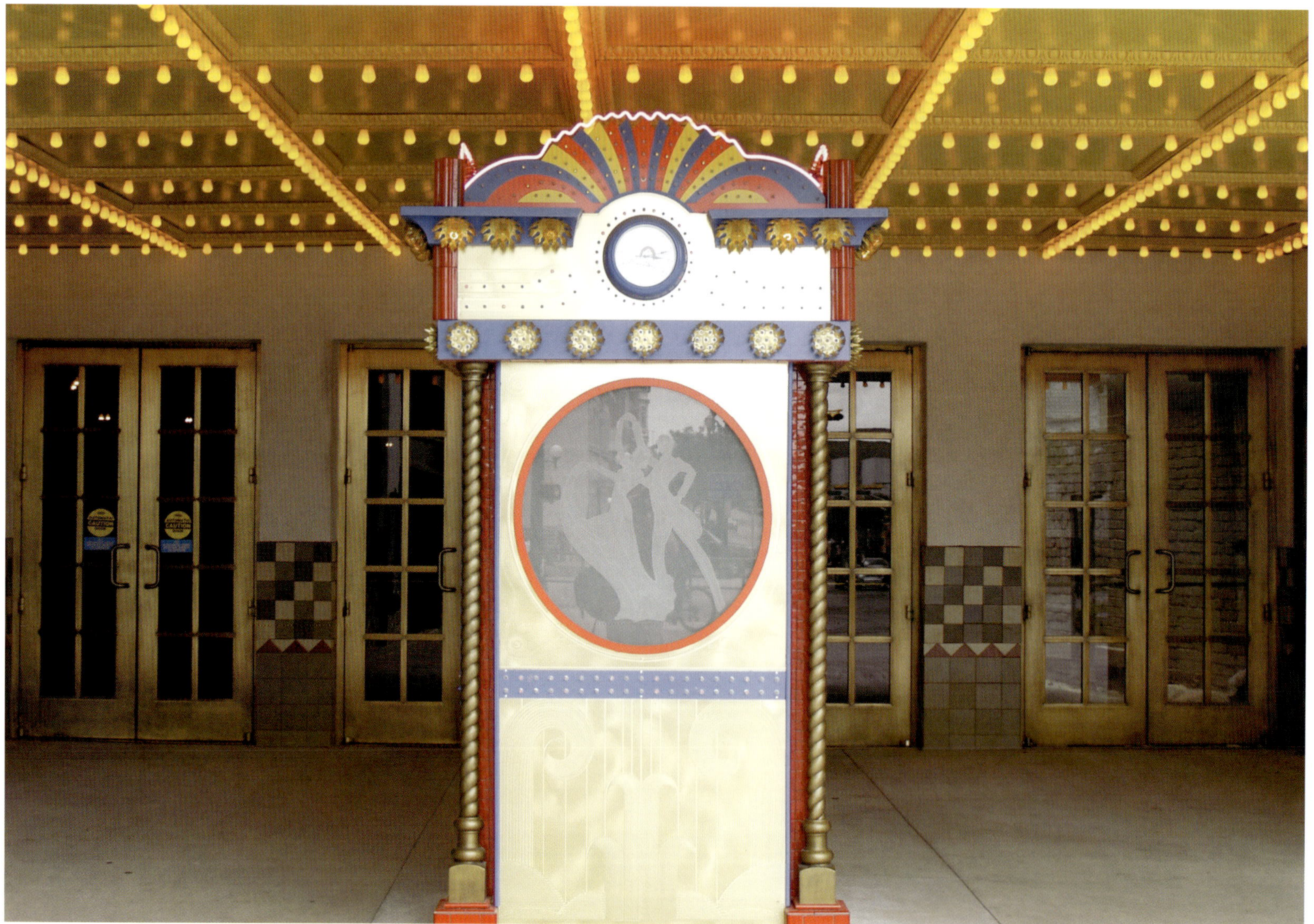

Showtime at the Plaza.
At the center of a growing El Paso was the Plaza Theatre, which opened September 12, 1930, to a capacity crowd of 2,410. It was advertised as the largest theater of its kind between Dallas and Los Angeles. Designed as a modern film house with the flexibility of presenting stage shows, the Plaza eventually hosted popular traveling shows and movies, becoming a fixture in the lives of theater-goers for generations to come.

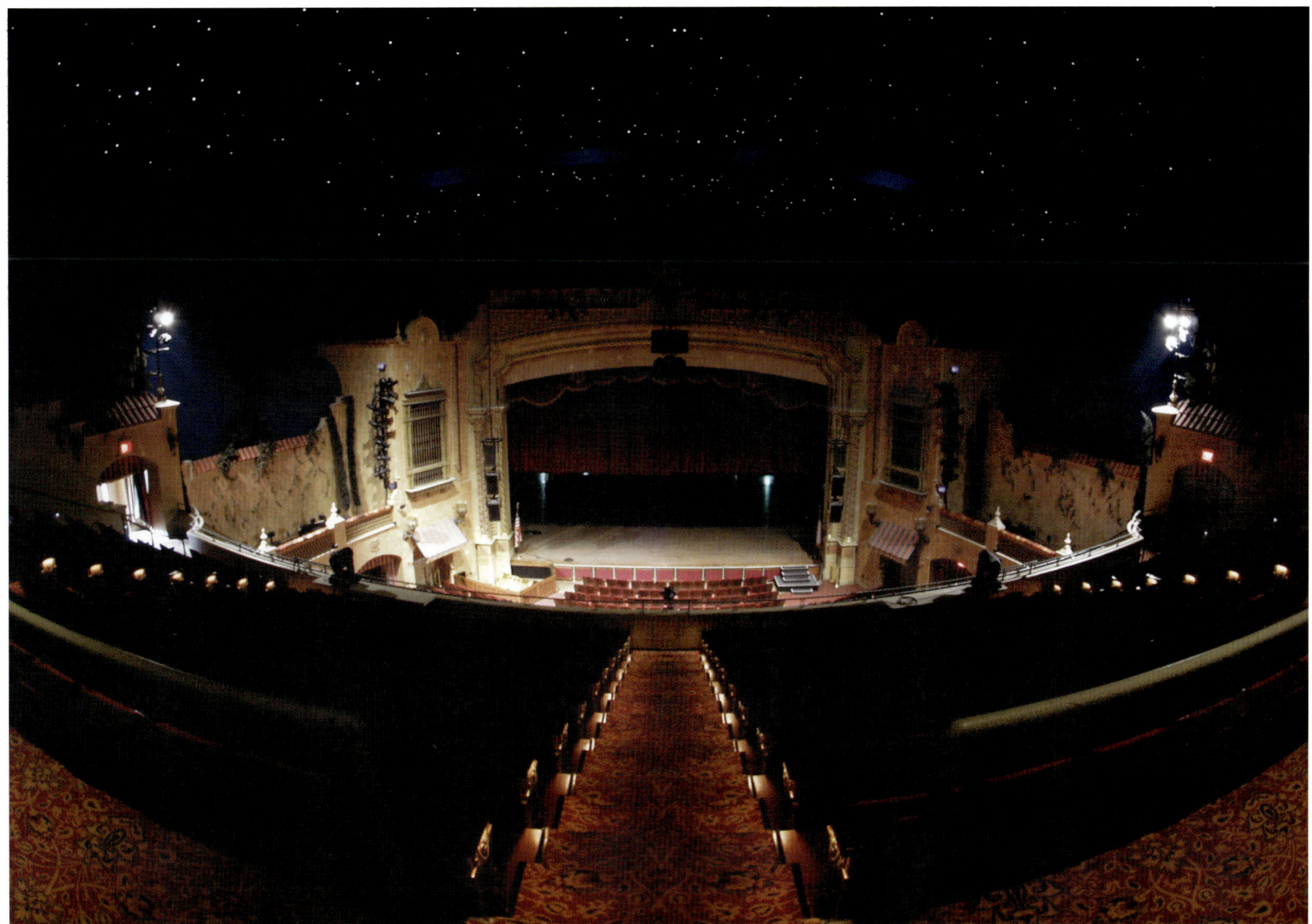

Plaza Theatre.
Like many historical structures, the Plaza Theatre had lost some of its original splendor. Furnishings and art had been removed and the façade had been altered, yet the interior structure appears as it has for close to seventy years. On July 30, 2002, the City of El Paso formally approved a public/private partnership with the El Paso Community Foundation to restore the Plaza Theatre to its original splendor and it is again El Paso's showplace of the Southwest.

My El Paso is pointing up and beyond.
It dares you to fly.

— SUZIE AZAR, PILOT AND EL PASO'S FIRST FEMALE MAYOR

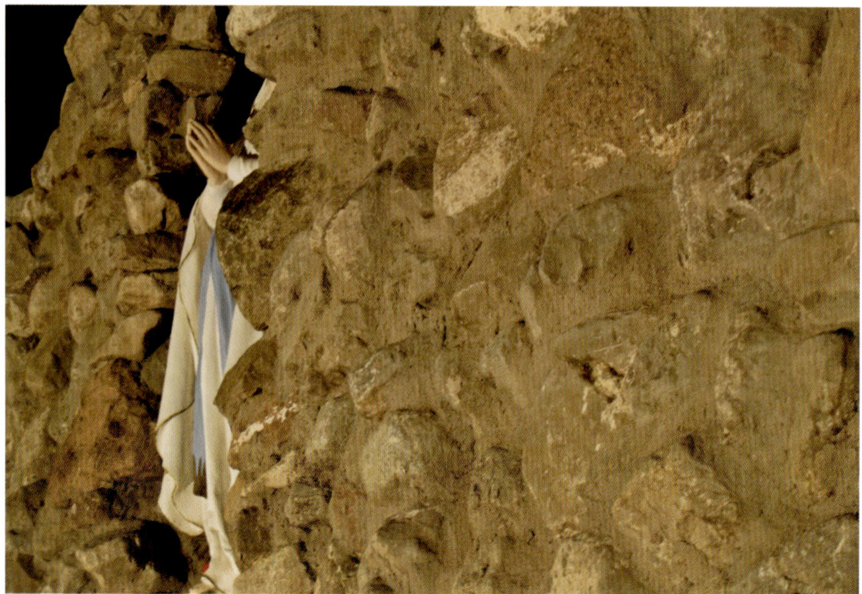

San Elizario Mission.

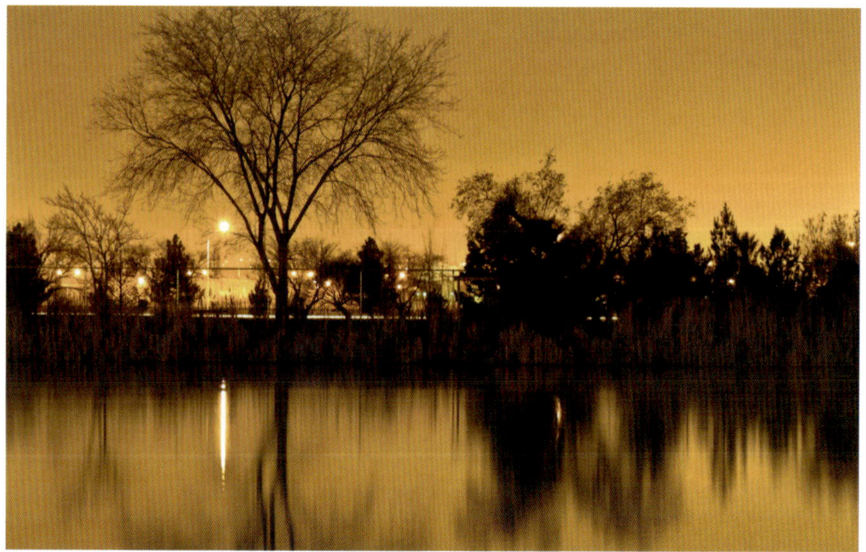

Ascarate Lake at dusk.

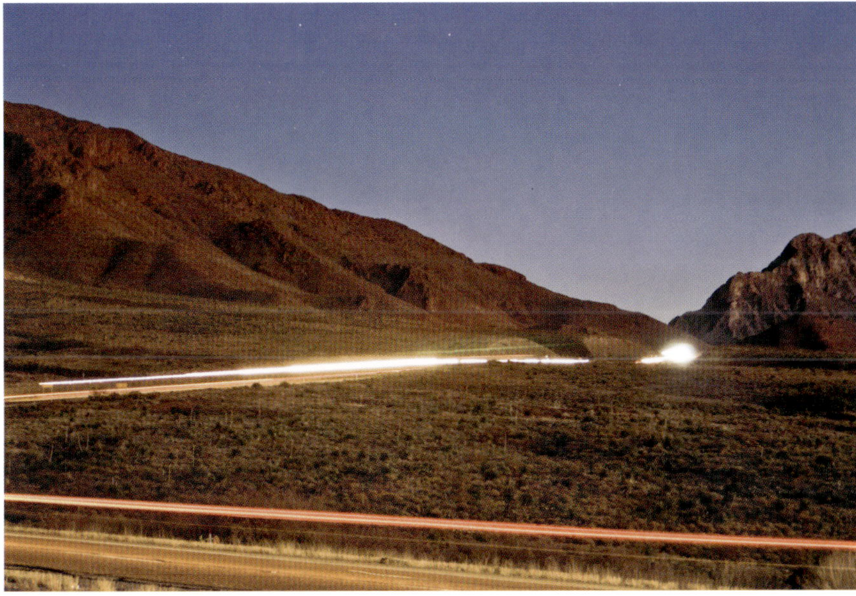

Transmountain at the Blue Hour.

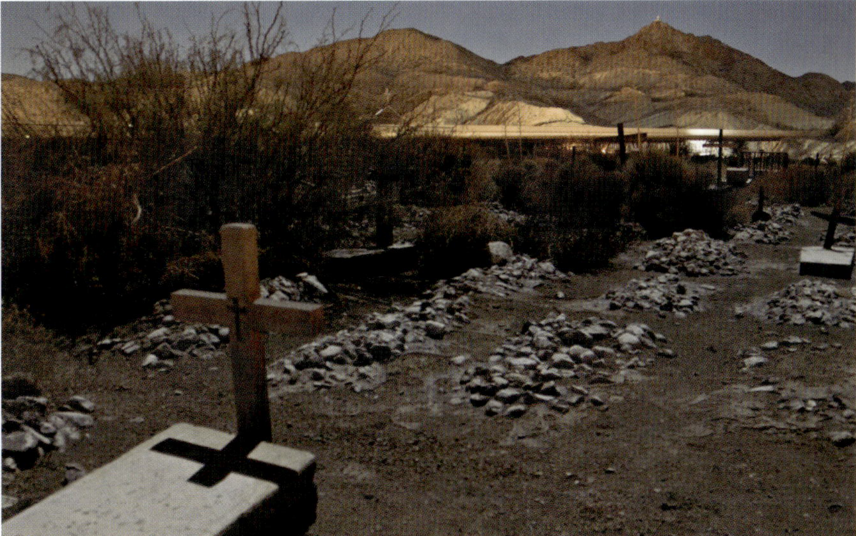

Smelter Cemetery under the full moon.

My El Paso is the foundation of our inspired past, our exciting present and our promising future. My El Paso is the origin of my roots and my proud heritage. And, it is the legacy of my family's hopes and my grandchildren's dreams.

—THE HONORABLE SILVESTRE REYES,
UNITED STATES HOUSE OF REPRESENTATIVES,
DISTRICT 16

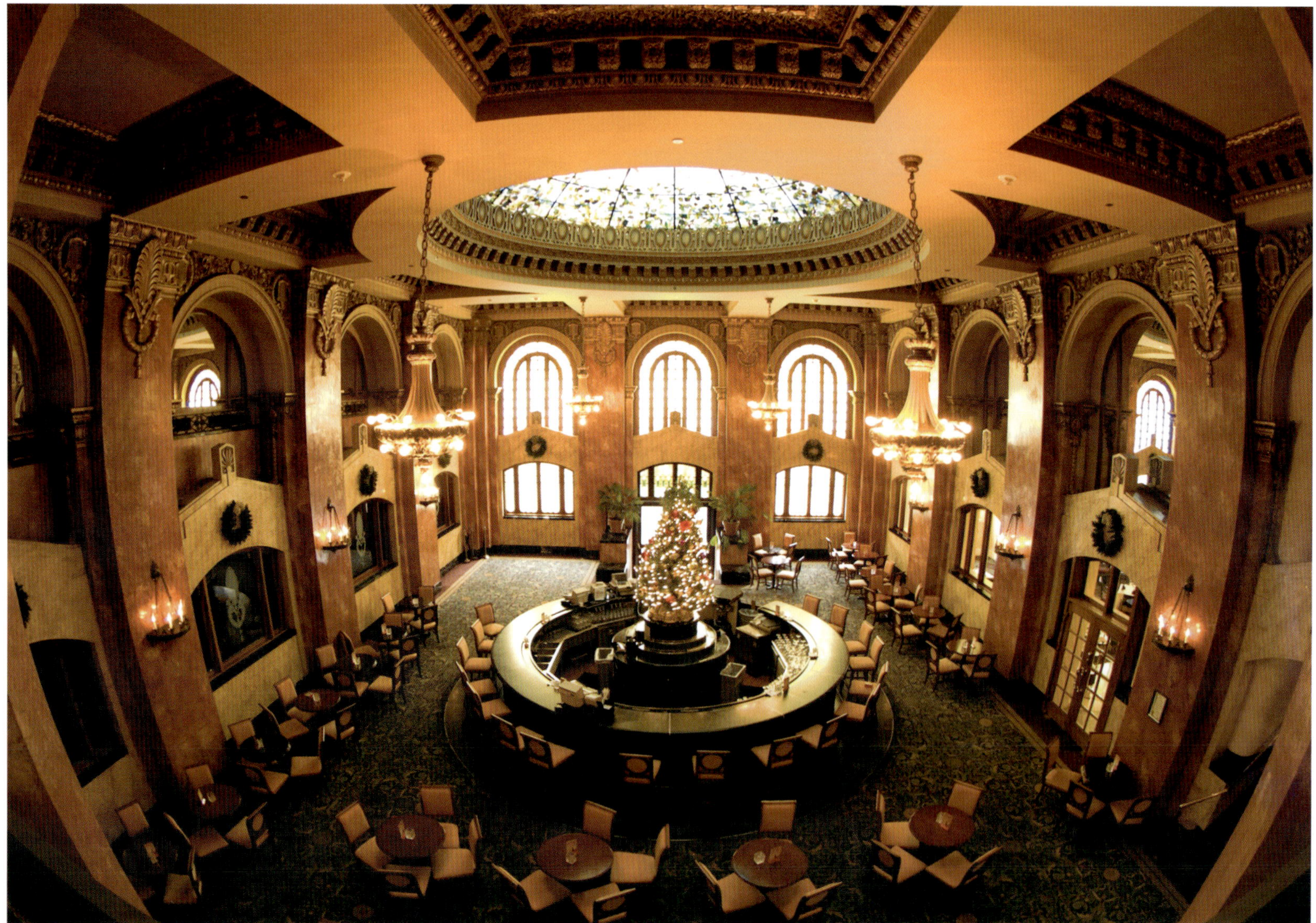

Camino Real Hotel.
The Paso del Norte Hotel, opened in 1912, is now known to El Pasoans as the Camino Real Hotel. Owner Zach White traveled to San Francisco to inspect buildings that had survived the 1906 earthquake so that similar features could be used. The hotel also makes use of fireproof gypsum from New Mexico for the interior partitions. The original nine floors were capped with a tenth floor ballroom in 1922, all designed by Henry C. Trost.

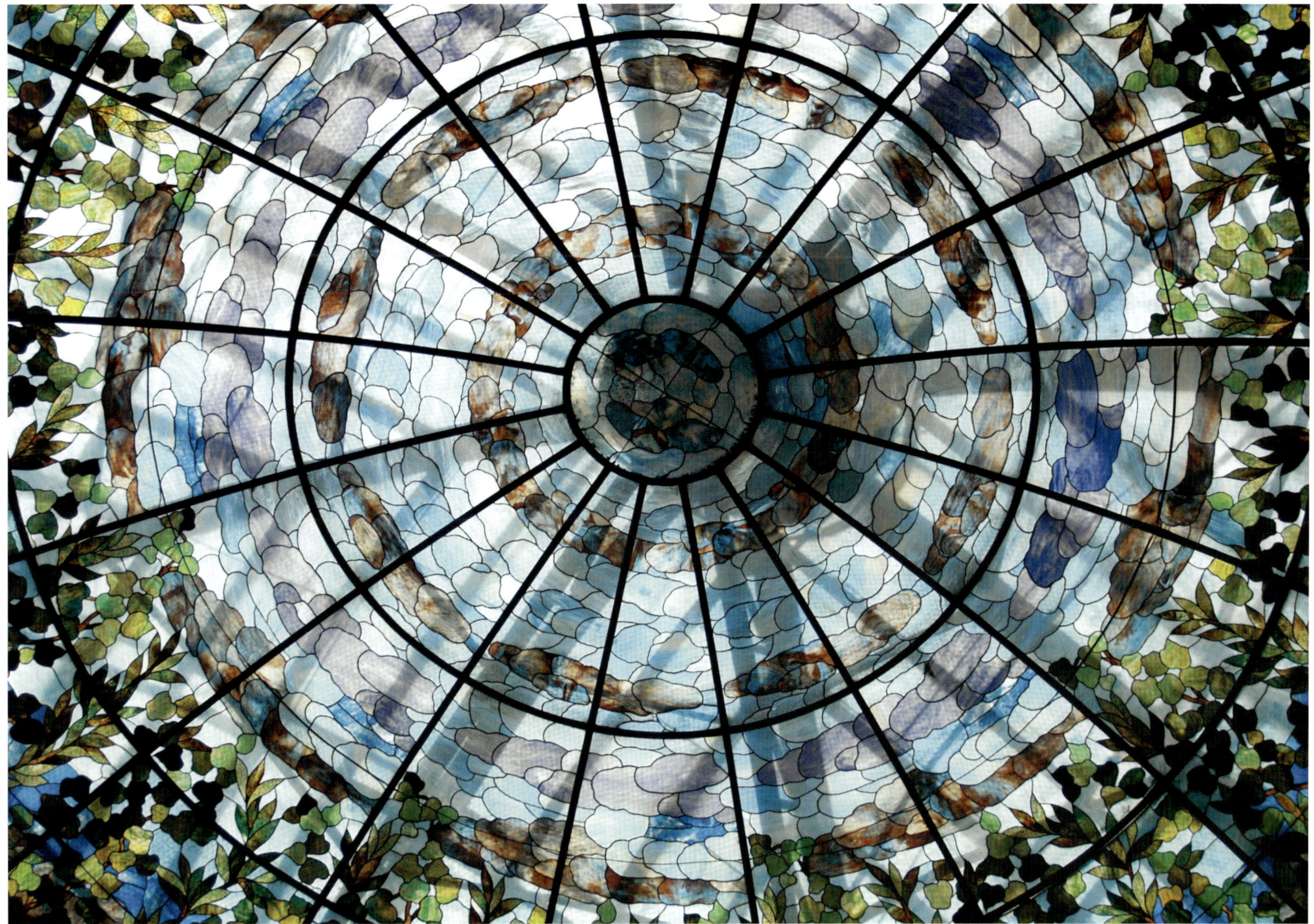

Tiffany Dome, Camino Real Hotel.
The world famous Dome Bar provides the perfect ambiance for an unforgettable evening. One can enjoy a cocktail under the breathtaking Tiffany stained class dome, which is twenty-five feet in diameter and is suspended by wires.

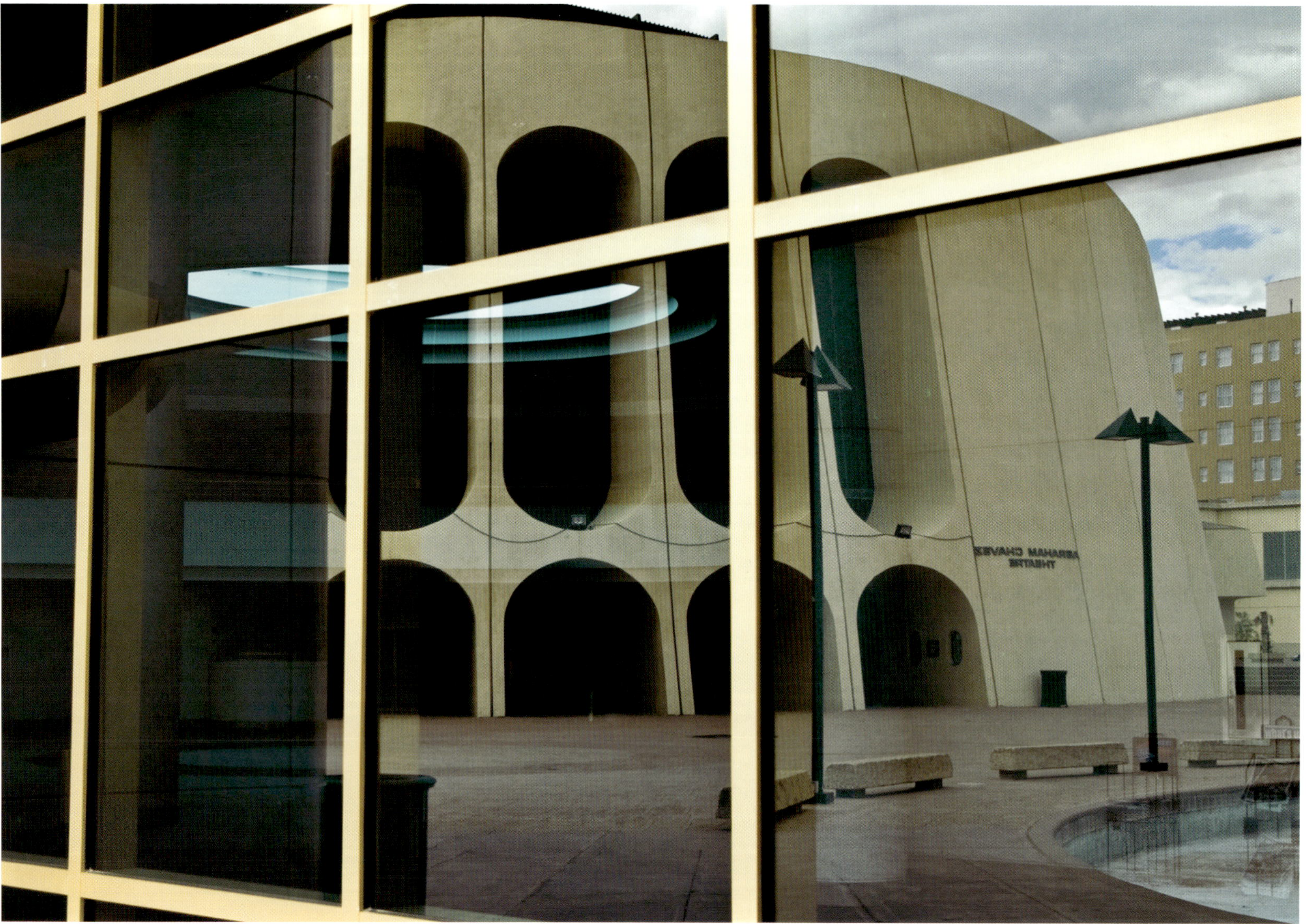

Abraham Chavez Theatre.
Located adjacent to the El Paso Convention & Performing Arts Center, the Abraham Chavez Theater welcomes patrons with a three-story high glass windowed entry and unique sombrero-shaped architecture making it a distinct feature on El Paso's southwestern landscape.

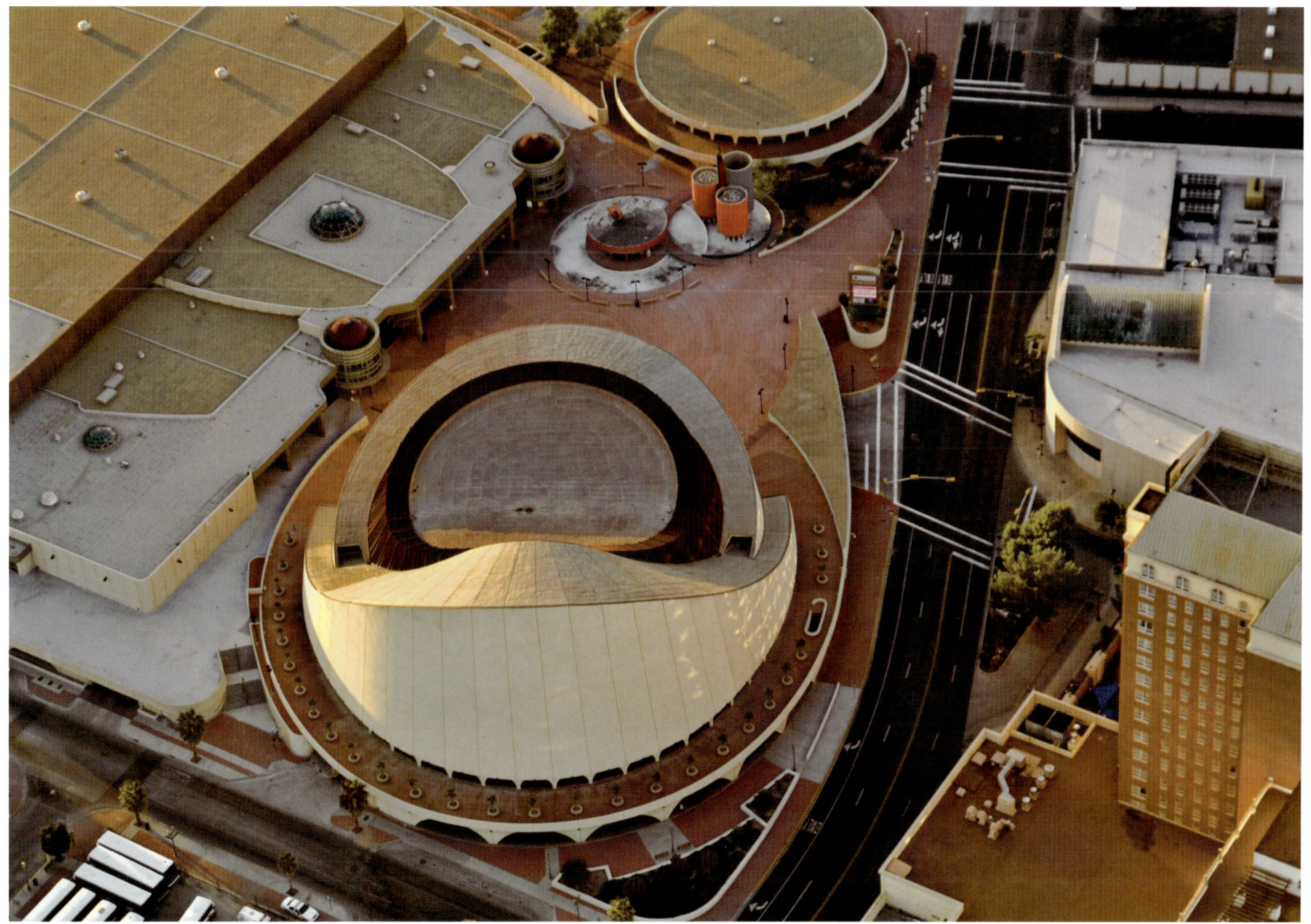

Abraham Chavez Theatre and Civic Center Plaza.
Abraham Chavez Theatre, known simply as Chavez Theatre, is a 2,500-seat concert hall located in El Paso, Texas. It is adjacent to Williams Convention Center. Its exterior resembles a sombrero and features a three-story glass main entrance.

El Paso City Hall.
As a key part of the City's pursuit to become a high-performing, customer focused organization, the City day to day embraces the core values of El Paso – Excellence, Integrity, Respect, and Accountability.

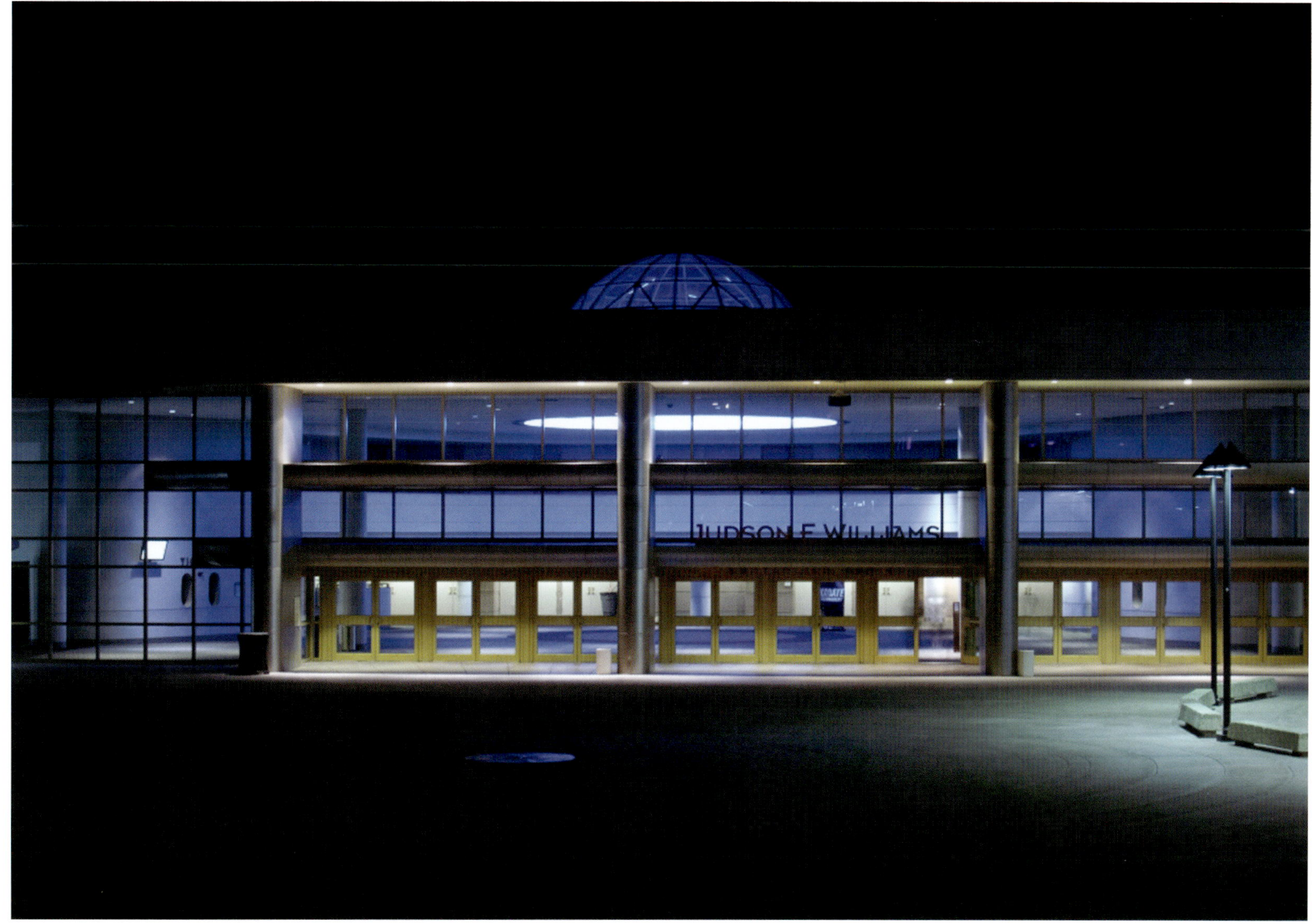

Judson F. Williams Convention Center. Downtown El Paso.
The beautiful Judson F. Williams Convention Center was newly remodeled and expanded in May, 2002. This addition to downtown center offers state-of-the-art meeting rooms and high quality services for a host of conventions and community activities held in El Paso each year.

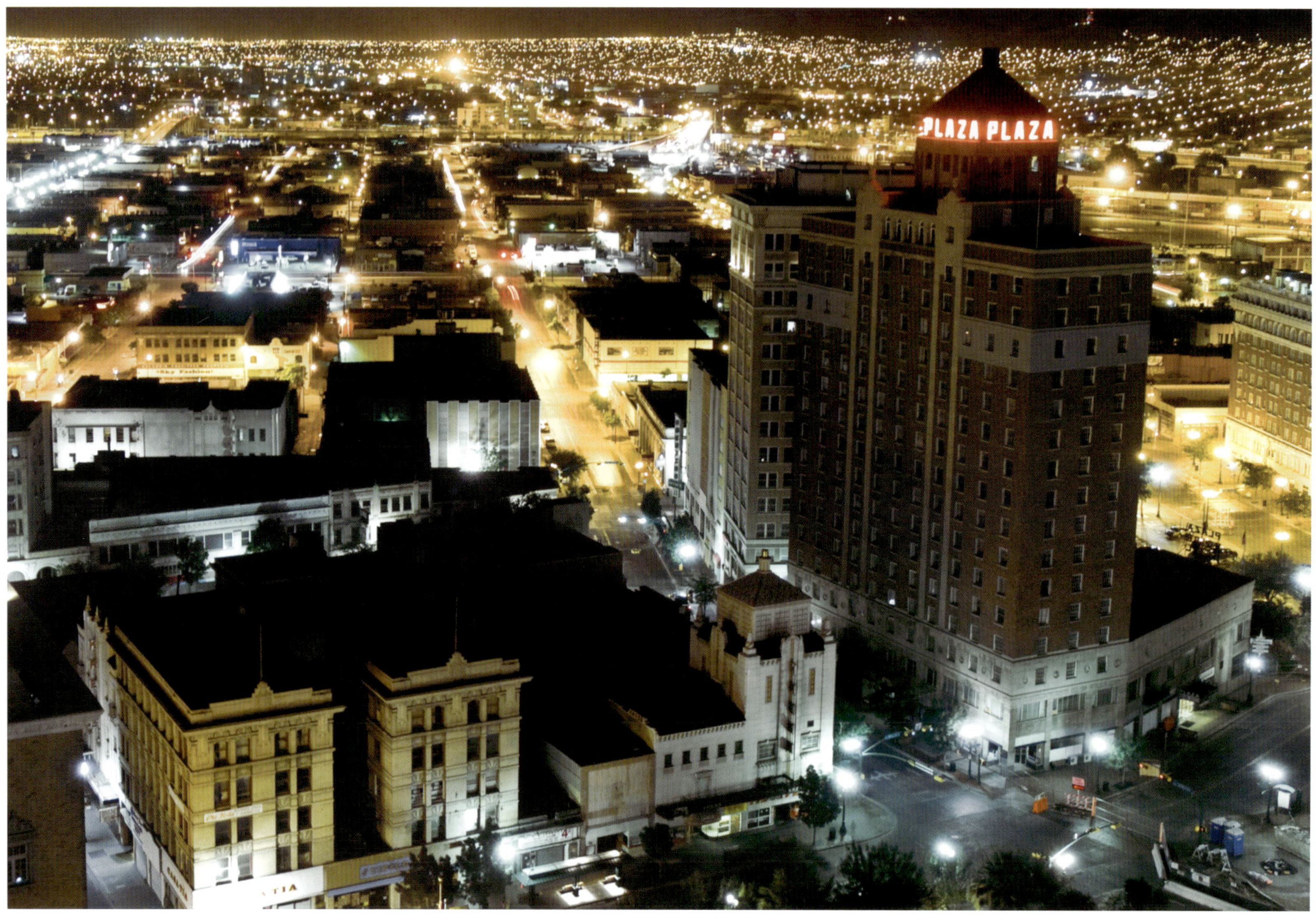

The Core of Downtown El Paso.
The Mexican Revolution (1910-1920) began in 1910 and Ciudad Juárez was the focus of intense fighting. Occasionally, stray shots killed civilians on the El Paso side. El Paso became a center of intrigue as various exiled leaders, including Victoriano Huerta and Pancho Villa, were seen in the city. Many El Pasoans witnessed the revolution first hand atop Hotel del Norte in downtown El Paso.

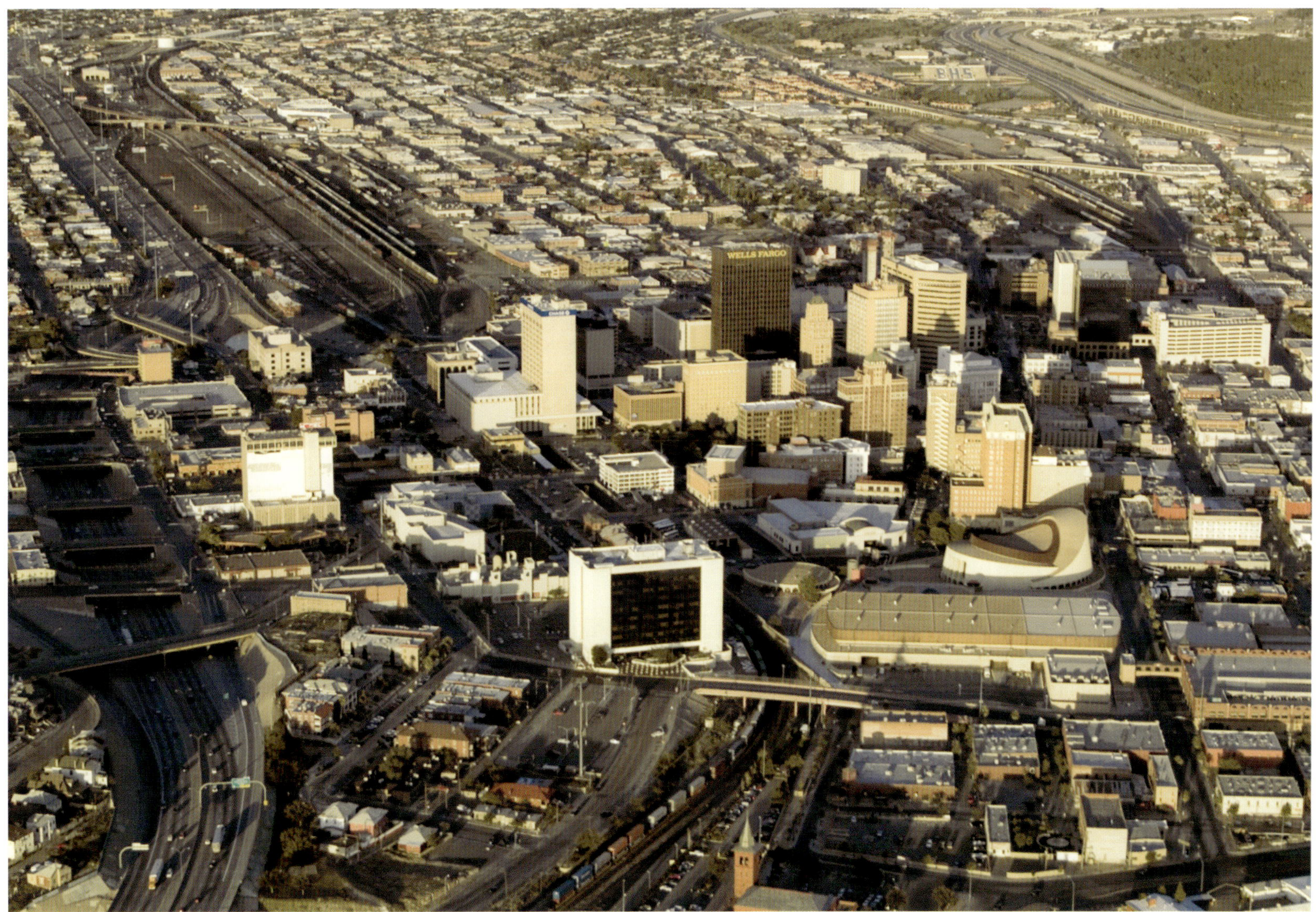

El Paso Downtown.
From the gun fighting days on the streets in the late 1800s to today's modern business dealings this area has always been the heart of El Paso.

My El Paso is where I live, where I love, where I'm happy.

— NICHOLE AYOUB HUGHES,
TELEVISION NEWS ANCHOR

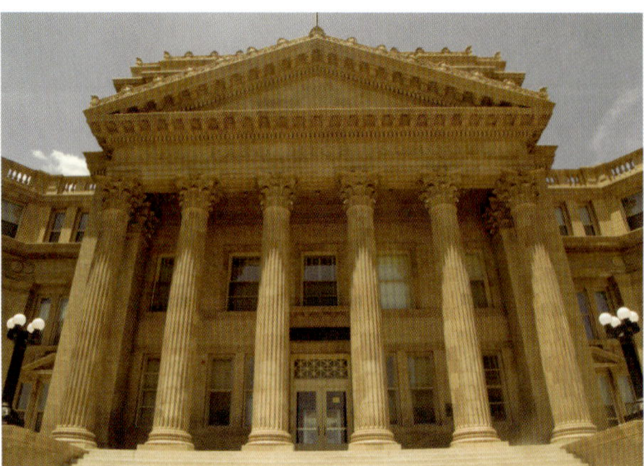

El Paso High School.
El Paso High School is the oldest operating high school in El Paso. "The Lady on the Hill" sits on a mountainside at the foot of the Franklin Mountains overlooking the central portion of the city and its boundary with Ciudad Juarez, Mexico. The school stands out prominently on the horizon commanding a view of the city. Trost & Trost, Architects.

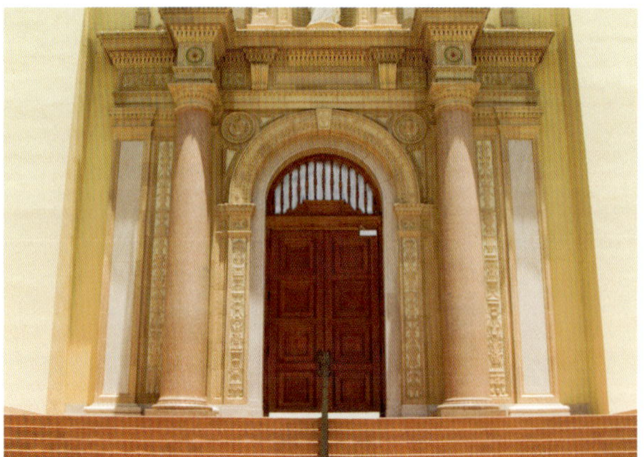

Loretto Academy.
Loretto Academy is a prime example of the Mission Revival Style, which was an architectural movement that began in the late 19th century and drew inspiration from the early Spanish missions in California. Trost & Trost, Architects.

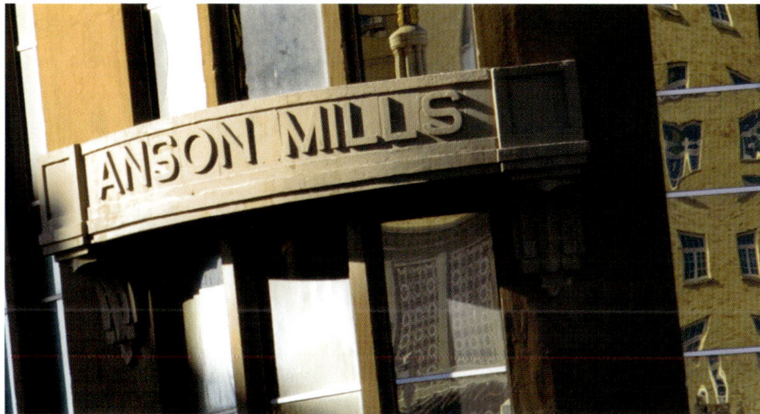

Anson Mills Building.
Built in 1910-1911, the building was only the second concrete-frame skyscraper in the United States and one of the largest all-concrete buildings. At 145 feet, the twelve-story Mills Building was the tallest building in El Paso when completed. Trost & Trost, Architects.

My El Paso is an undiscovered treasure of art and artists.

— DONALD BEENE, PRESIDENT,
EL PASO ART ASSOCIATION

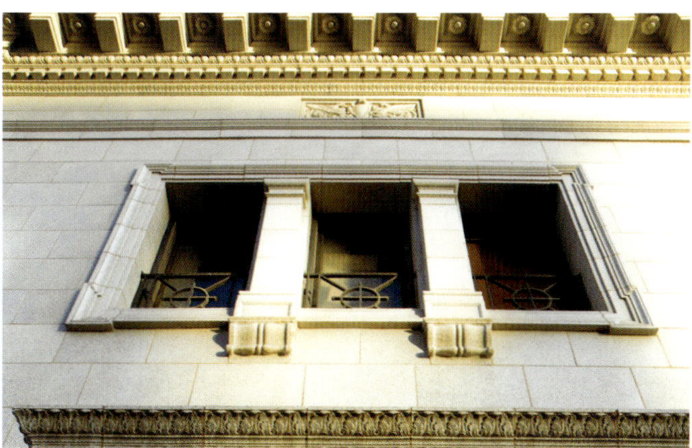

State National Bank.
Built in 1922 by Trost & Trost Architects & Engineers, an architecture firm based in El Paso, Texas from 1903–1933. Trost & Trost was responsible for many of the historic buildings in El Paso that still stand today. Many of the buildings designed by Trost & Trost display an influence from the Chicago school of architecture, especially the work of Louis Sullivan. Henry Trost had lived in Chicago between 1888 and 1896 and worked as a draftsman for the firm of Adler & Sullivan during that period.

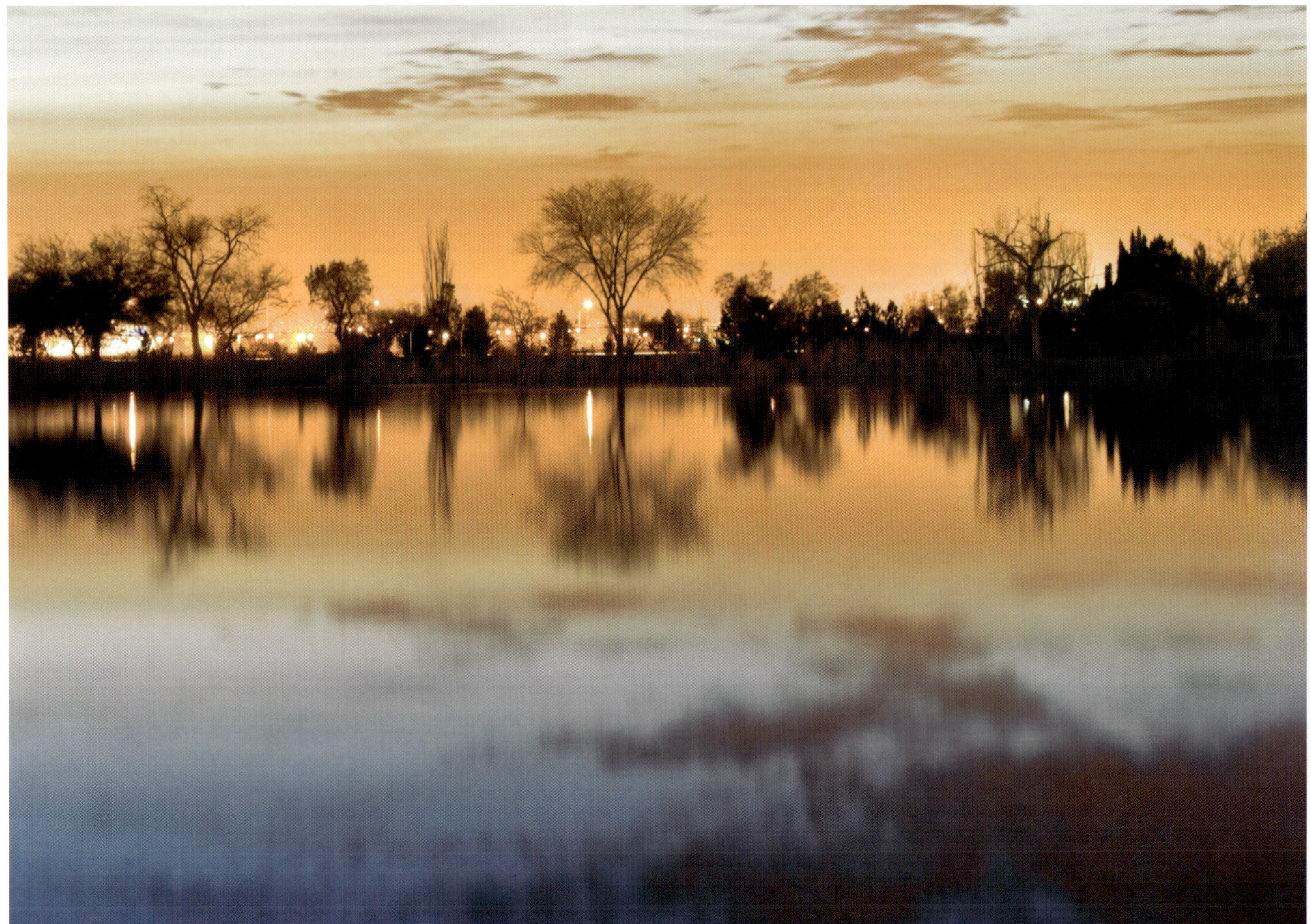

Dusk at Ascarate.
Ascarate Park is the largest public use recreational park in El Paso County, at 448 total acres with forty-eight acres of water surface. Two-hundred-eighty acres of the park are utilized as a public golf course and the rest (152 acres) is dedicated to sports, picnicking, and other recreational activities.

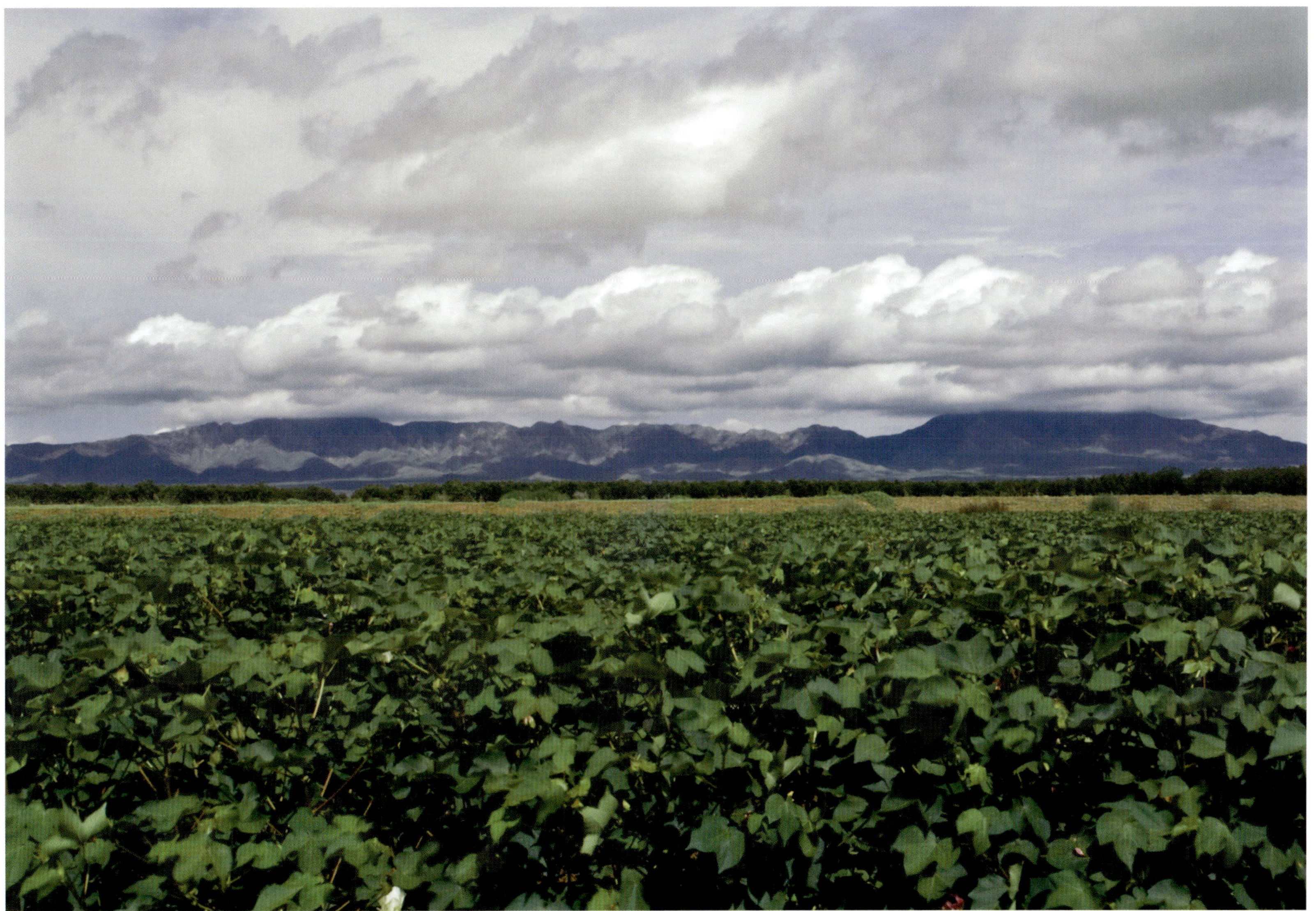

Upper Valley cotton fields and the Franklin Mountains.
The valley of the Rio Grande winds like a green snake through the brown desert of El Paso, forming the enormous border between the State of Texas and Mexico. By providing water, cover, comfort, and sustenance in an otherwise arid land, this green corridor has been a lifeline for animals for eons and for humans for a few thousand years.

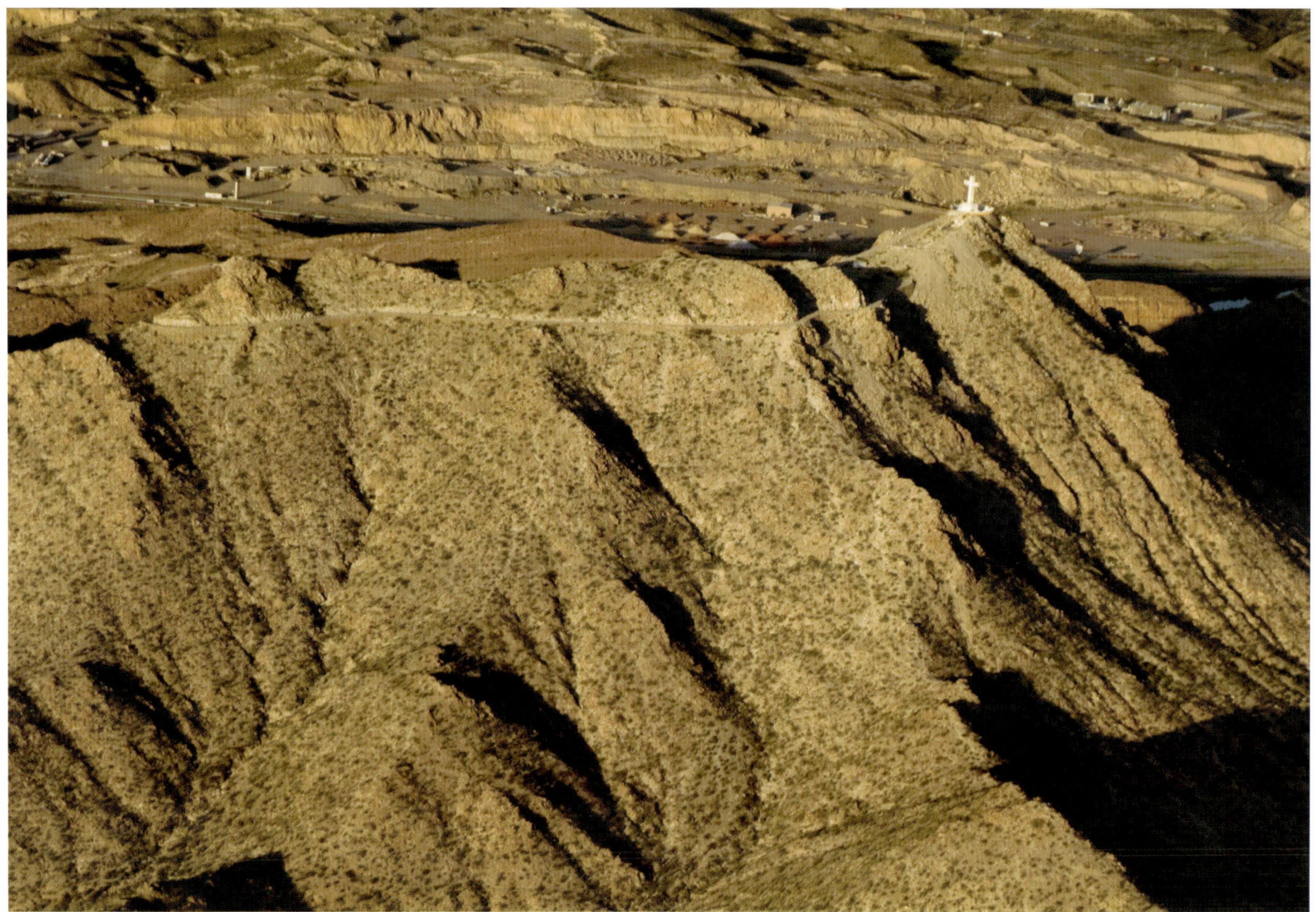

Mount Cristo Rey.
Urbici José Soler y Manonelles (1890-1953) was born in Ferran, Lleida, Spain, and died in Anapra, New Mexico, at the foot of Mount Cristo Rey. Soler is remembered chiefly for a monumental statue of Christ atop Mount Cristo Rey, completed in 1939. The statue was inspired by a papal call for mementoes of the nineteenth centennial of Christ. The project was begun at the behest of Father Lourdes Costa, pastor of the Smeltertown parish, which covered both the New Mexico and the Texas sides of the Rio Grande.

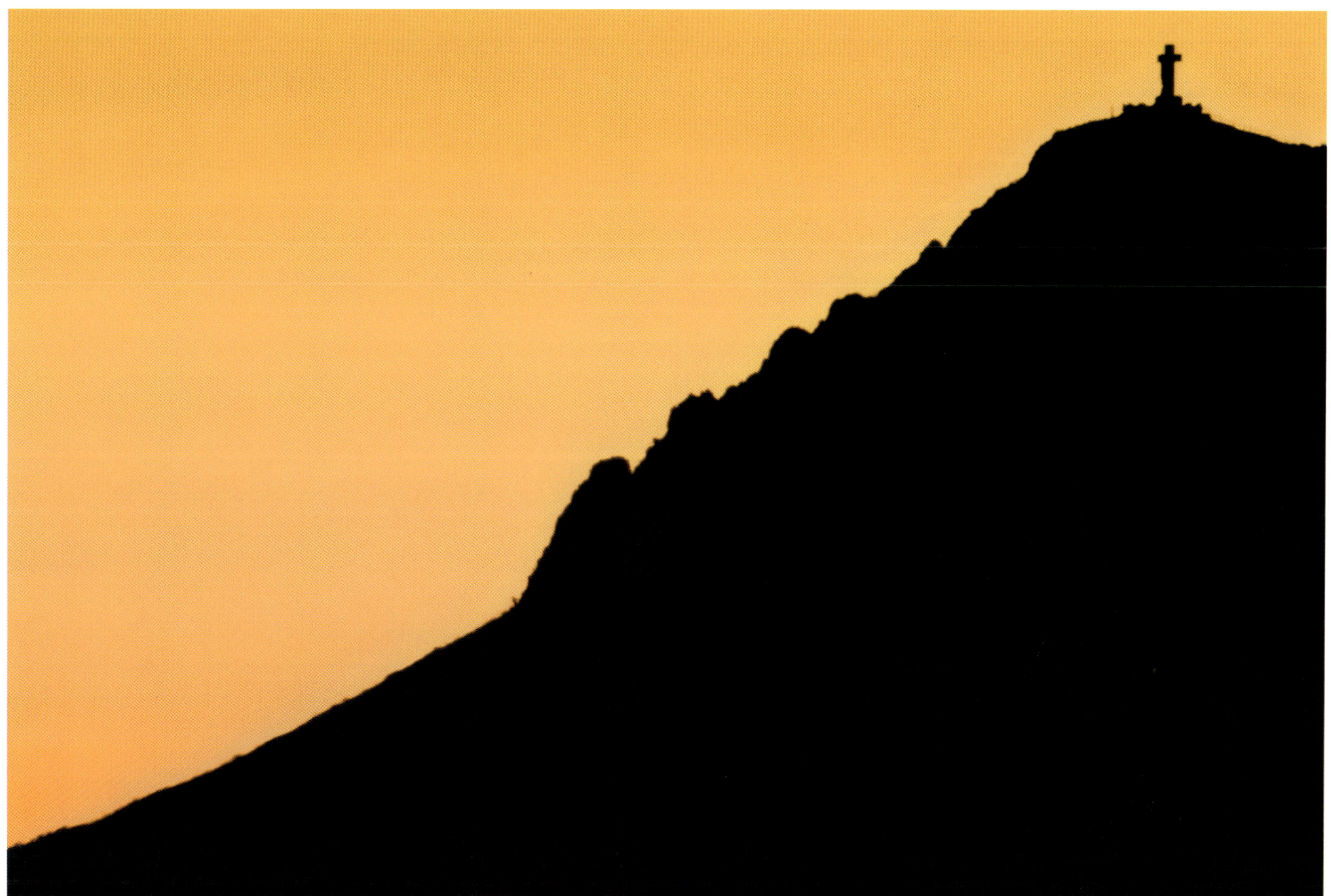

Monumental Statue of Christ.
The statue is 33.5 feet tall on a 9-foot base and is composed of concrete, steel, and Cordovan cream limestone, which was quarried near Austin, Texas. The blocks were chosen by Soler and winched up the mountain. Soler carved it on site with an air chisel. The head of the statue is elongated so that the figure appears of natural proportions when viewed from below. The statue is not technically a crucifix, as the palms of Christ face downward in a gesture of blessing. The statue was completed in 1939 and dedicated in 1940. The diocese ran short of money, but Soler completed the front of *Cristo Rey* with his own funds.

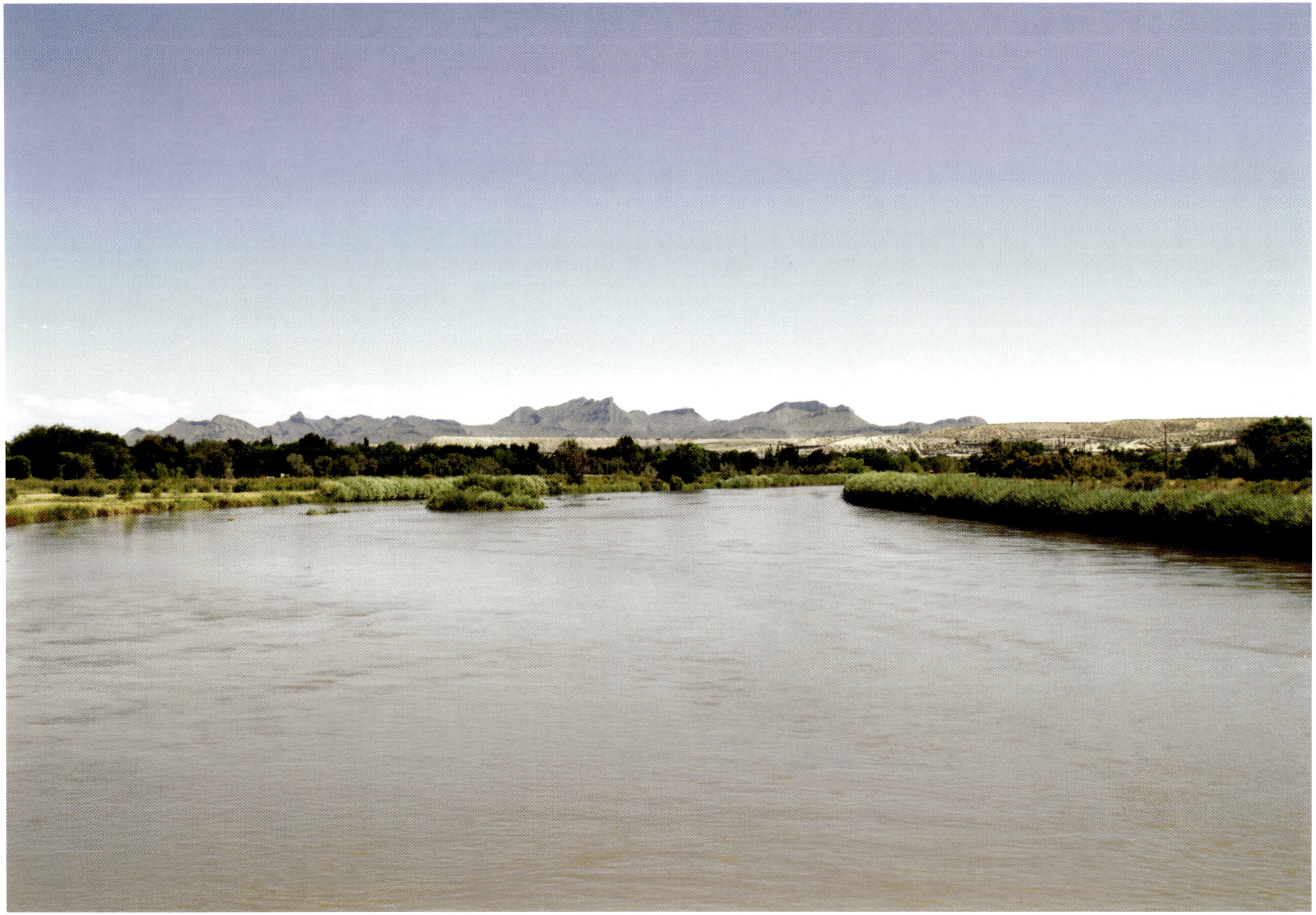

The Mighty Rio.
The Rio Grande River has, since 1848, marked the boundary between Mexico and the United States from the twin cities of El Paso, Texas, and Ciudad Juárez, Chihuahua, to the Gulf of Mexico. *Río Grande* is Spanish for "Big River" and *Río Grande del Norte* means "Great Northern River" (literally "Great River of the North"). In Mexico it is known as *Río Bravo, bravo* meaning fierce.

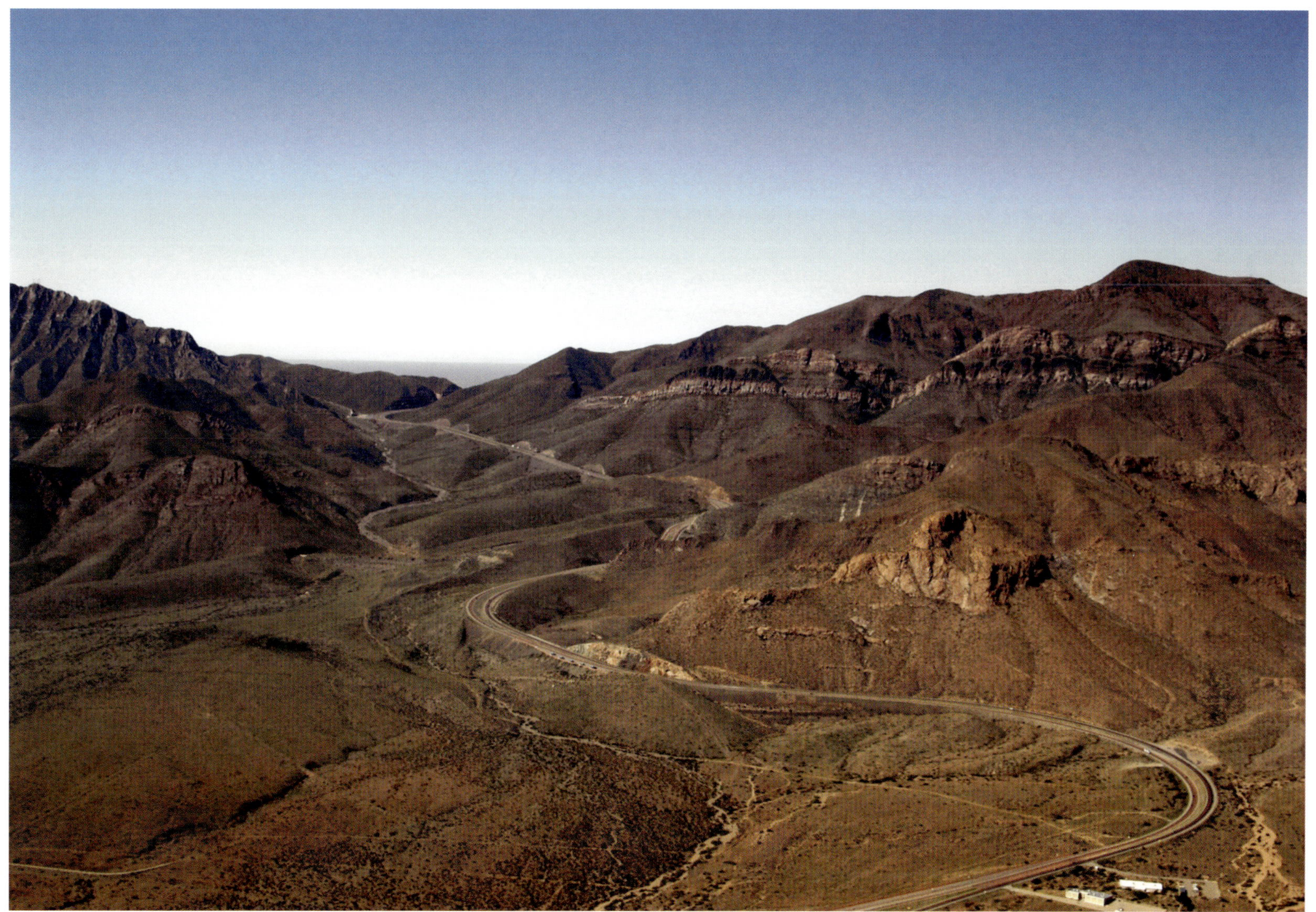

Transmountain Road through the Franklins.
The highest peak is North Franklin Mountain at 7,912 feet or 2,192 meters. Much of the range is part of the Franklin Mountains State Park. The mountains are composed primarily of sedimentary rock with some igneous intrusions. Geologists refer to them as tilted-block fault mountains and in them can be found billion-year-old Precambrian rocks, the oldest in Texas.

Morning Glow.
Full Moon – Moon Set – 5:00 a.m. – Transmountain Road.

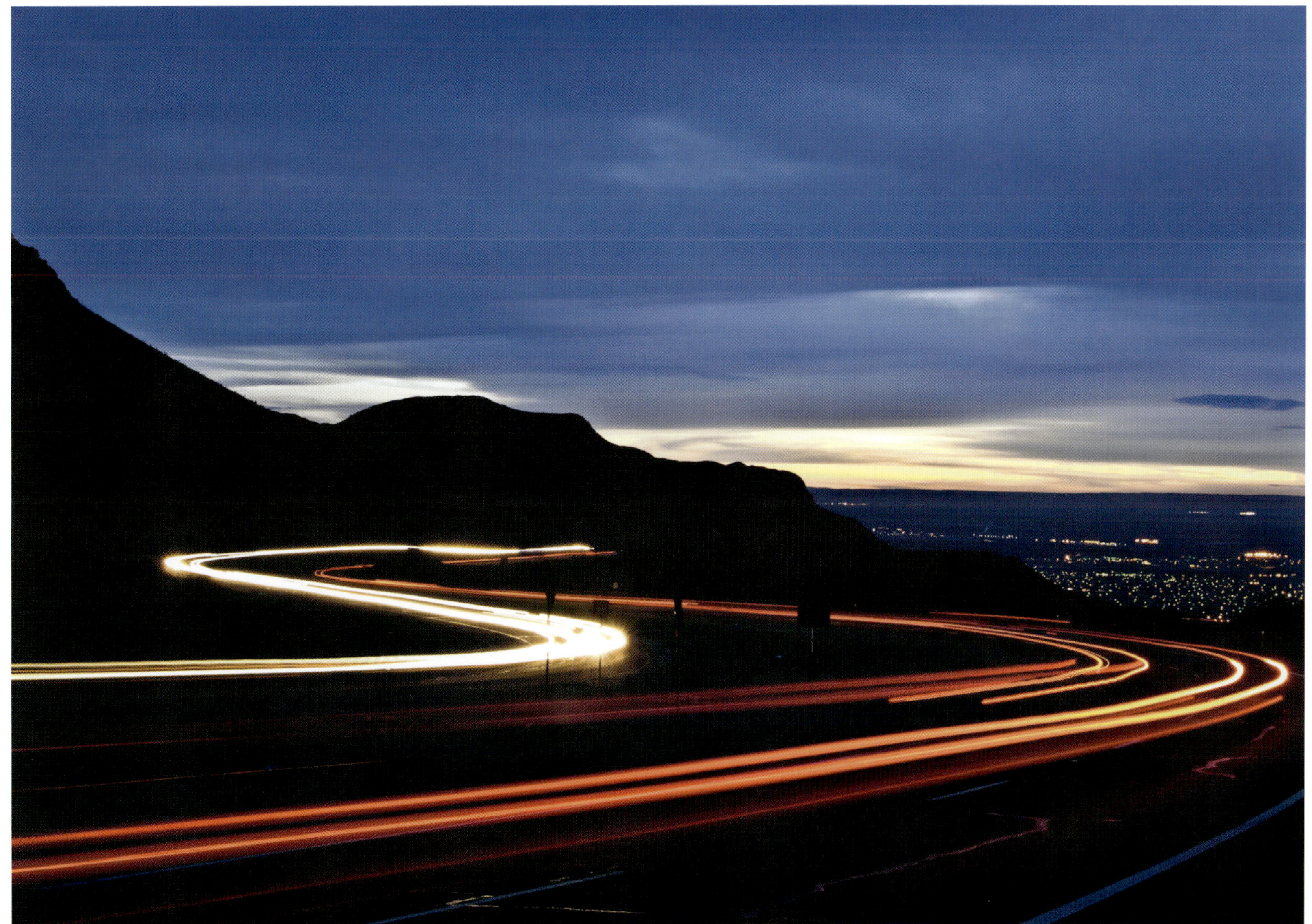

Transmountain Road.
The 24,000-acre Franklin Mountains State Park is the largest urban park in the United States and resides entirely in El Paso, extending from the north and neatly dividing the city into several sections.

My El Paso is constantly evolving. It is brilliant, with blinding sunlight that illuminates the skies. It is chaotic, with an abundant energy that comes from two worlds and two cultures constantly colliding. It is beautiful, with a collection of smiles unique to this corner of the world.

— MARIBEL VILLALVA, EL PASO HOLOCAUST MUSEUM

El Paso Winds.

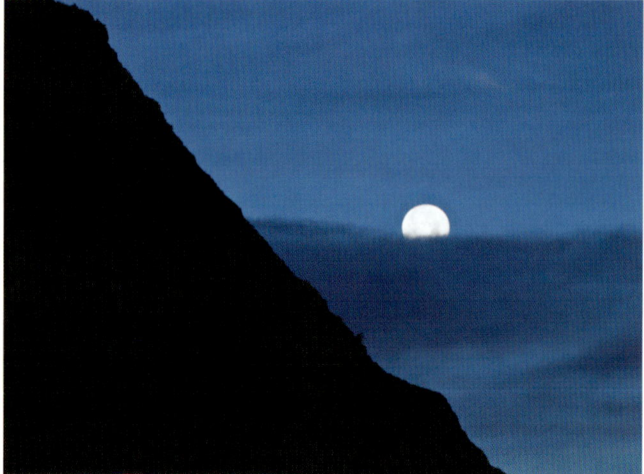

Moon Set.

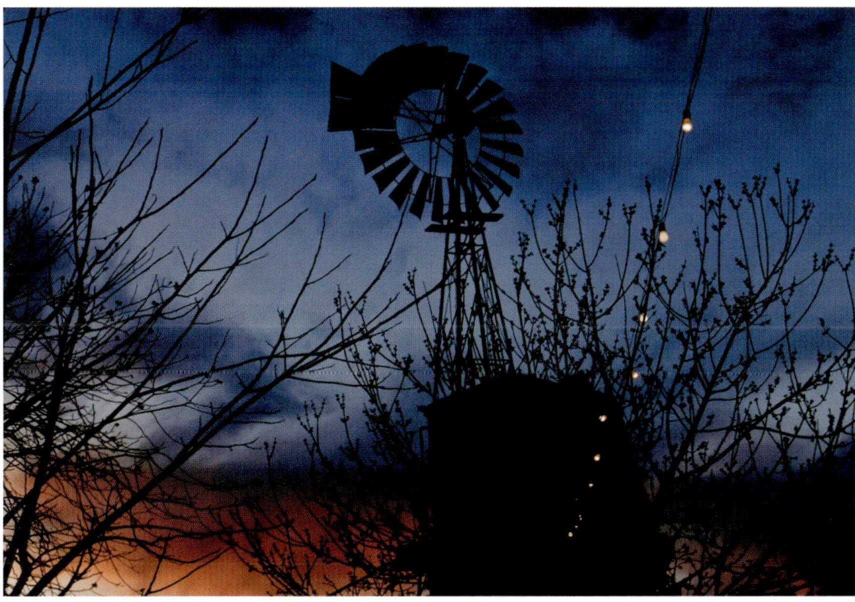

Ardovino's Desert Crossing.

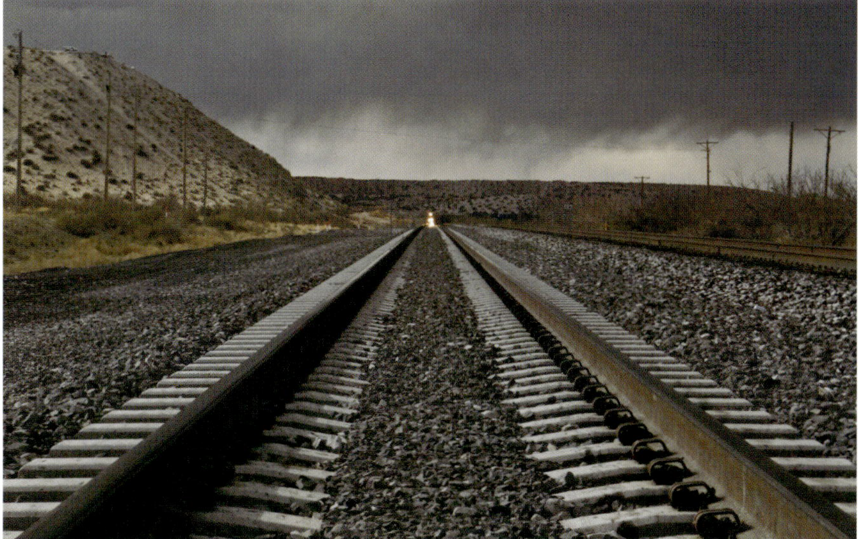

Anapra Rails.

My El Paso is big ideas, a deep breath, and a fast beat. It's the unfinished story in us all.

— MARK PAULDA, PHOTOGRAPHER

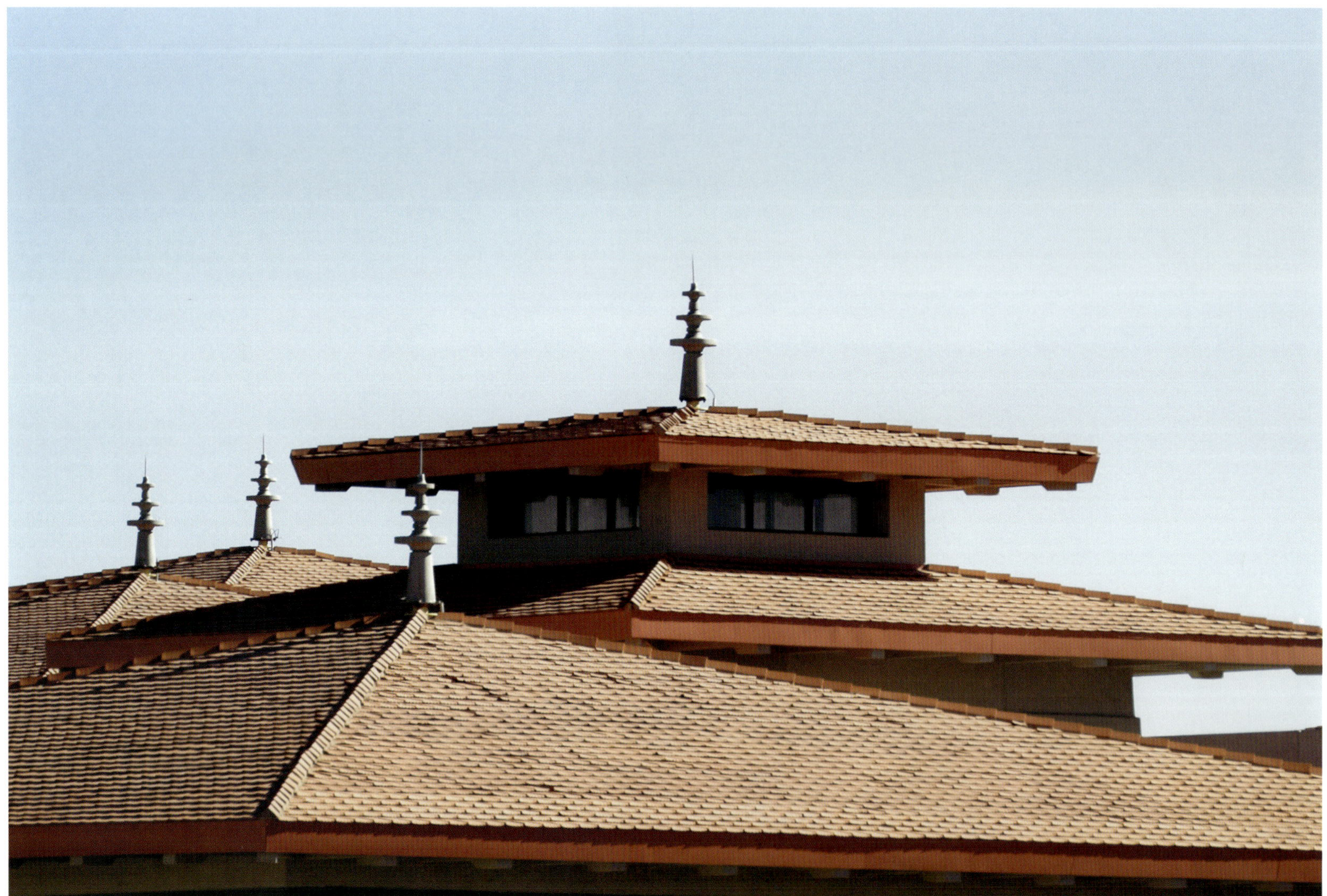

Bhutanese Architecture.
The University of Texas at El Paso's campus is modeled after Bhutanese monasteries, or Dzong architecture, also similar to Tibetan architecture (the university hosts the Chenrezig Himalayan Cultural Center of El Paso).

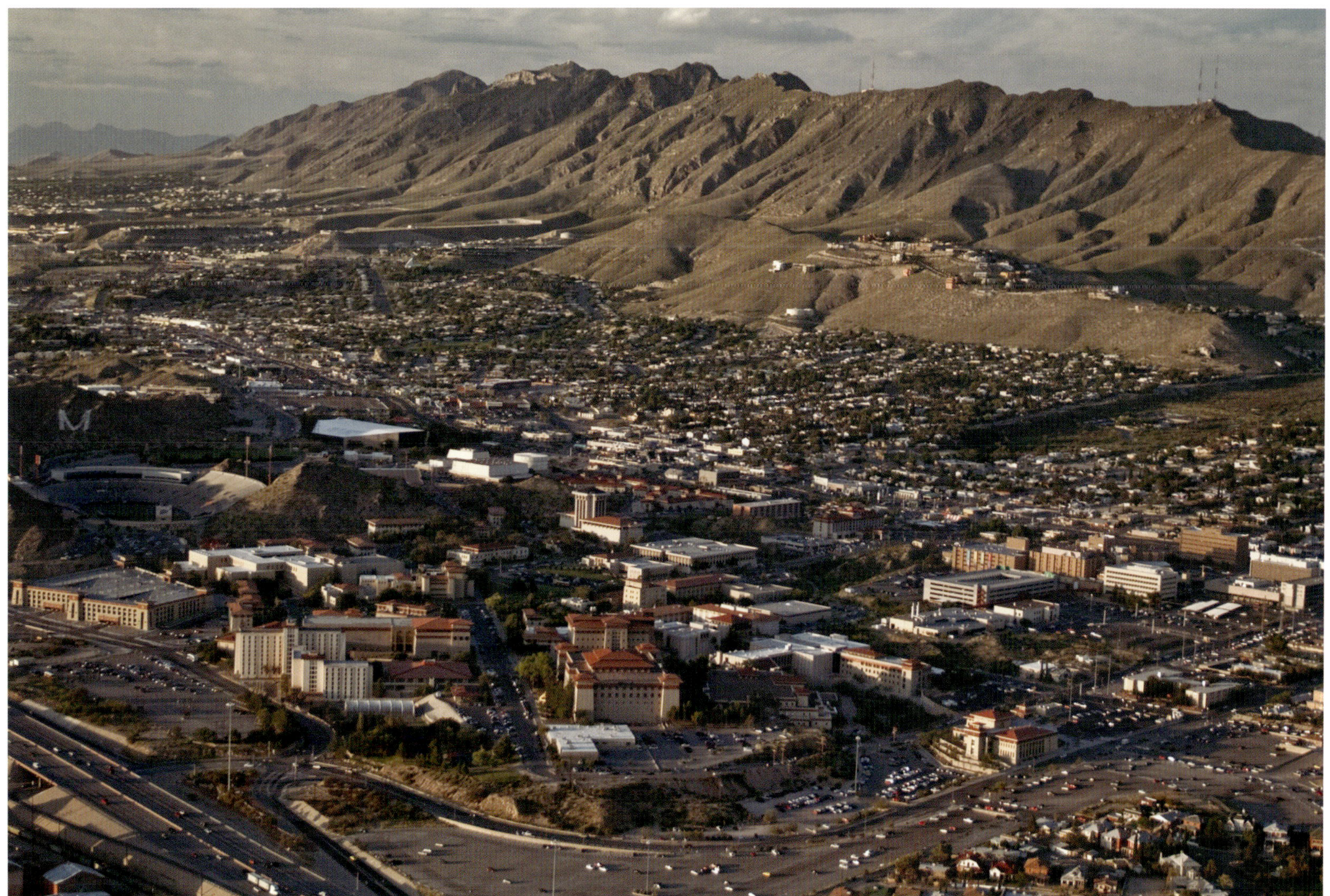

UTEP Glow.
The University of Texas at El Paso, popularly known as UTEP, is a public, coeducational university, and it is a member of the University of Texas system. The school is located on the northern bank of the Rio Grande, in El Paso, Texas, and is the largest university in the nation with a majority Mexican American student population. Founded in 1914 as The Texas State School of Mines and Metallurgy, a mineshaft still exists on the mountainous desert campus. It is composed of buildings of Bhutanese architecture, with massive sloping walls and overhanging roofs.

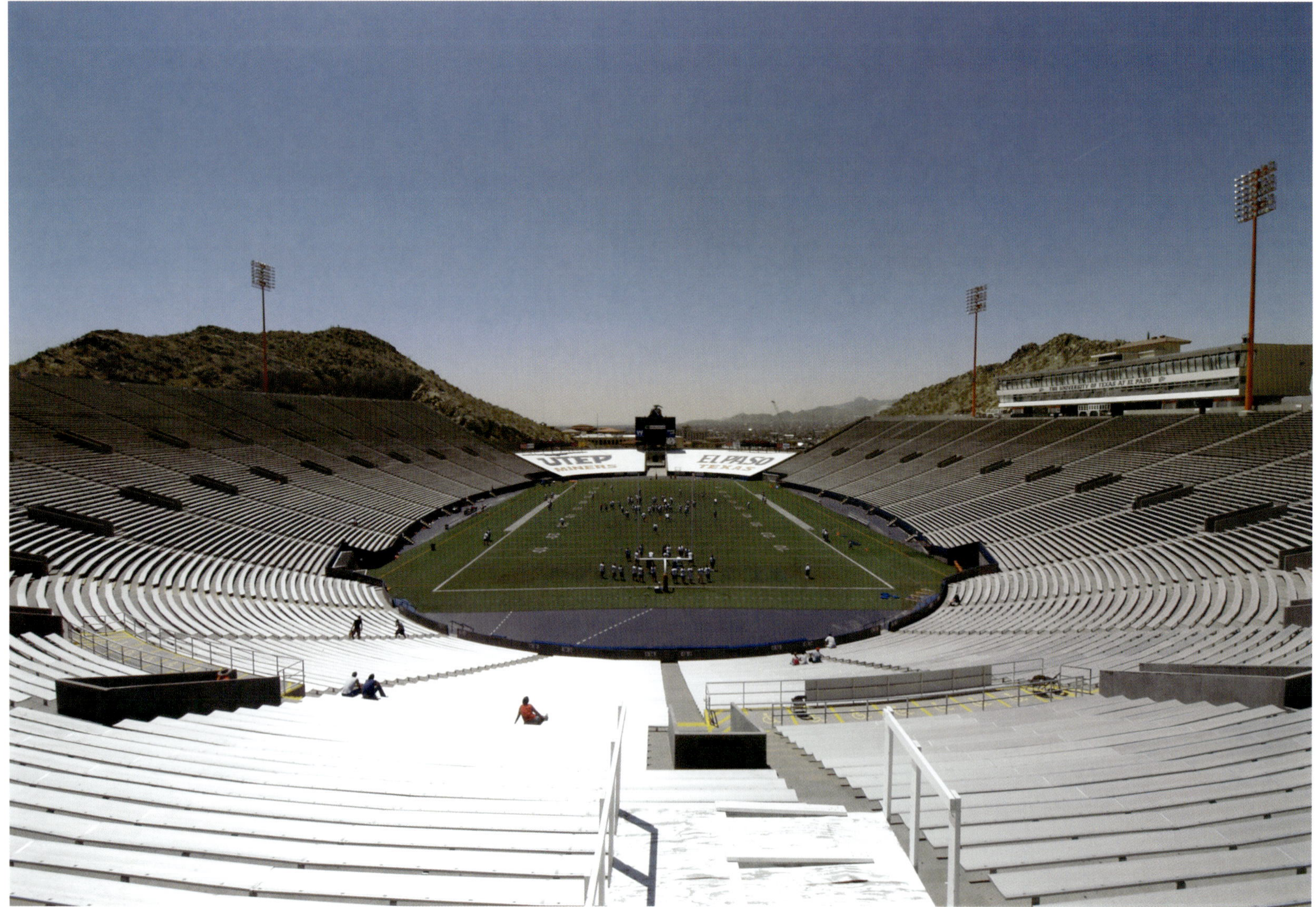

Sun Bowl.
The Sun Bowl is an outdoor football stadium on the campus of the University of Texas at El Paso. It is home to the UTEP Miners of Conference USA (formerly of the WAC), and the late December college football bowl game, The Brut Sun Bowl. The stadium was opened in 1963 and has a current seating capacity of 51,500.

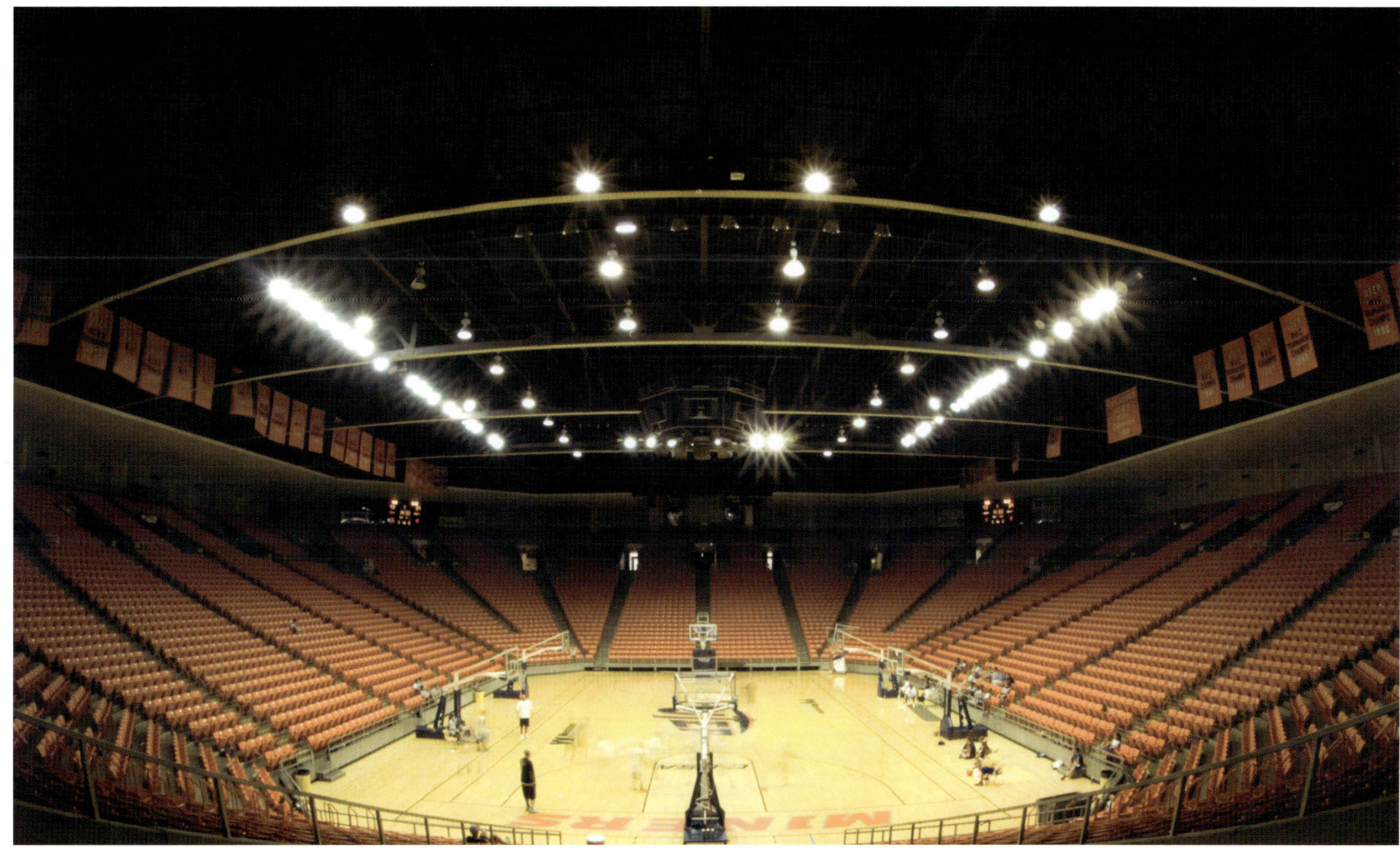

Don Haskins Center.
In the mid-1950s, UTEP, then called Texas Western College, became the first college in a southern state to integrate its intercollegiate athletic teams. Although the campus population was less than 1 percent African American, in 1966 basketball coach Don Haskins and his Texas Western team thrilled portions of the nation by winning the NCAA Men's Basketball Championship with an all-black starting lineup, thus breaking an unspoken barrier and transforming the history of college basketball.

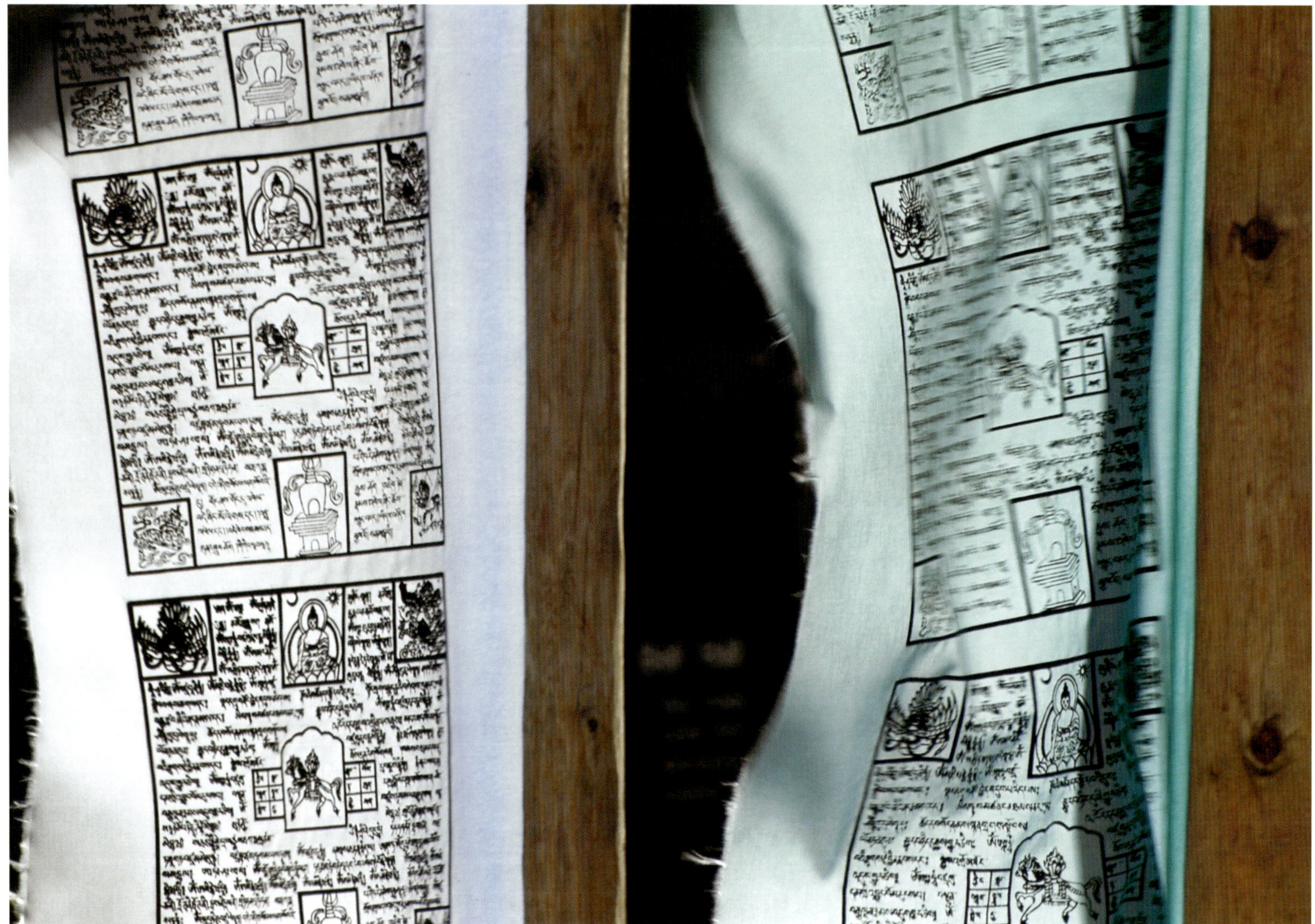

Bhutanese Prayer Flags.
Prayer flags flutter on the hillside of UTEP's Centennial Museum offering up prayers to benefit all nearby sentient beings. In Bhutan houses fly a small white flag on the roof indicating the owner has made offering payments to appease the local god.

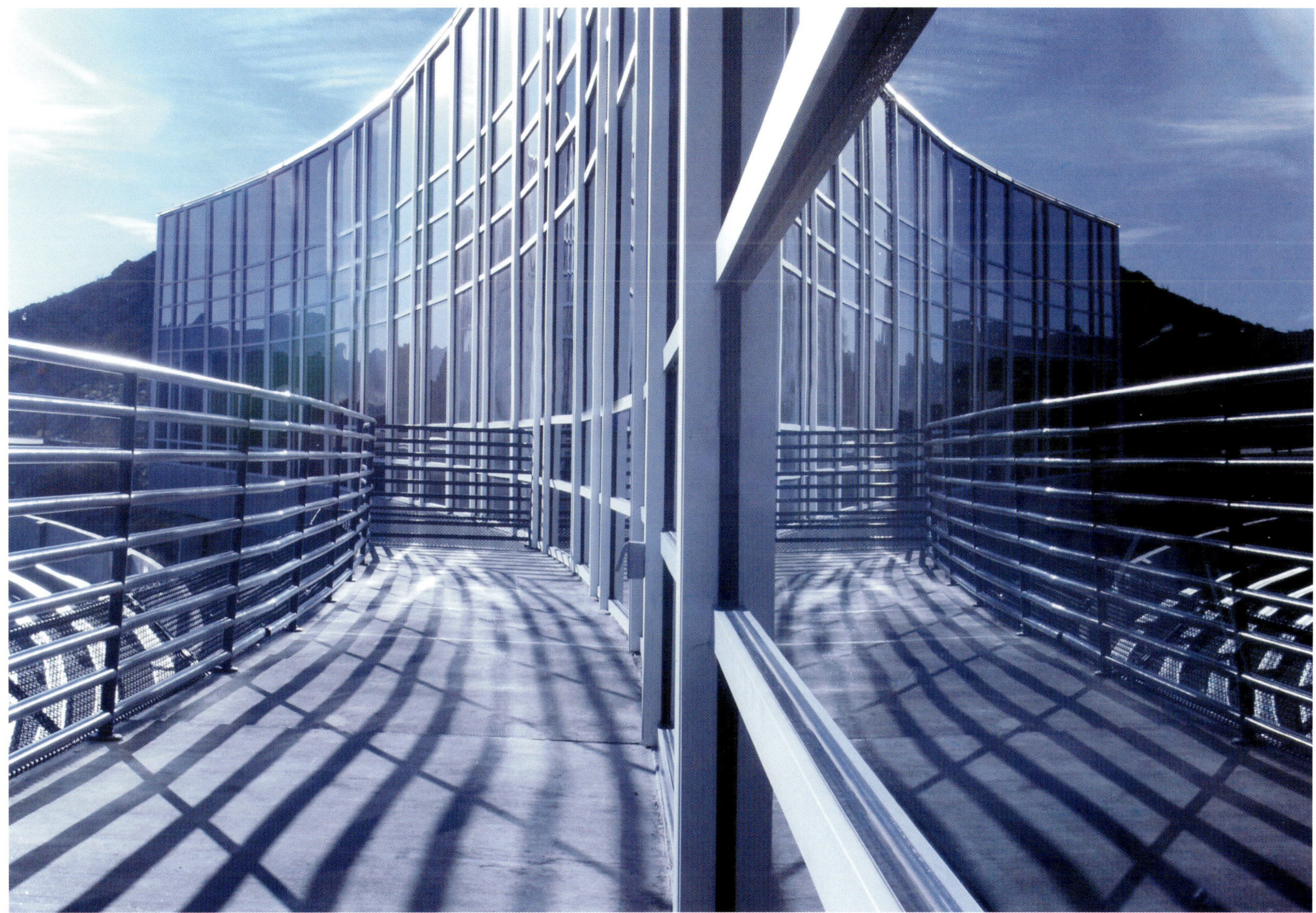

Larry Durham Sports Center.
In 2002, the $11 million Larry K. Durham Sports Center at UTEP's Sun Bowl opened for the first time.

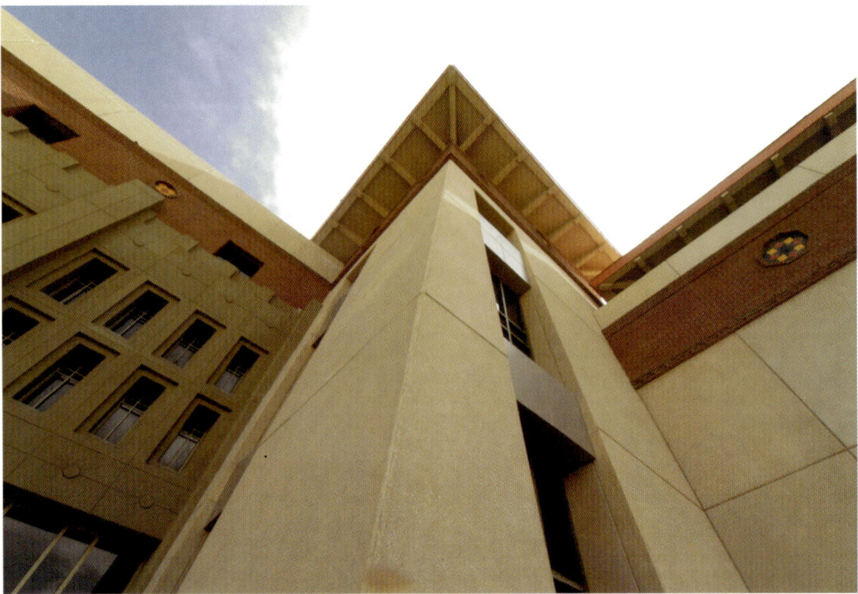

University of Texas at El Paso.

My El Paso is the joy I feel each day as I head from Kern Place toward my office and catch sight of the UTEP campus in the early morning light, with the Juarez Mountains in the background. From this perspective, the interconnectedness of El Paso and Juárez appears as it always should be ... seamless, graceful, and extraordinarily beautiful. And the UTEP campus stands as a proud beacon of opportunity for our collective prosperity through education.

— DR. DIANA NATALICIO,
PRESIDENT, UNIVERSITY OF TEXAS AT EL PASO

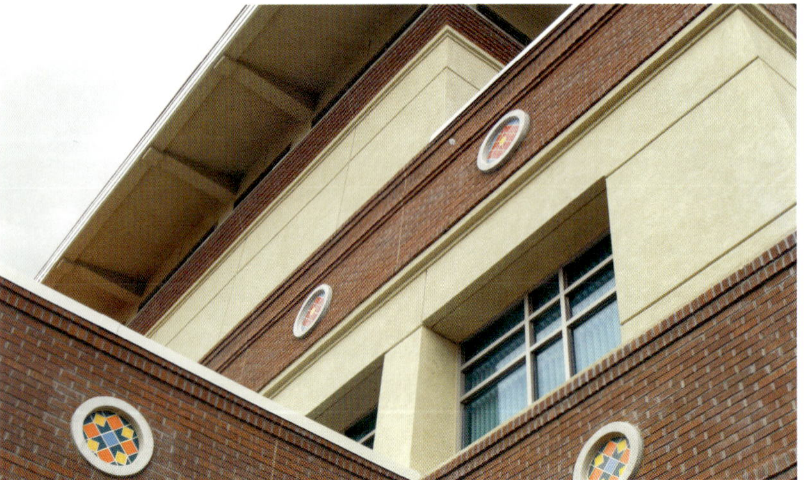

University of Texas at El Paso.

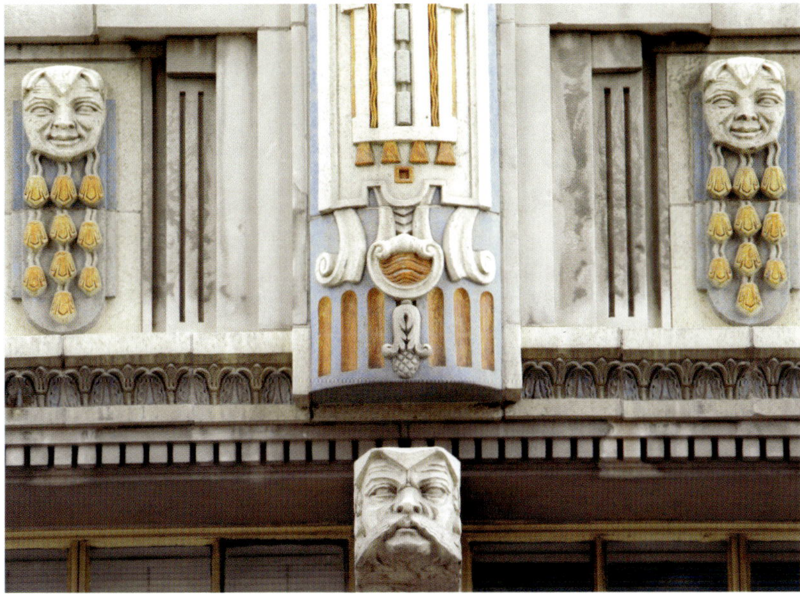

O.T. Bassett Tower.

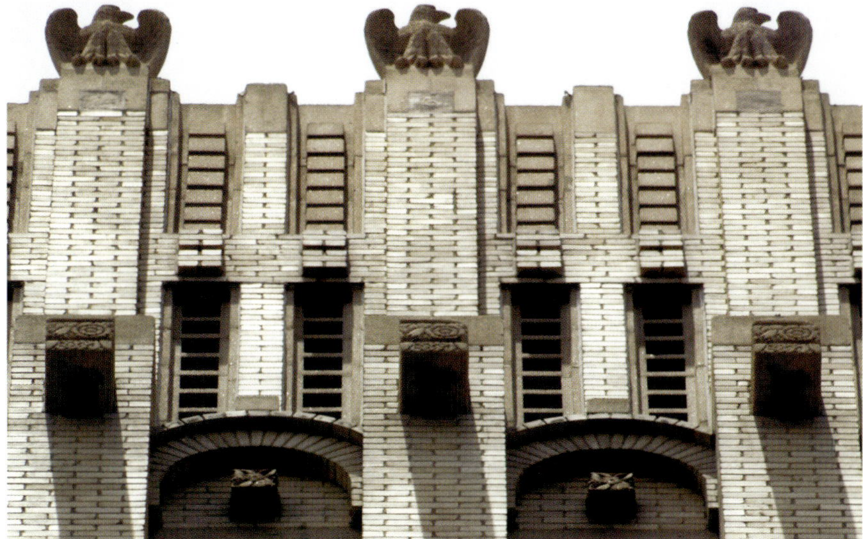

O.T. Bassett Tower.

My El Paso is cool desert rides in the early, early morning … hot! hot! hot! in the middle of the day … and cosmopolitans at Jaxon's as the sun eases below the horizon.

— SUZANNE MICHAELS, PRINCIPAL AND OWNER OF SUZANNE MICHAELS COMMUNICATIONS

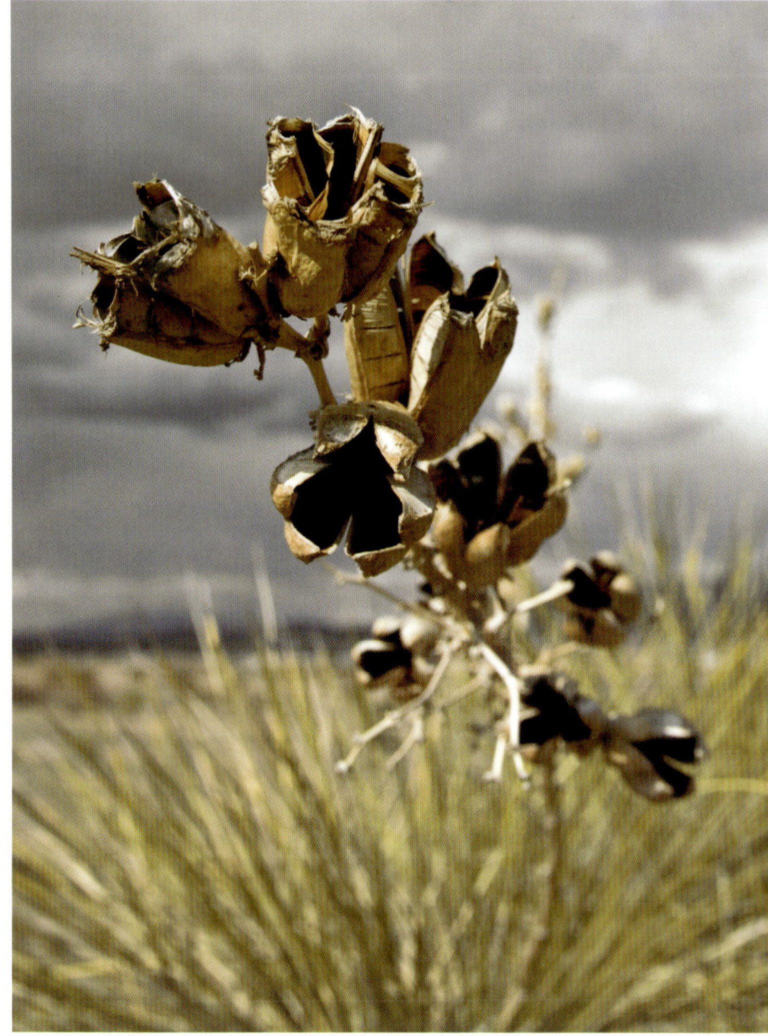

Yucca.

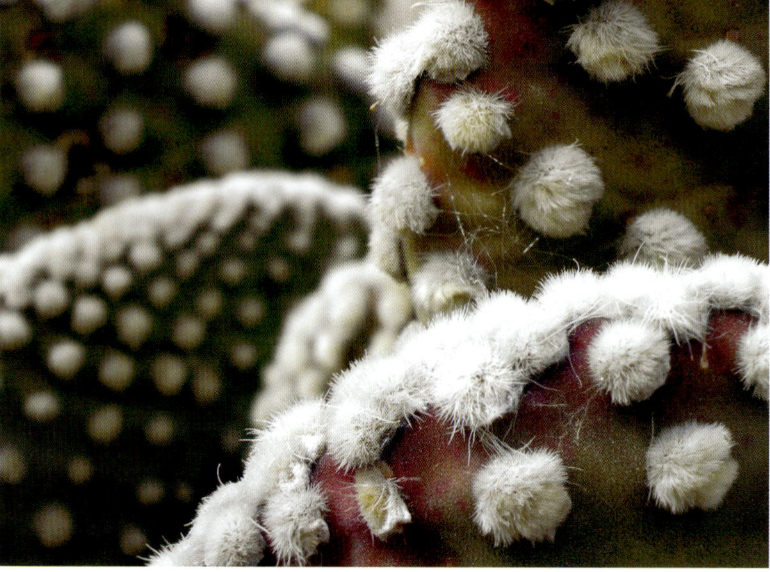

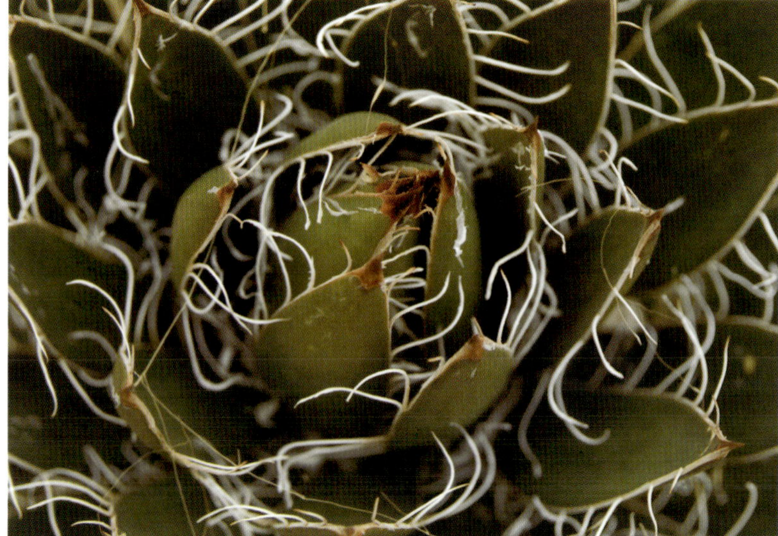

Cacti are distinctive and unusual plants, which are adapted to extremely arid and hot environments, showing a wide range of anatomical and physiological features which conserve water. Their stems have adapted to become photosynthetic and succulent, while the leaves have become the spines for which cacti are well known.

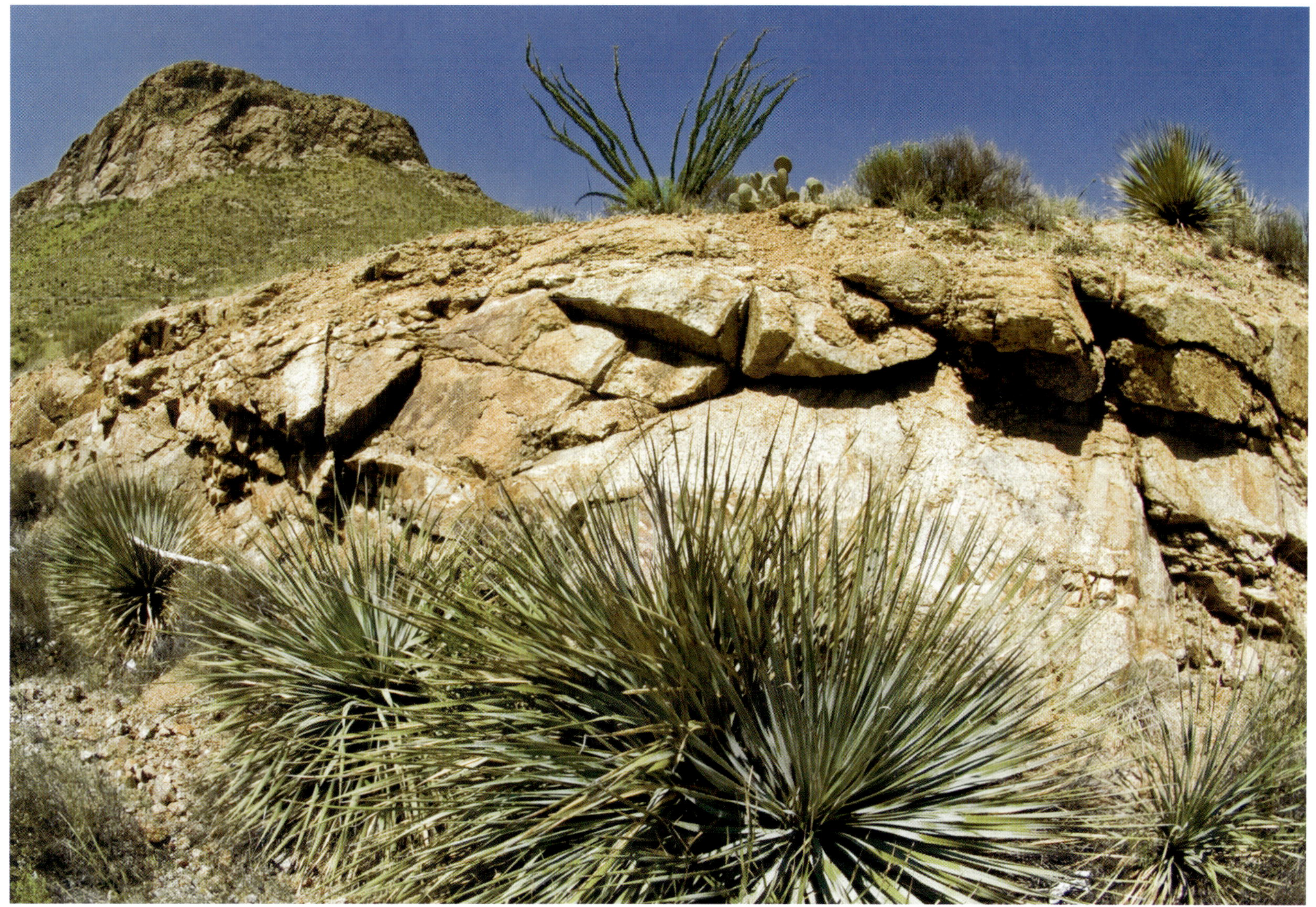

Franklin Mountains.
The Chihuahuan Desert is a desert that straddles the U.S.–Mexico border. On the U.S. side it occupies the valleys and basins of central and southern New Mexico, Texas west of the Pecos River and southeastern Arizona. South of the border, it covers the northern half of the Mexican state of Chihuahua, most of Coahuila, northeast portion of Durango, extreme northern portion of Zacatecas, and small western portions of Nuevo León. It is the third largest desert entirely within the western hemisphere and second largest in North America, after the Great Basin Desert.

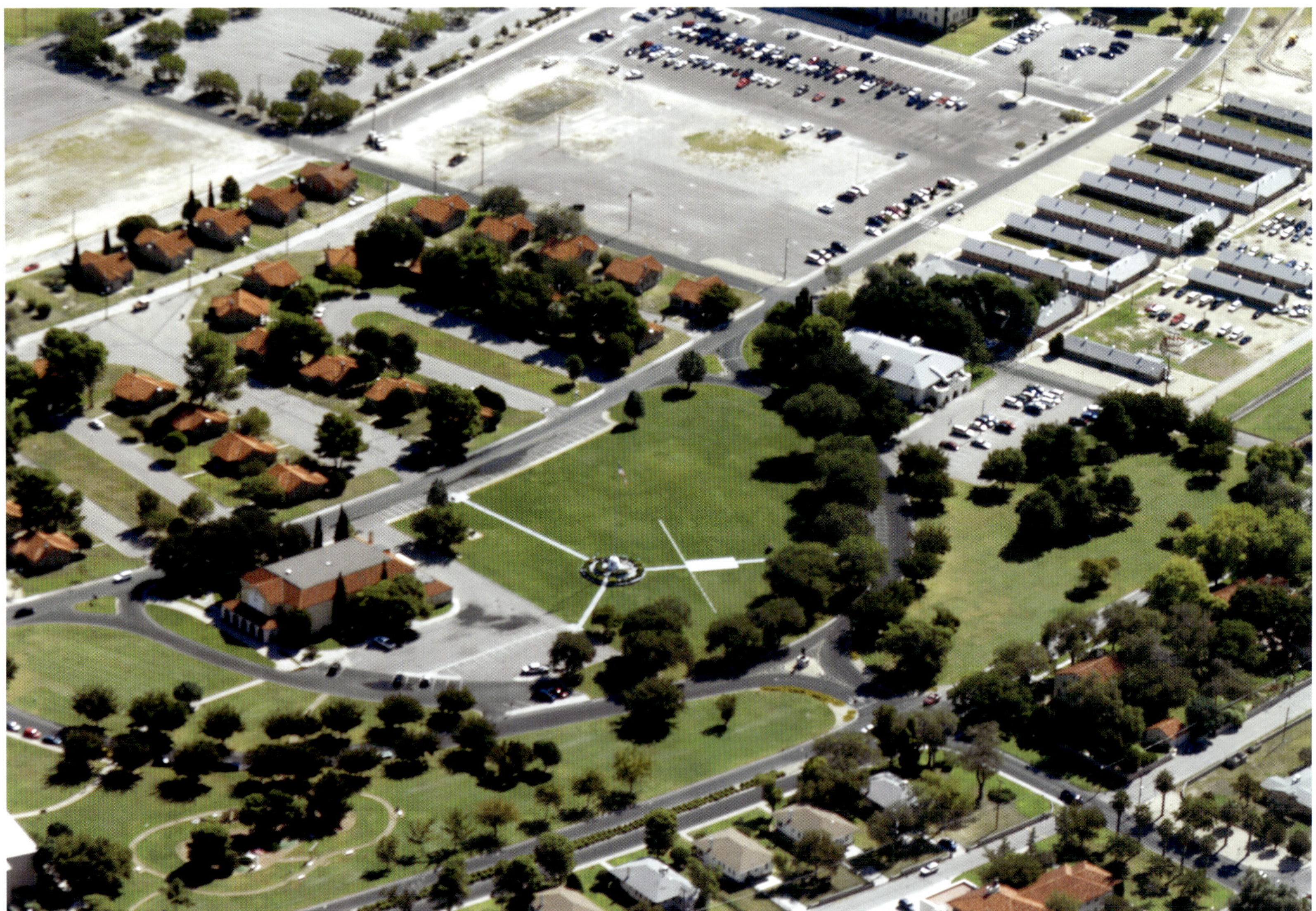

Fort Bliss From Above.
Fort Bliss today is vastly different from the original post created in 1849 to guard the area from Indian and Mexican raids. The mission of Fort Bliss has changed to providing anti-aircraft and missile defense capabilities, a role that Fort Bliss retains. As the largest military base in the continental United States, Fort Bliss is also uniquely suited to conduct live fire exercises of nearly every type of military weapon in the current U.S. Army arsenal.

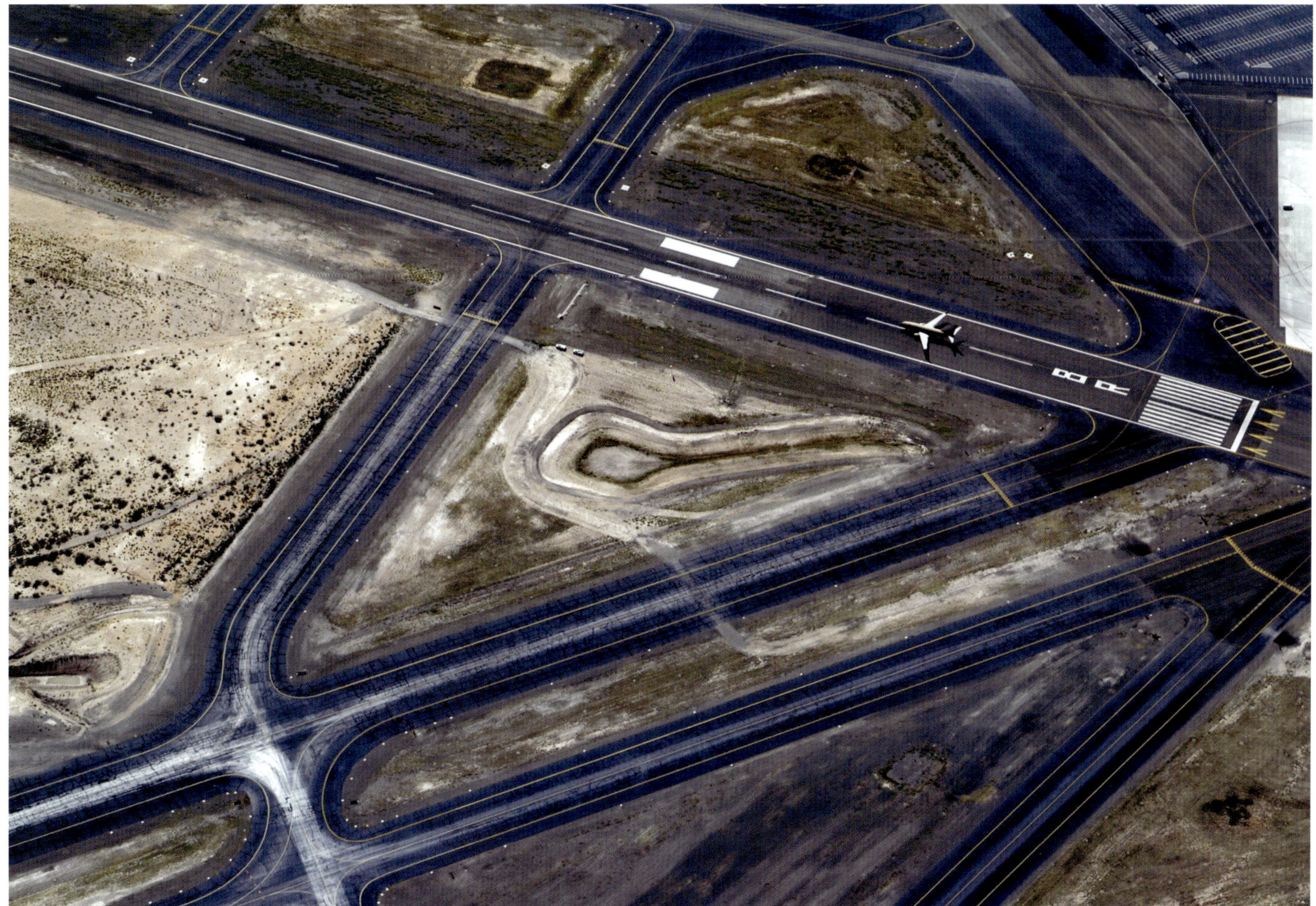

El Paso International Airport.
The El Paso International Airport was originally constructed as Standard Airport, constructed by Standard Airlines in 1929 for transcontinental airmail service. Standard Airlines became a division of American Airlines in the 1930s. In 1936, American Airlines "swapped" airports with the city of El Paso, and the El Paso International Airport was born.

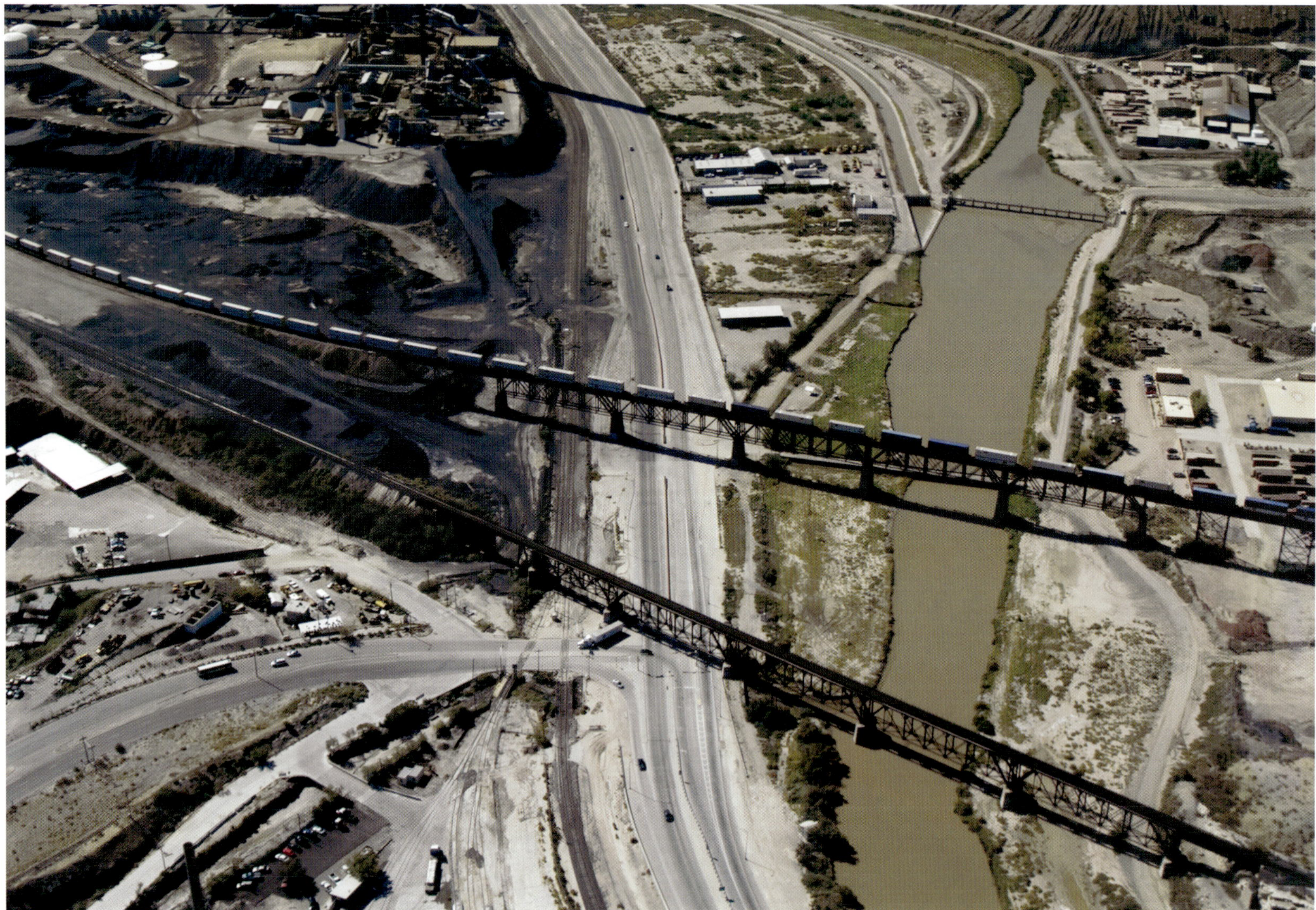

Crossing the Rio.
Executive Center at Paisano.

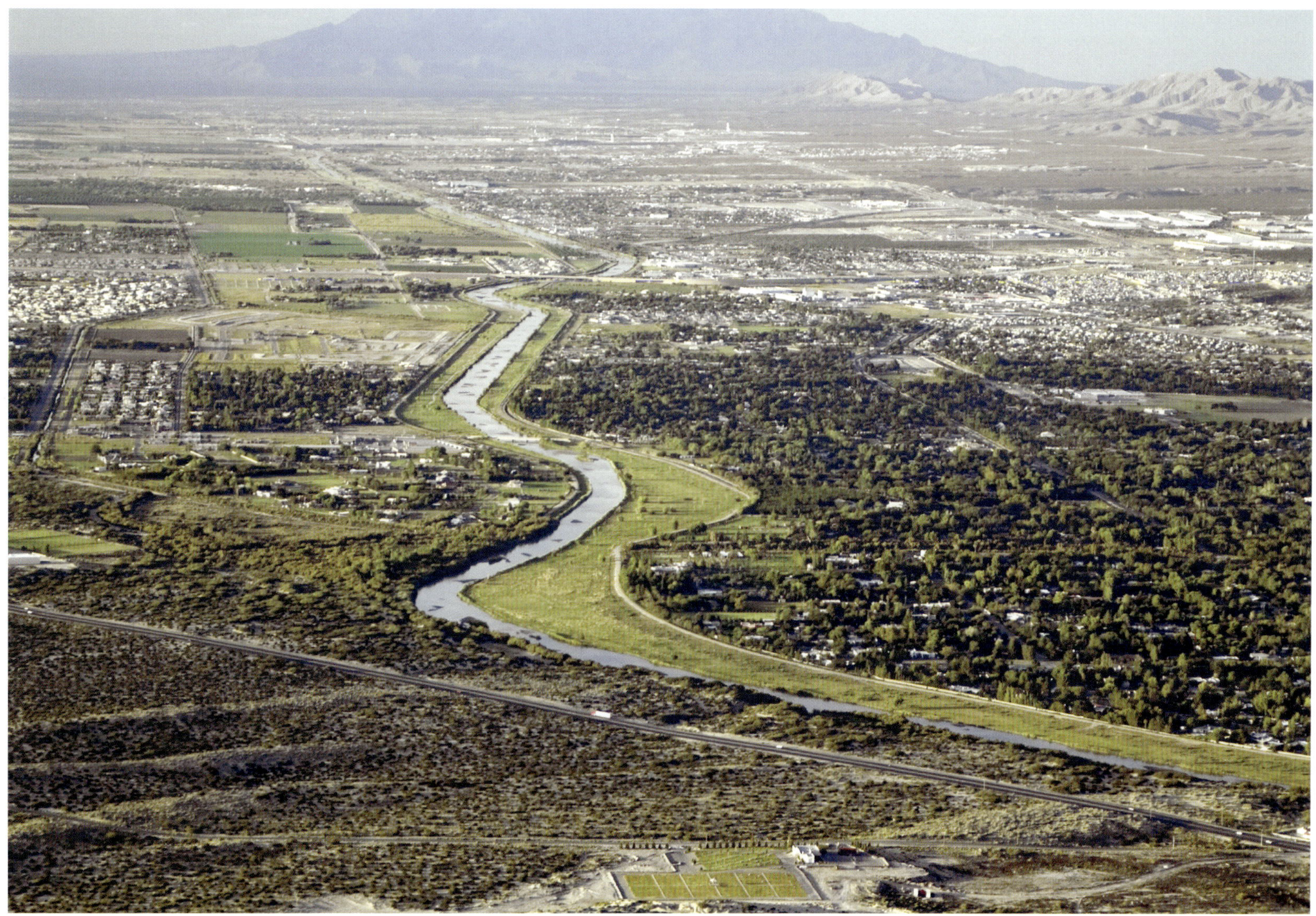

Winding Rio.

The Rio Grande, the fifth longest river of North America and the twentieth longest in the world, forms the entire border between the U.S. state of Texas and Mexico. It flows 1,760 miles (2,830 km) from its sources in the southern Rocky Mountains of southwestern Colorado to the Gulf of Mexico.

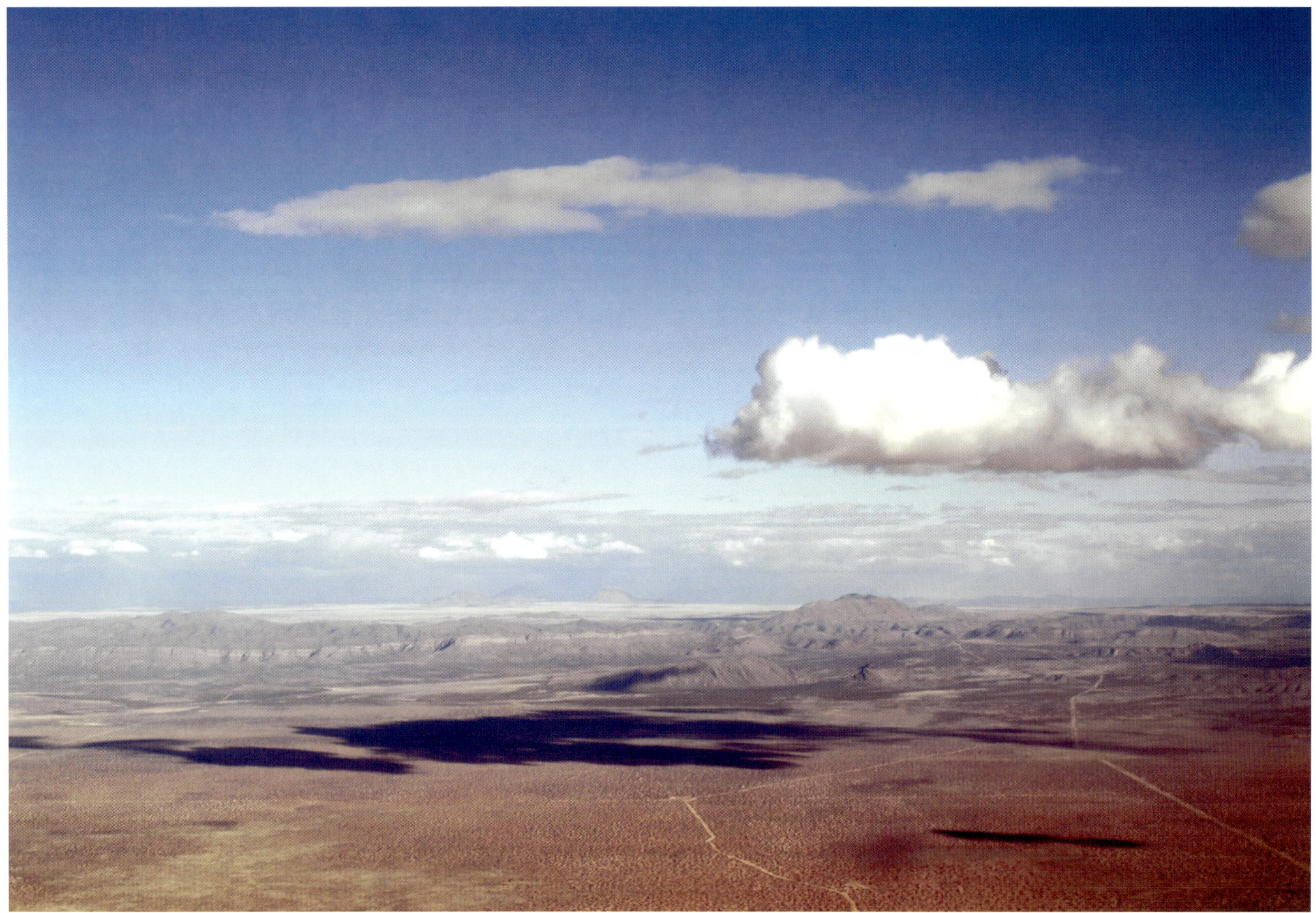

My West Texas Backyard.
West Texas is a region that has more in common geographically with the Southwestern United States than it does with the rest of the state. The area is known for its natural beauty and has many small mountain ranges. This part of Texas is in the Northern Chihuahua Desert, and the high mountain areas have a climate that many find pleasant: cold nights but warm afternoons in winter, hot days but cool nights in the summer. West Texas has a much lower population density than the rest of the state.

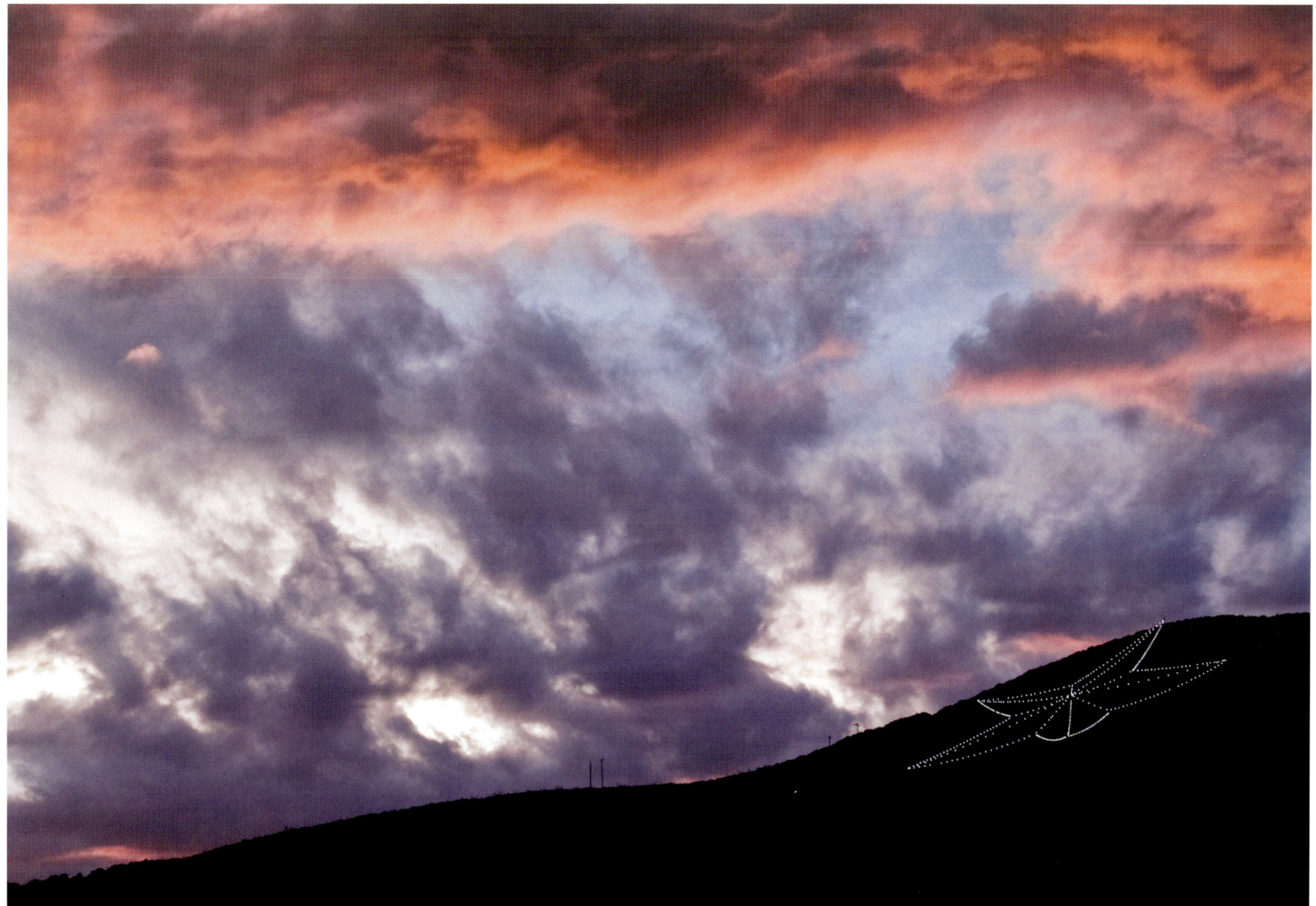

Star Once Again.
Today the star stands at 459 feet long, 278 feet wide and uses 459 (150 W) lights. The poles, which vary in height from twelve to fifteen feet, start at the mountain top and run down to a point about 300 feet above Scenic Drive. The star sits at an angle of 30 degrees and appears to be "perfect" when viewed from the focal point at the intersection of Texas and Alameda Avenues.

My El Paso is filled with hot places and cool spaces and awesome diversity.

— KATHERINE BRENNAND, EL PASO ARTS LEADER

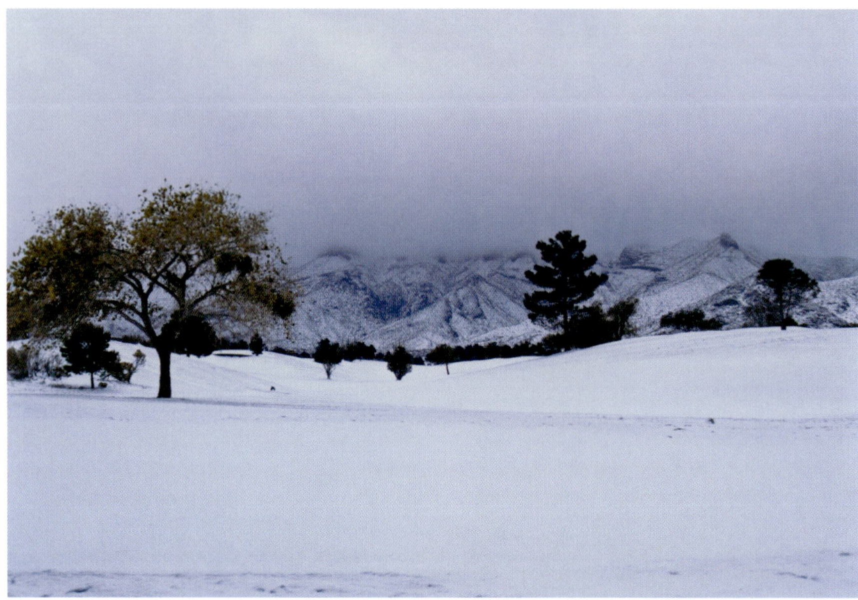

Snow Day.

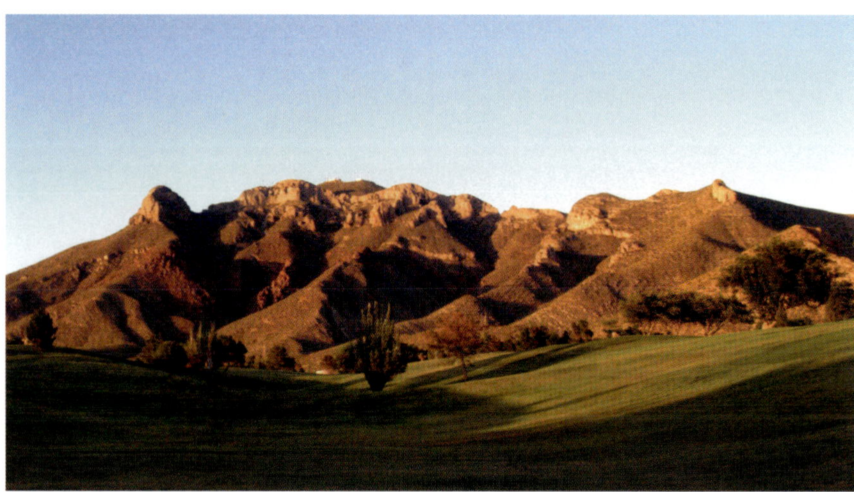

Coronado Country Club.

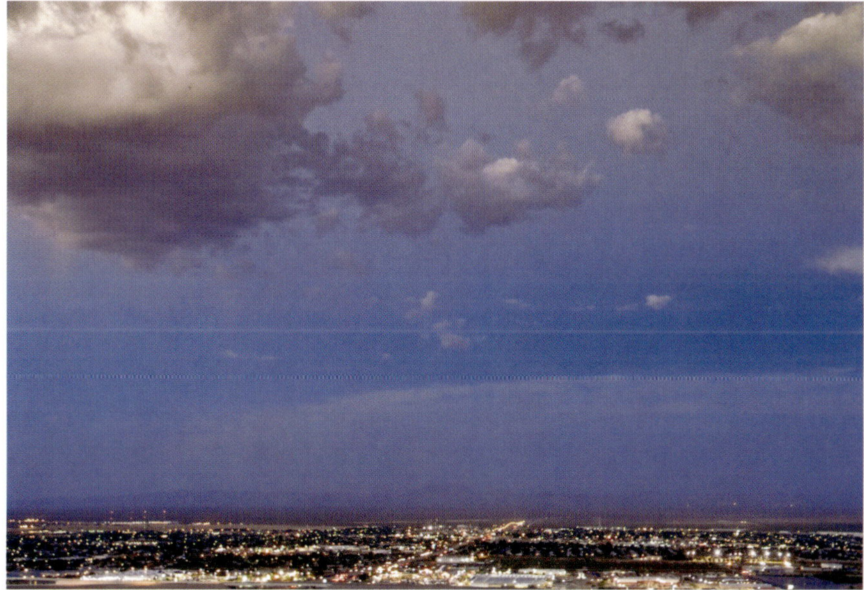

Northeast and Beyond.

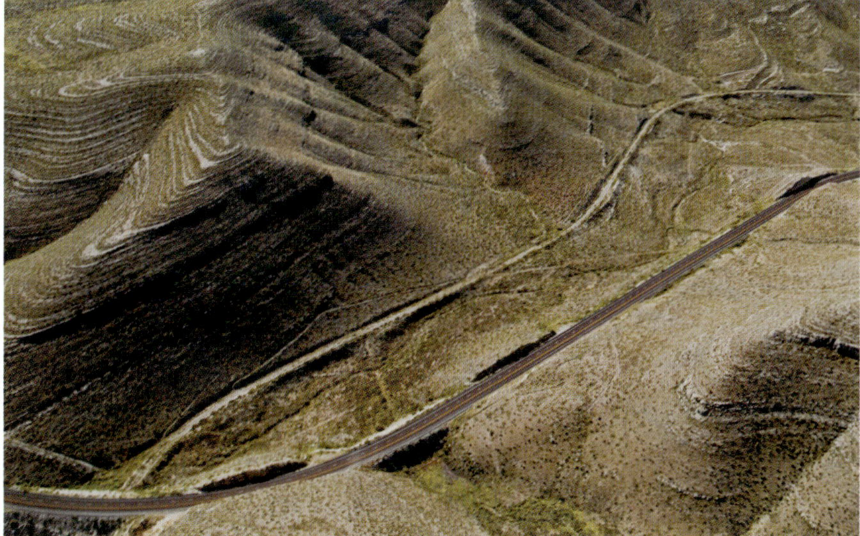

Through the Huecos.

My El Paso is a time capsule without a clock.

— RYAN PERRY, WARRIOR POET

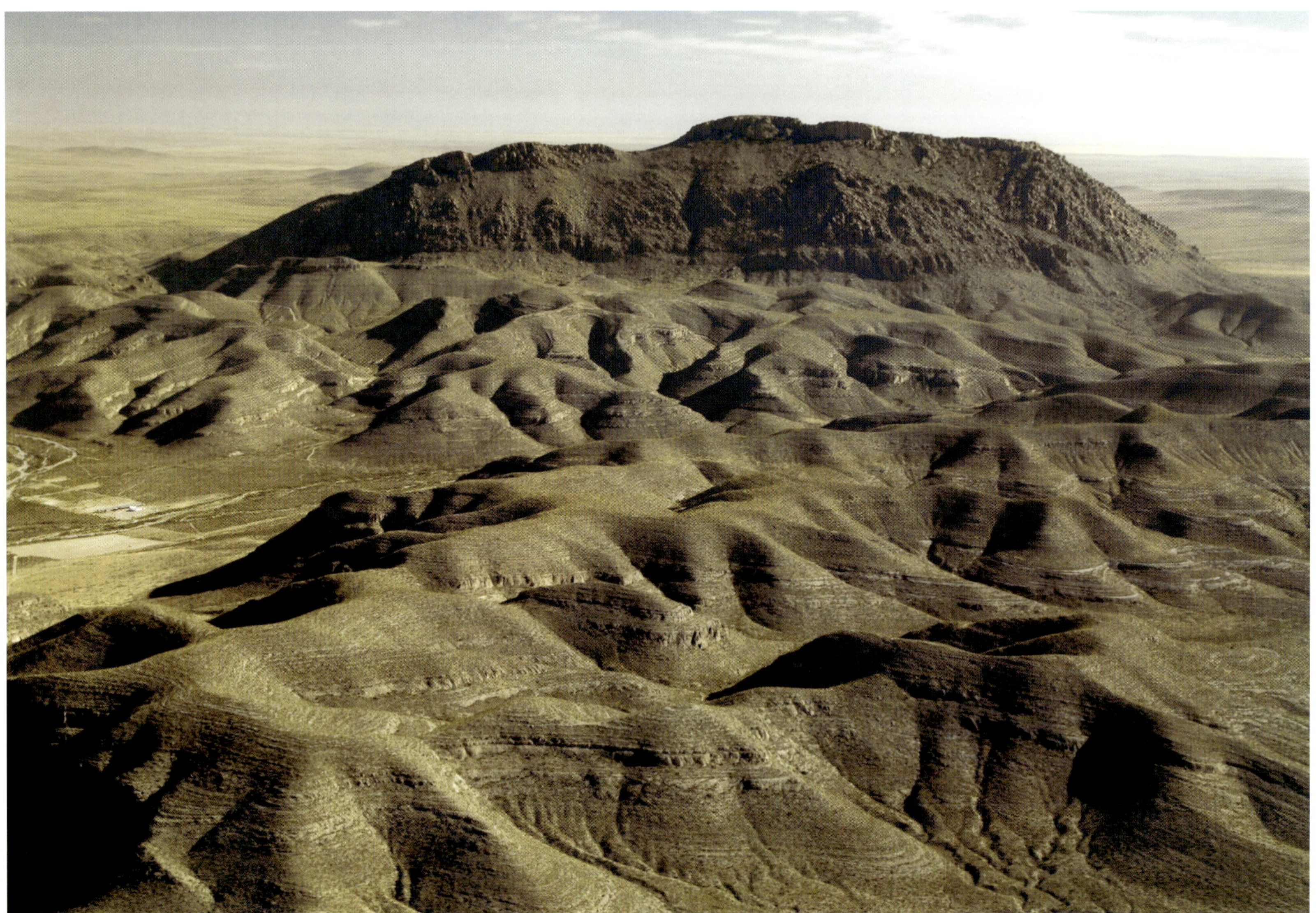

Hueco Mountains.
The Hueco Mountains are a range that rises in southern Otero County, New Mexico, and extend twenty-seven miles south into Texas, generally along the El Paso-Hudspeth County line just east of the city of El Paso. The highest point of the range is the Cerro Alto (6,787 feet) in Hudspeth County.

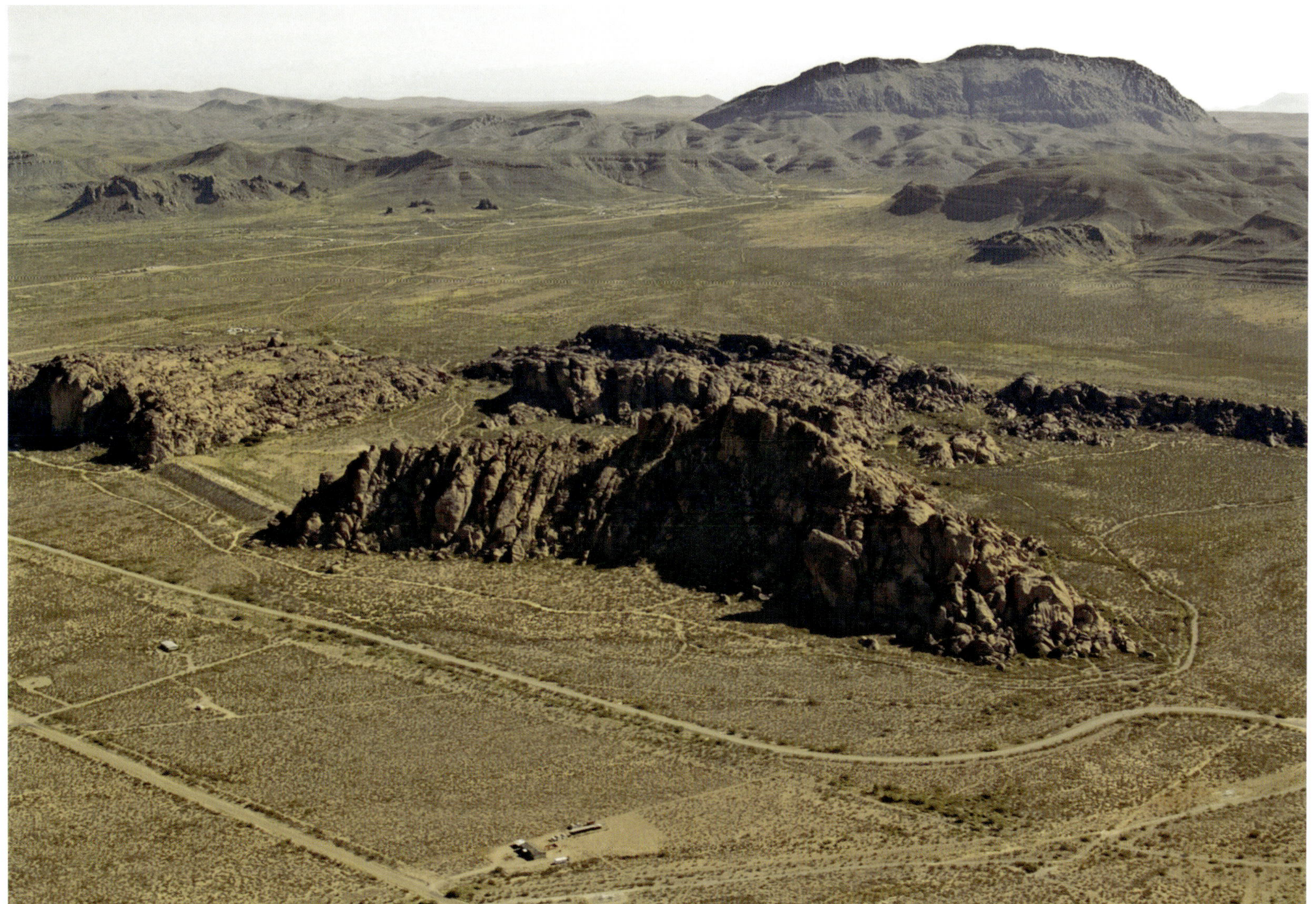

Hueco Tanks State Historical Site.
This site is named for the natural rock basins in its granite outcroppings that capture rainwater, a precious resource in the Chihuahuan Desert environment. For millennia, people seeking life-giving water and the diverse plants and animals that could be found here left curious and beautiful paintings on the rocks. Today this ancient site preserves more than 2,000 pictographs that are a wonder to behold.

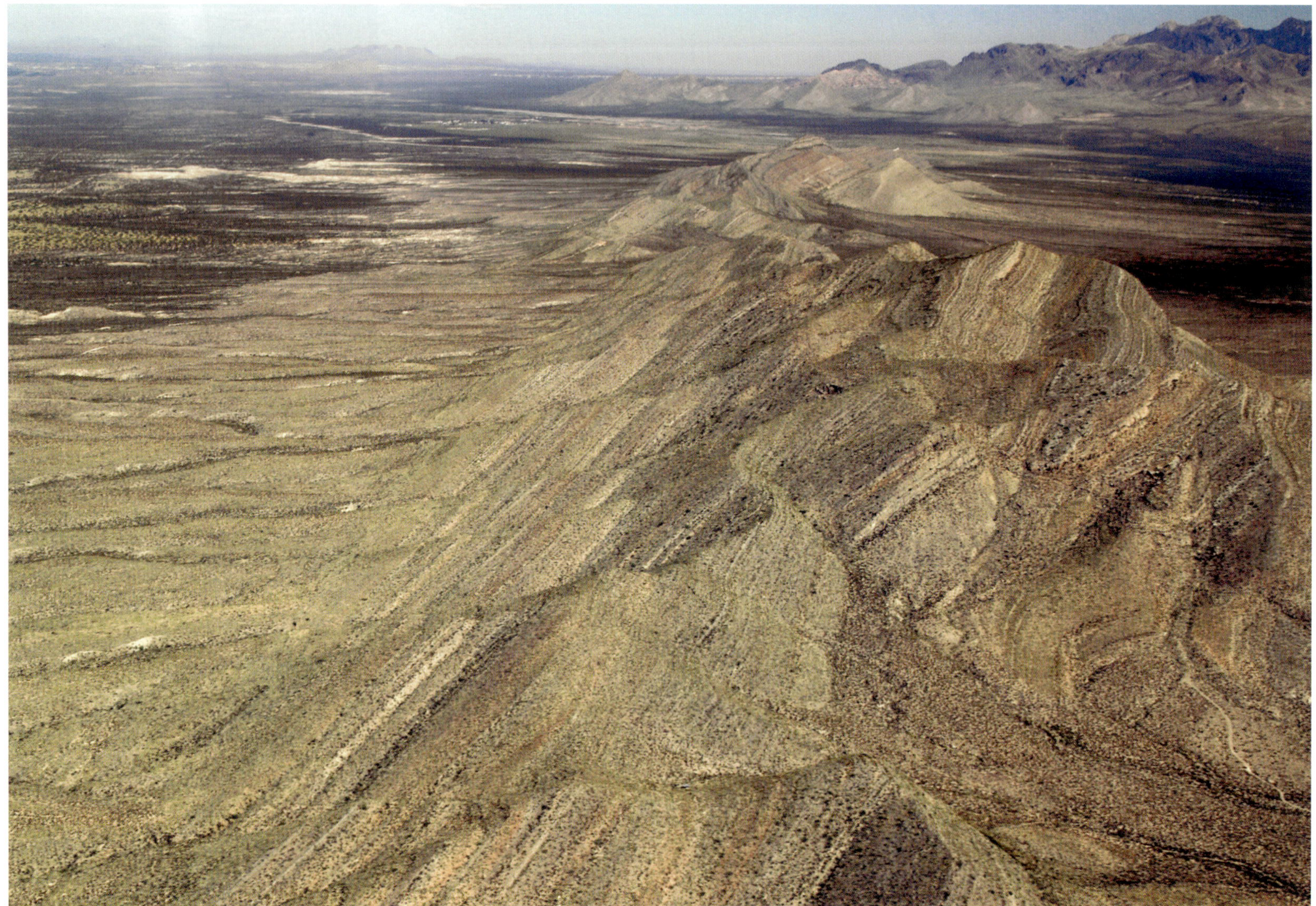

Anthony Gap.
The Anthony Gap is situated at the northern edge of El Paso's Franklin Mountains and the southern edge of Southern New Mexico's Organ Mountains. The gap is known as the Anthony Gap due to its proximity to the community of Anthony, New Mexico.

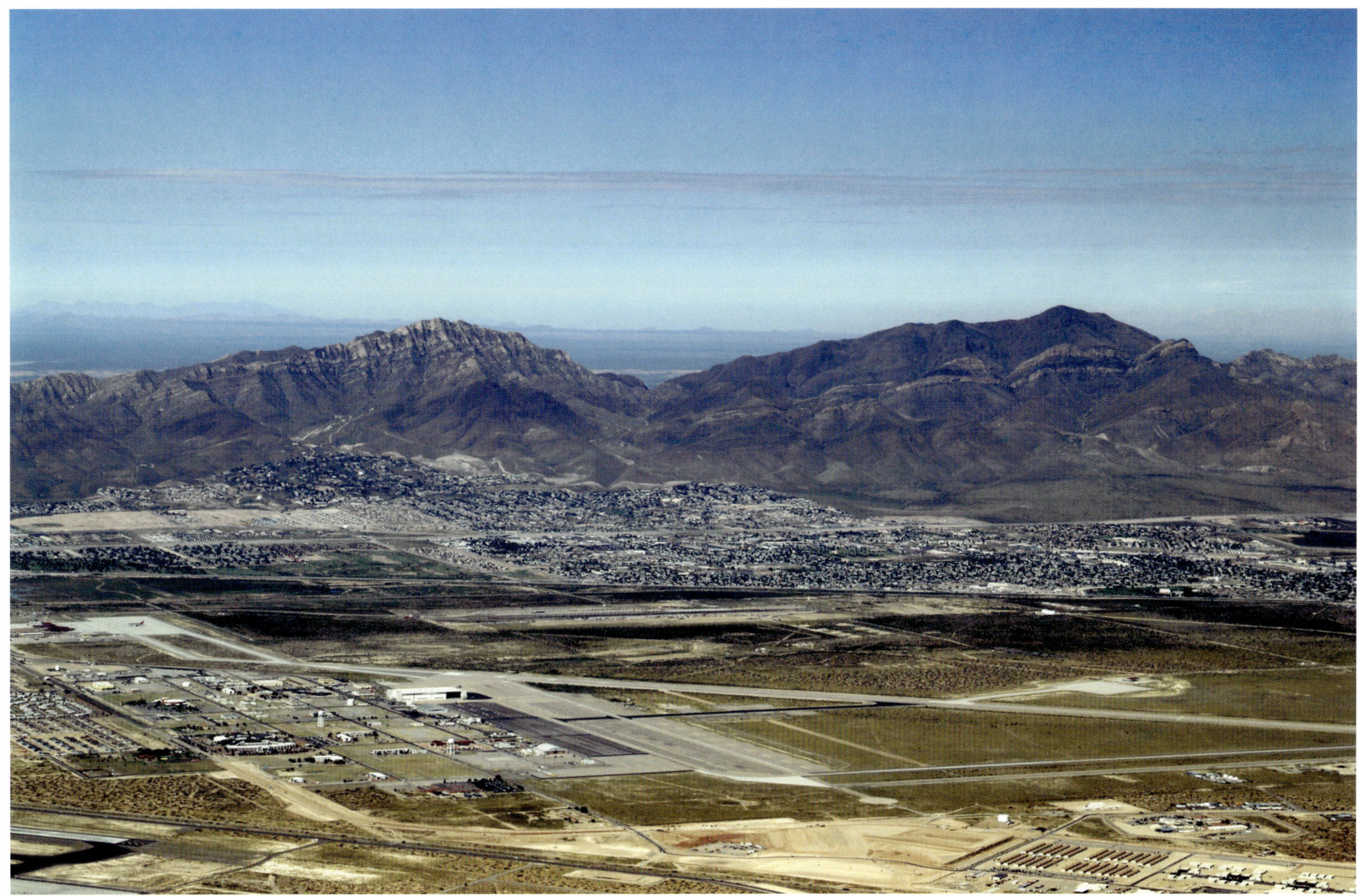

El Paso Del Norte.
As they approached the Rio Grande from the south, Spanish explorers in the colonial period viewed two mountain ranges rising out of the desert with a deep chasm between. They named this site El Paso del Norte (the Pass of the North), and it became the location of two future border cities, Ciudad Juárez on the south or right bank of the Rio Grande and El Paso, Texas, on the opposite side of the river. The arrival of the first Spanish expedition at the Pass of the North in 1581 marked the beginning of more than 400 years of history in the El Paso area. It was followed in 1598 by the colonizing expedition under Juan de Oñate. On April 30, 1598, in a ceremony at a site near present-day San Elizario, Oñate took formal possession of the entire territory drained by the Rio Grande and brought Spanish civilization to the Pass of the North.

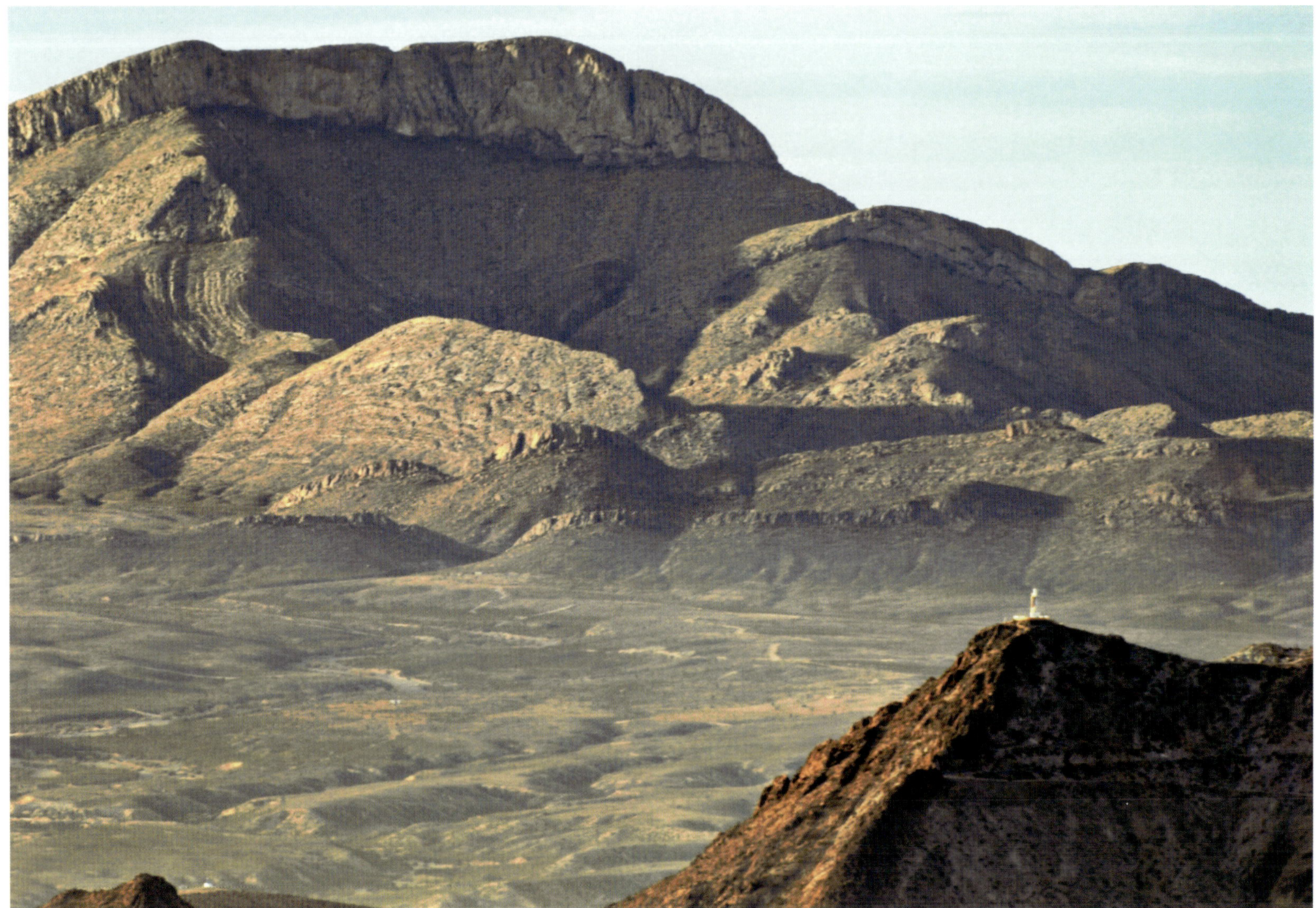

The Franklins – A Natural Divider.
The city's elevation is 3,800 feet above sea level. The rustic North Franklin Peak towers at 7,192 feet above sea level and is the highest peak in the city. The peak can be seen from sixty miles in all directions. According to the United States Census Bureau, the city has a total area of 250.5 square miles.

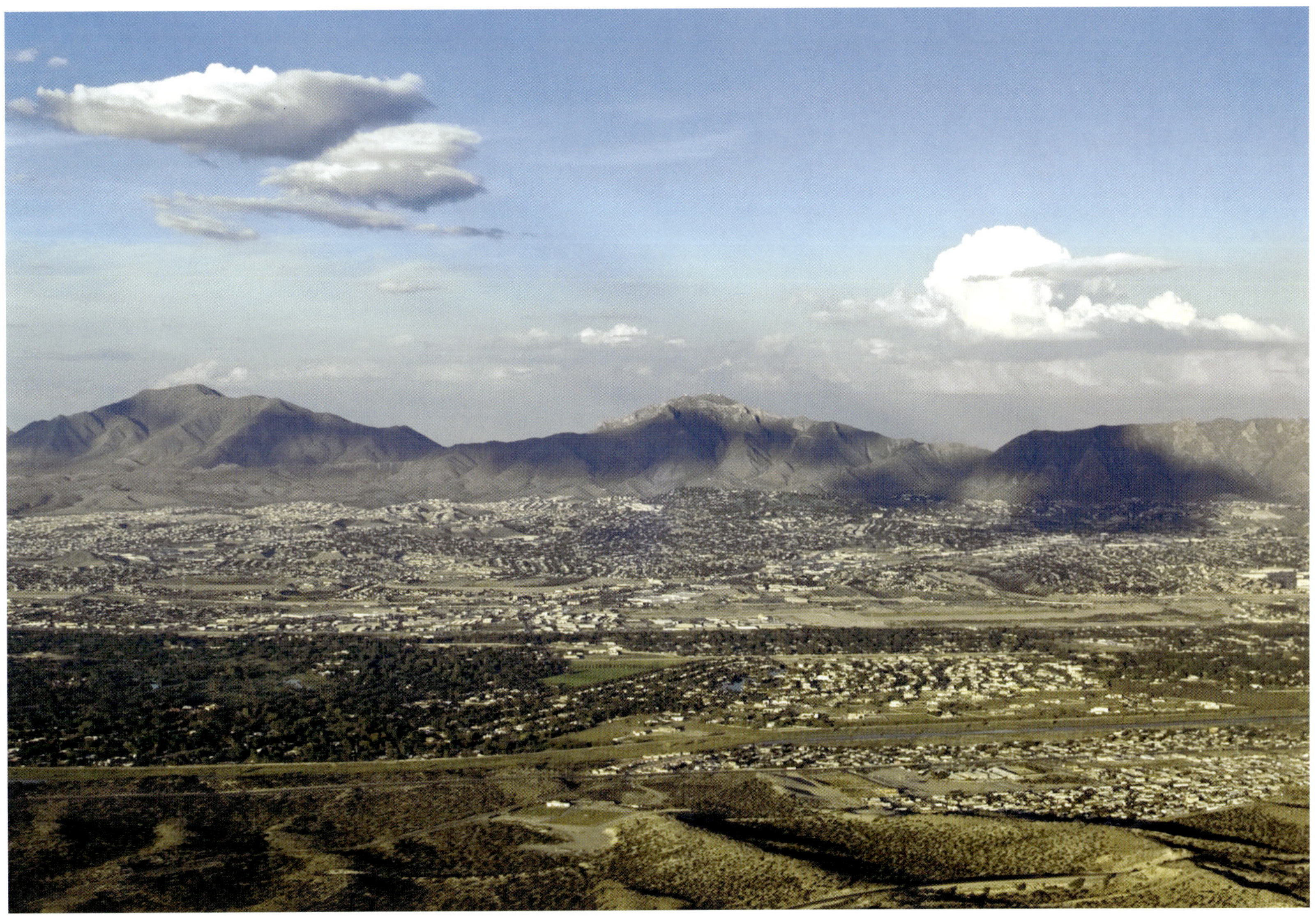

West El Paso.
El Paso lies at the intersection of three states (Texas, New Mexico, and Chihuahua) and two countries (the USA and Mexico). It is the only major Texas city on Mountain Time. When Ciudad Juárez was on Central Time, it was possible to celebrate New Year's twice in the same evening by travelling a very short distance across the state and into another country. Both cities are now on Mountain Time.

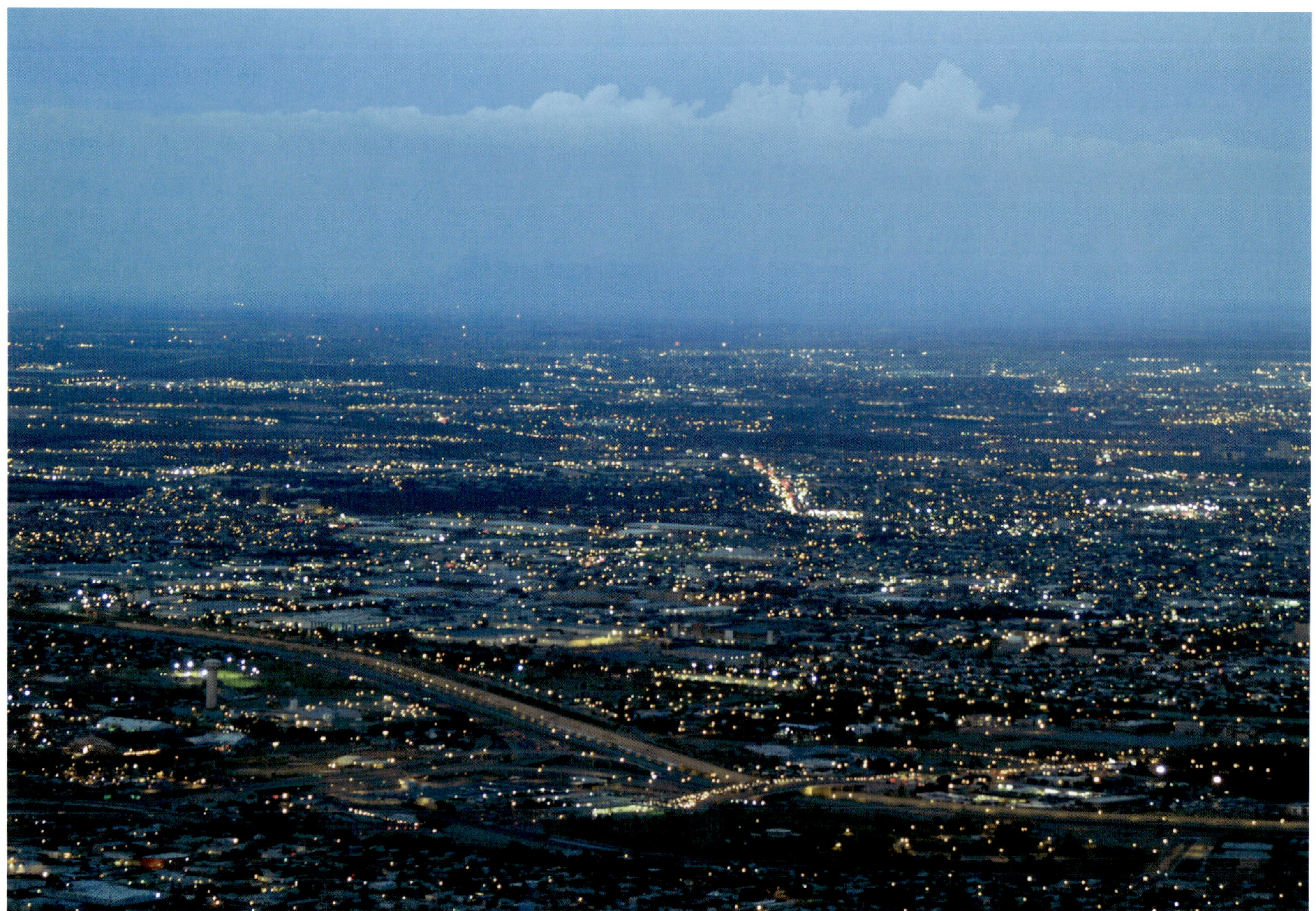

El Paso Dusk.
Scenic Drive. Topping off at 4,222 feet above sea level, the eighty-six-year-old El Paso landmark that's carved into the Franklin Mountains rivals any view in the United States.

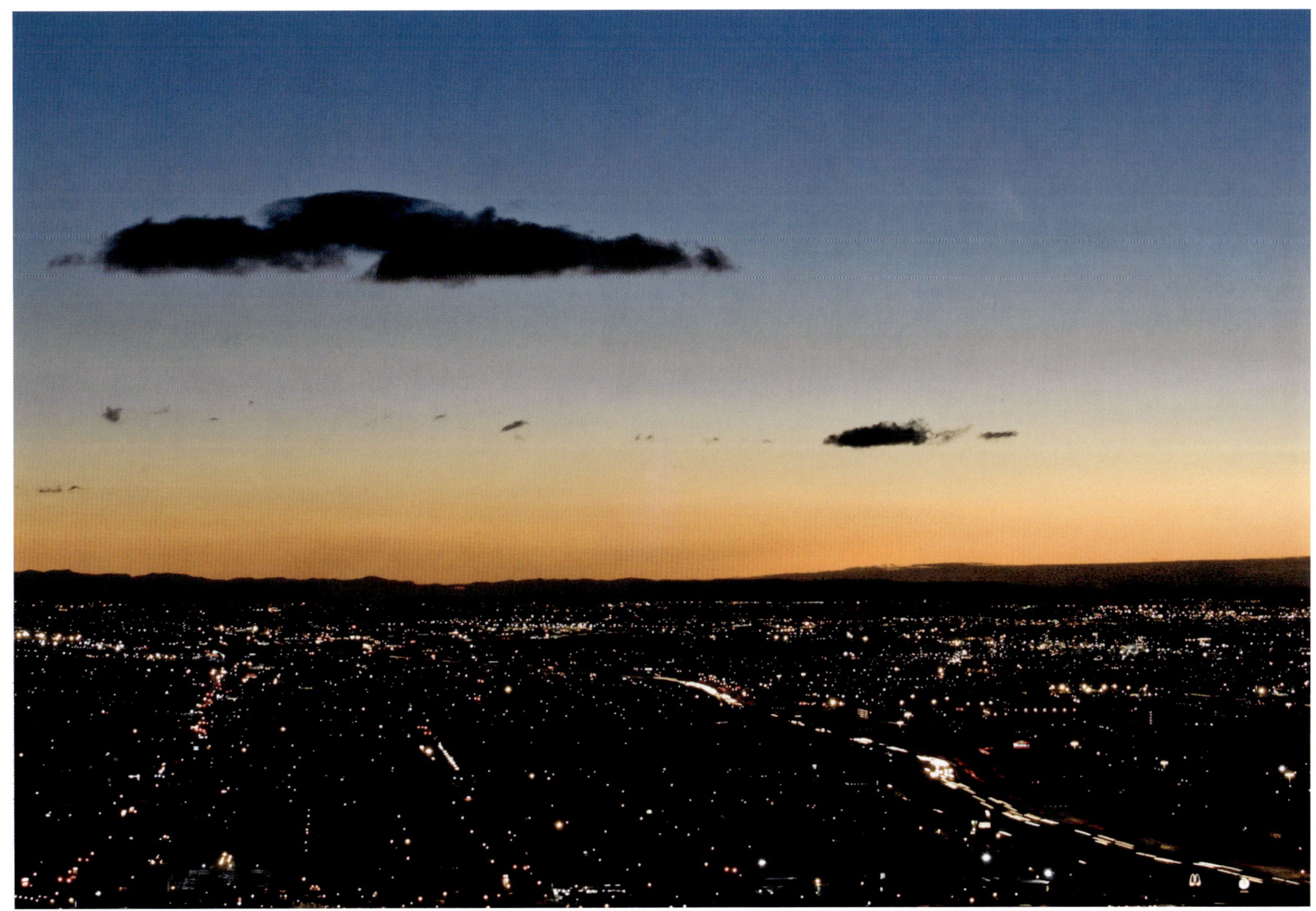

El Paso Wakes Up.
Construction on Scenic Drive began in 1920. An *El Paso Times* article from 1960 reported that in 1932, the two-lane road was paved with assistance from the Federal Emergency Relief Administration and the Texas Relief Commission to create a beautiful scenic route high above the city and to relieve unemployment in the city during the Depression.

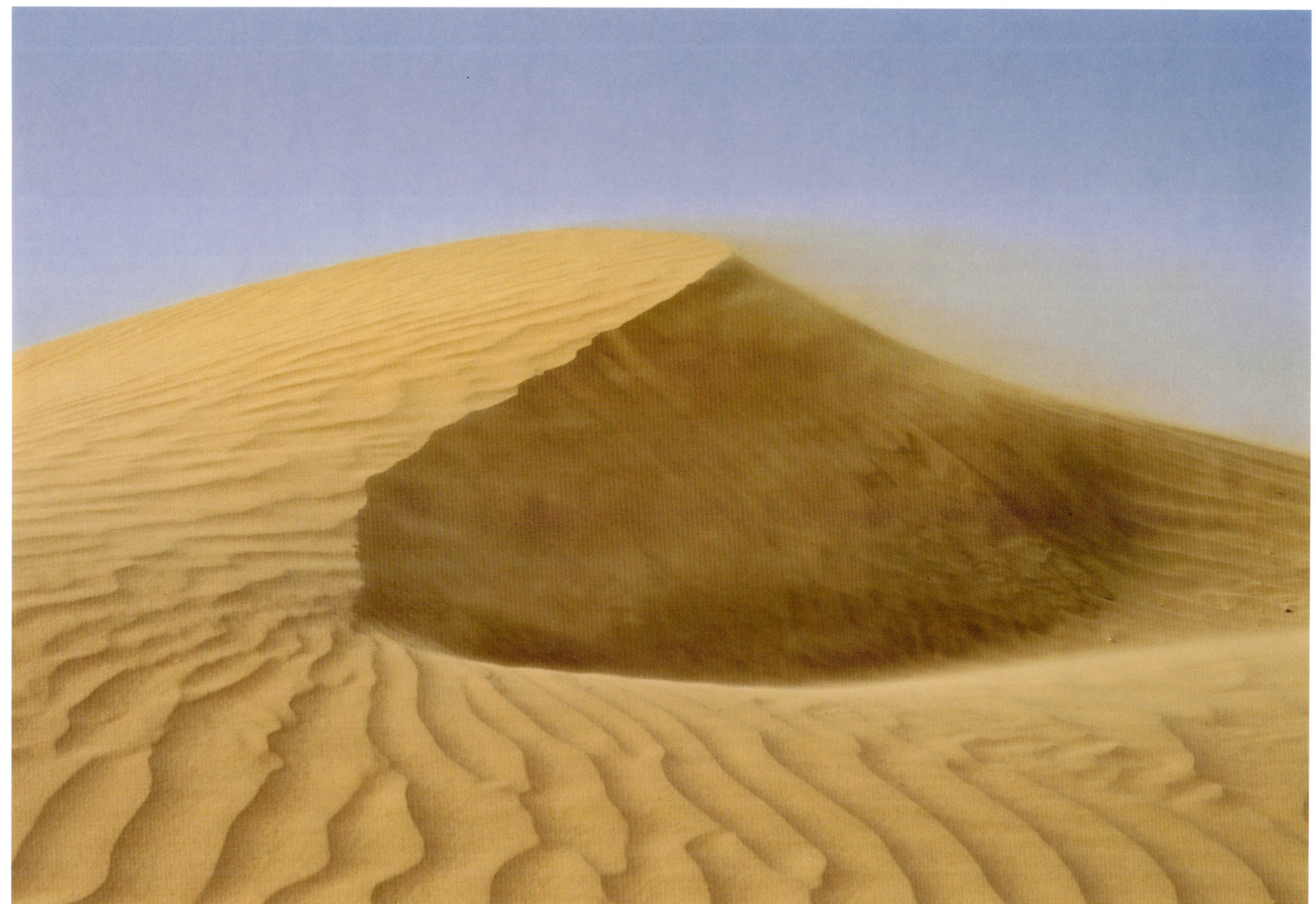

Wind Swept.
The Red Sand Dunes along Highway 62 is a popular area for four-wheeling and ATV riders.

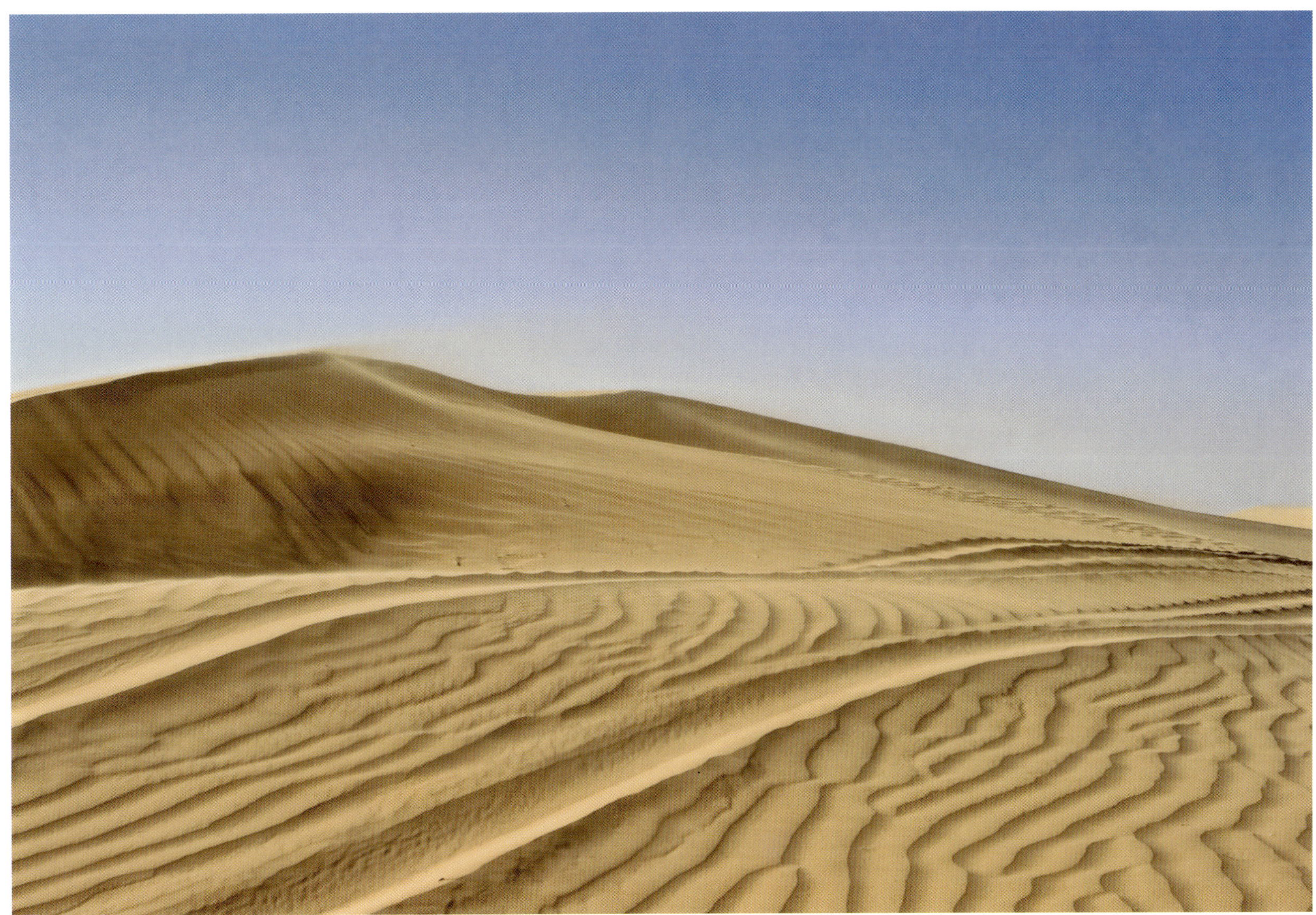

Red Sand Dunes – Far East El Paso.
Dunes are subject to different forms and sizes based on their interaction with the wind. Most kinds of dunes are longer on the windward side where the sand is pushed up the dune, and a shorter "slip face" in the lee of the wind. The "valley" or trough between dunes is called a *slack*. A "dune field" is an area covered by extensive sand dunes.

My El Paso is my place of refuge. My El Paso is my home and my heart.

— DR. KELLY OVERLEY,
VICE CHANCELLOR, TEXAS TECH UNIVERSITY

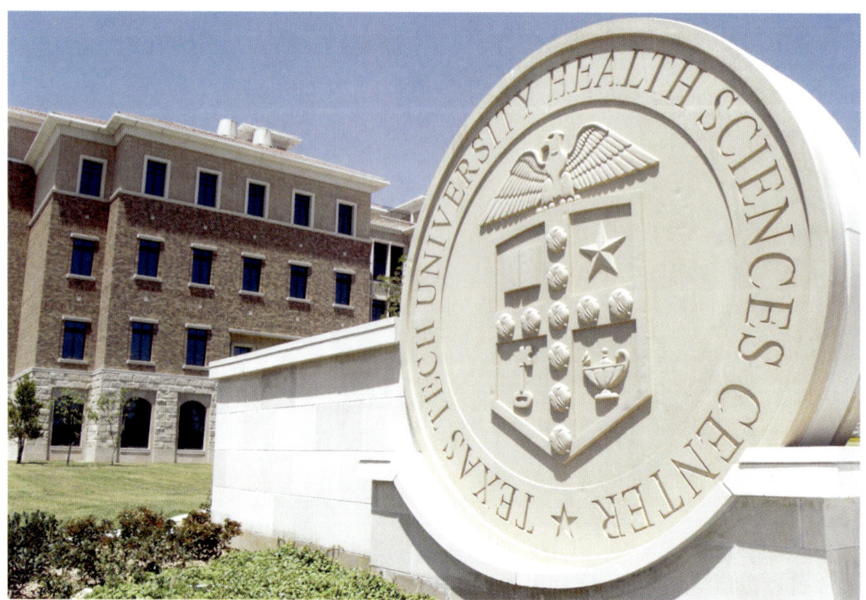

Texas Tech University Health Science Center.

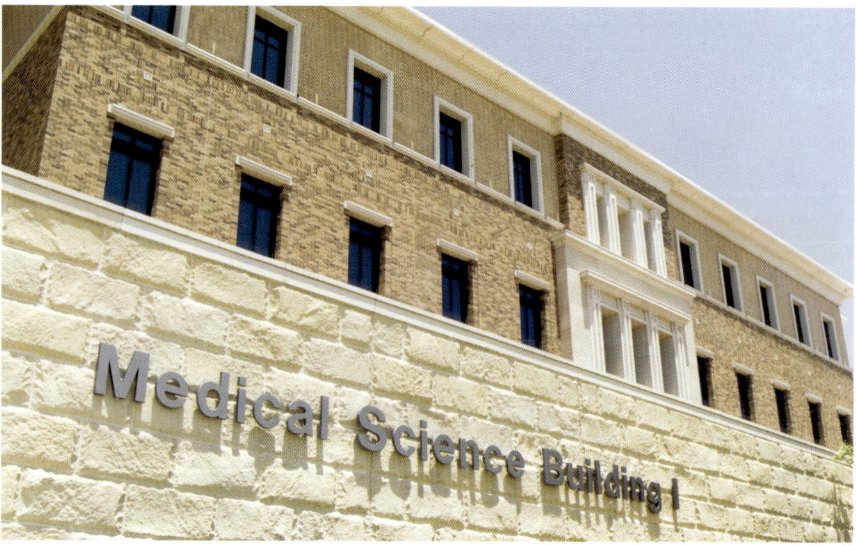

Texas Tech University Health Science Center.

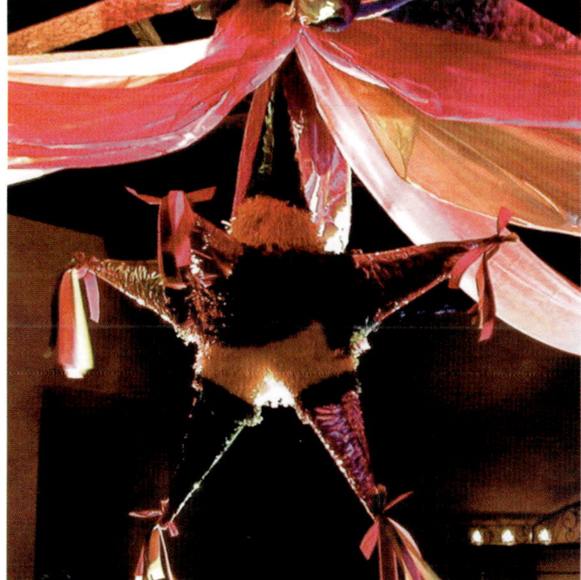

Piñata.

My El Paso is dry in climate and wet in culture.

— LISA DEGLIANTONI,
EDITOR, *EL PASO MAGAZINE*

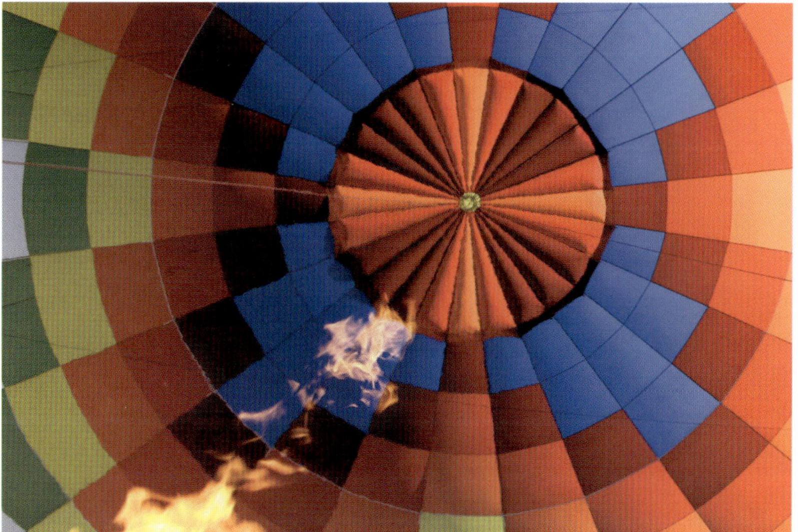

Fueling the Fire – Hot Air Ballooning.

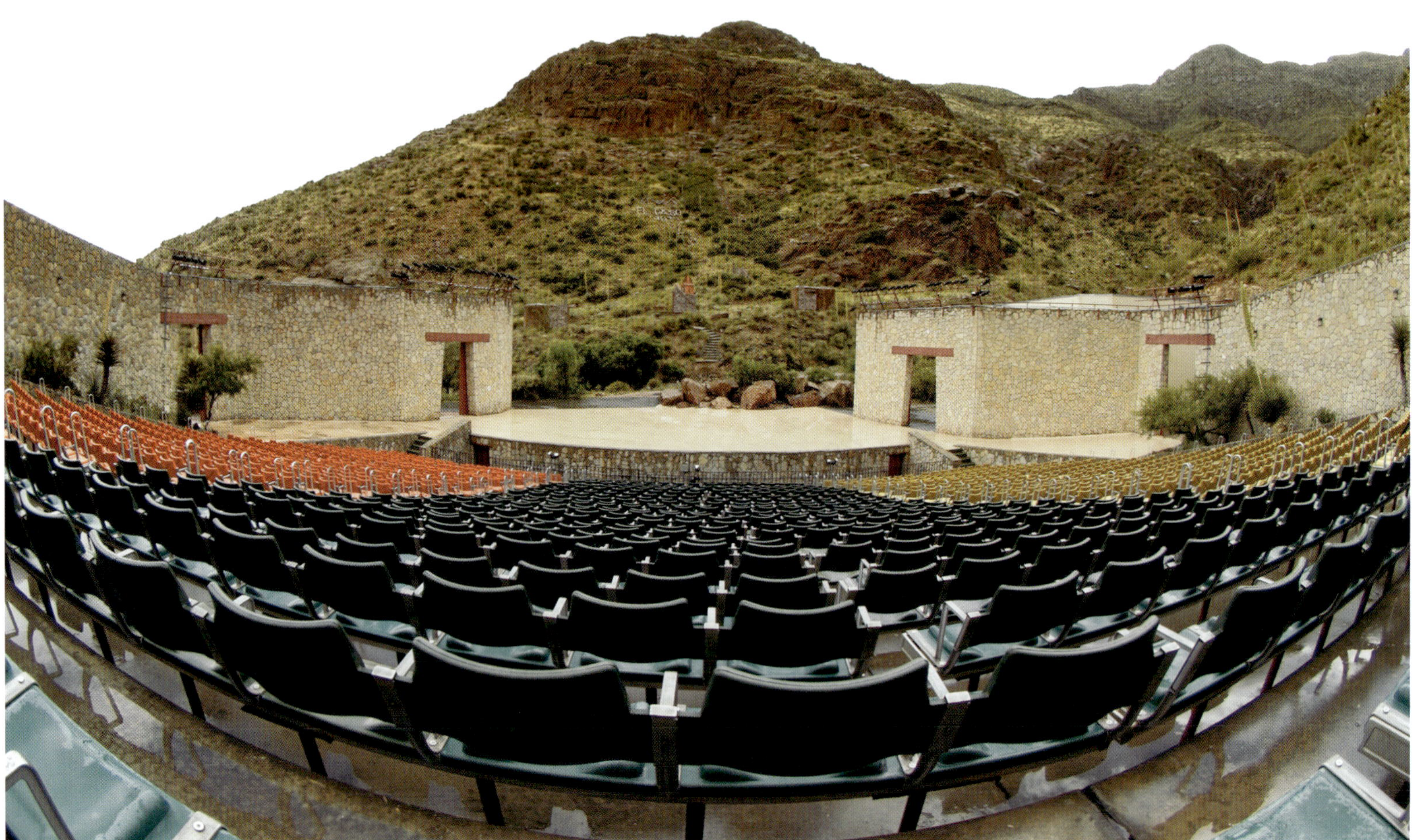

McKelligon Canyon Amphitheatre.
McKelligon Canyon is a ninety-acre park, located in the Franklin Mountains, open to hikers and picnickers. In the canyon, McKelligon Canyon Amphitheatre is surrounded on three sides by dramatic canyon walls; the 1,500-seat amphitheatre is used for concerts and special events, such as *Viva El Paso!*

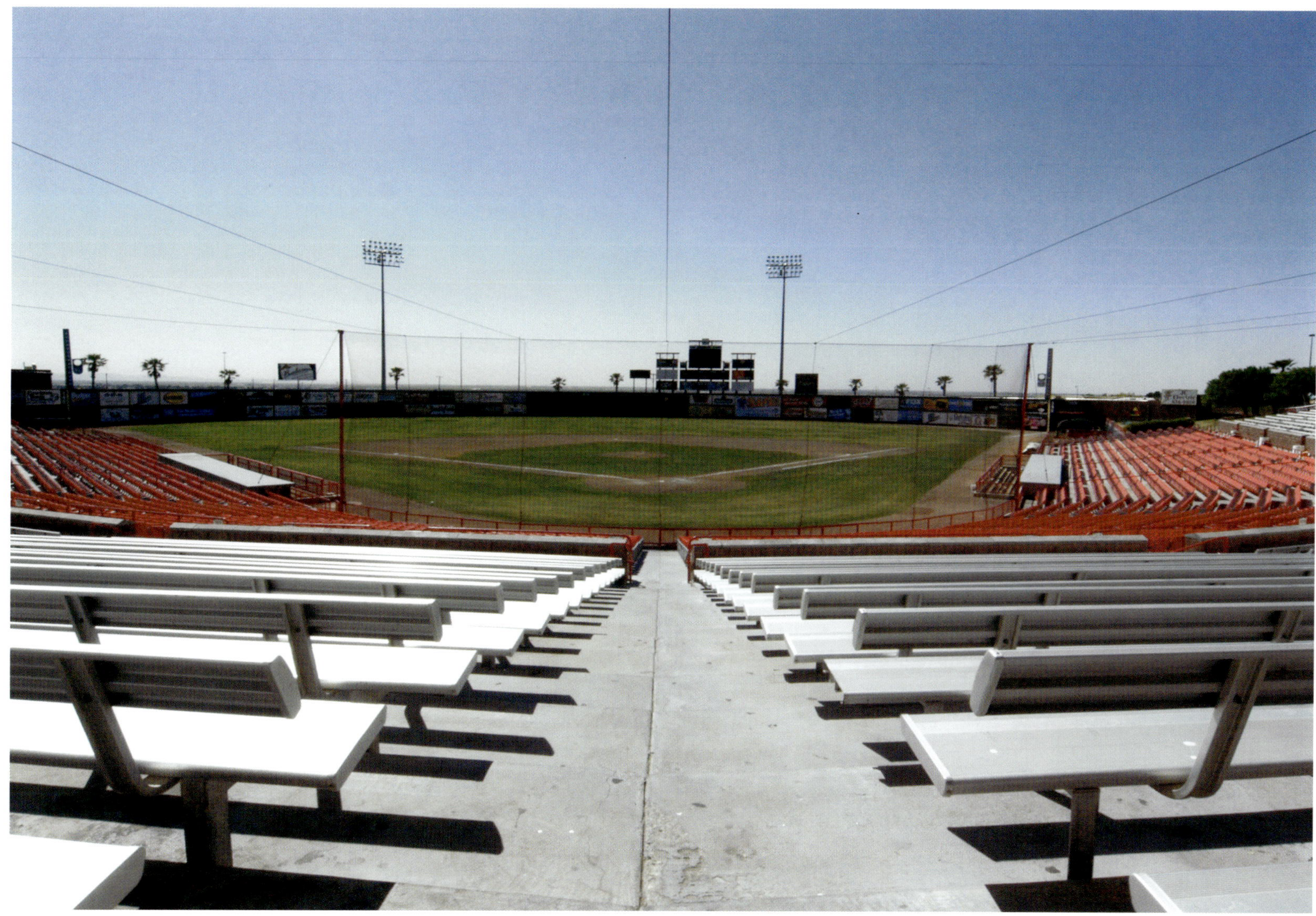

Cohen Stadium.

In 1922, Syd and Andy Cohen played baseball for the El Paso Mavericks and later played in the major leagues. Andy Cohen was a second baseman for the New York Giants, and Syd was a pitcher for several different teams in the American League, and was the last pitcher to strike out Babe Ruth. Syd also pitched in the Mexican leagues and later managed the Juarez team. Today, the El Paso Diablos minor league baseball team calls Cohen Stadium home.

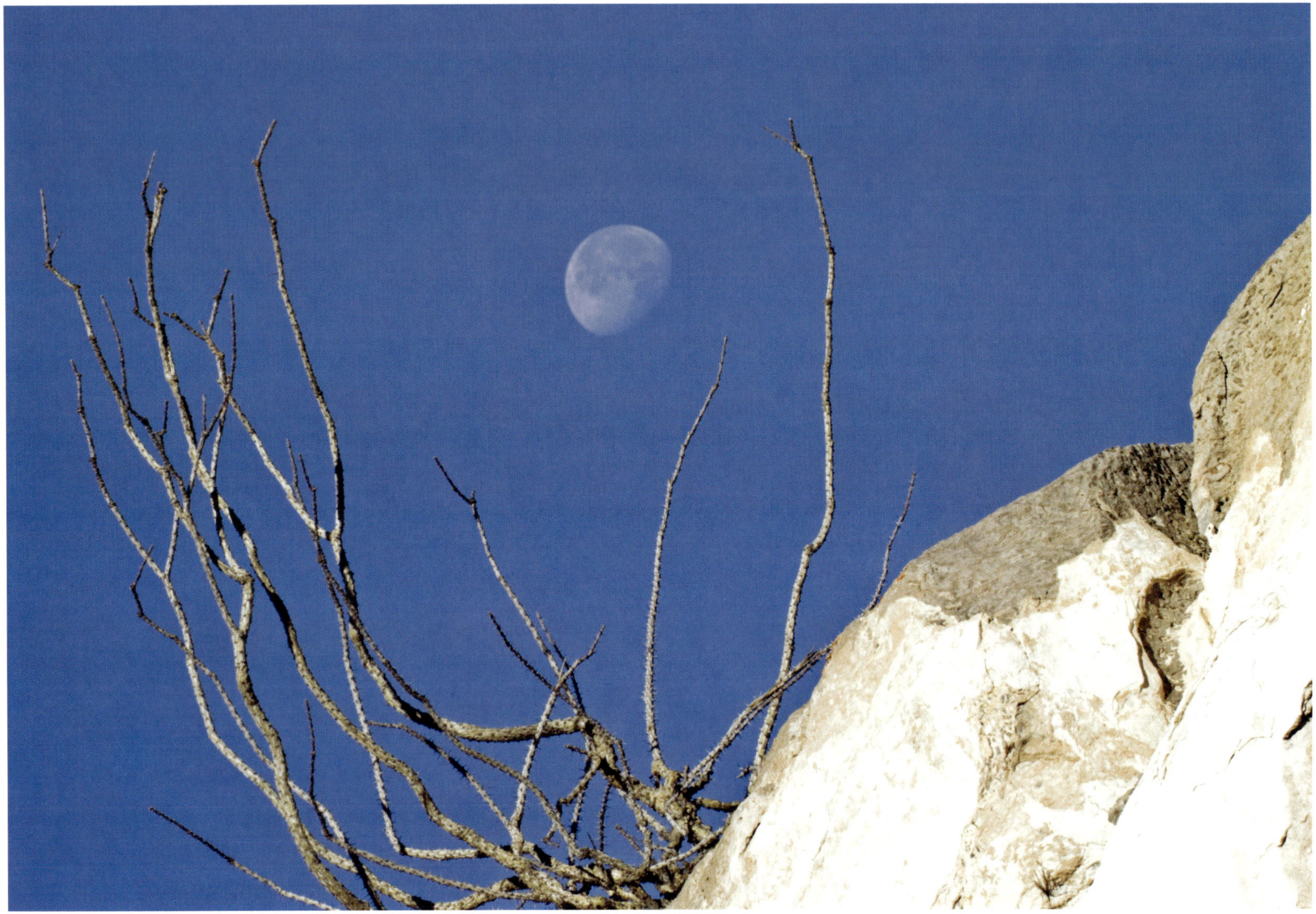

West Texas Forest.
The ocotillo (*Fouquieria splendens* – also called the coachwhip, Jacob's staff, and the vine cactus) is a curious, and unique desert plant of the southwestern United States and northern Mexico. For much of the year, the plant appears to be an arrangement of large spiny dead sticks, although closer examination reveals that the stems are partly green.

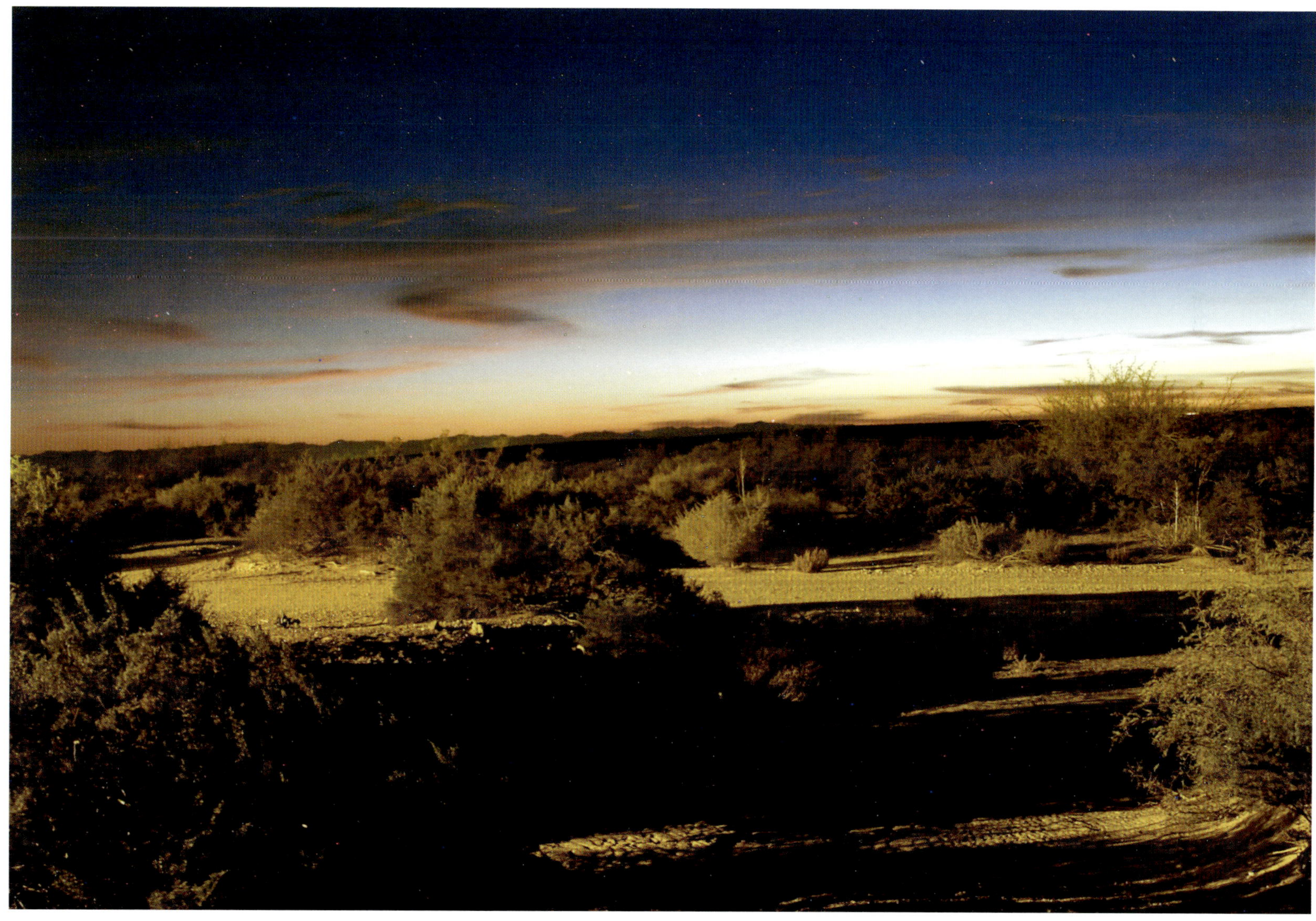

Life in the Desert.

West Texas, with its sparsely populated and relatively unpolluted land and its wide vast openness, has also become a destination for people looking to get away from urban life, and although it appears to be only lightly populated, there are many people who own vacation homes there.

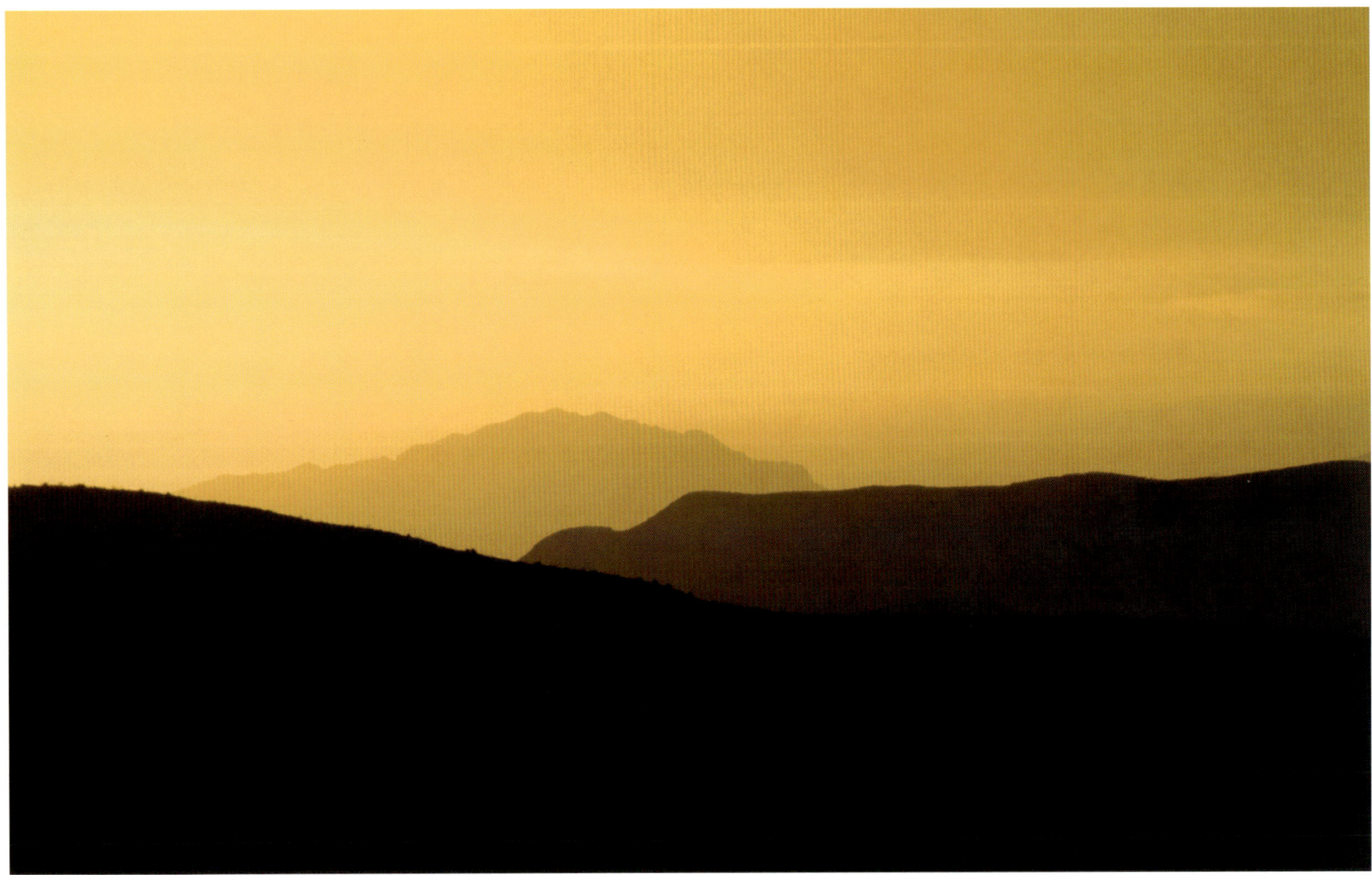

West Texas Drama.
The Franklin Mountains of Texas are a small range (twenty-three miles long, three miles wide) that extend from El Paso, Texas north into New Mexico. The Franklins were formed due to crustal extension related to the Cenozoic Rio Grande rift. Although the present topography of the range and adjoining basins is controlled by extension during rifting in the last ten million years, faults within the range also record deformation during the Laramide orogeny, between eighty-five and forty-five million years ago.

The highest peak is North Franklin Mountain at 7,192 feet. Much of the range is part of the Franklin Mountains State Park. The mountains are composed primarily of sedimentary rock with some igneous intrusions. Geologists refer to them as tilted-block fault mountains with billion-year-old Precambrian rocks inside, the oldest in Texas.

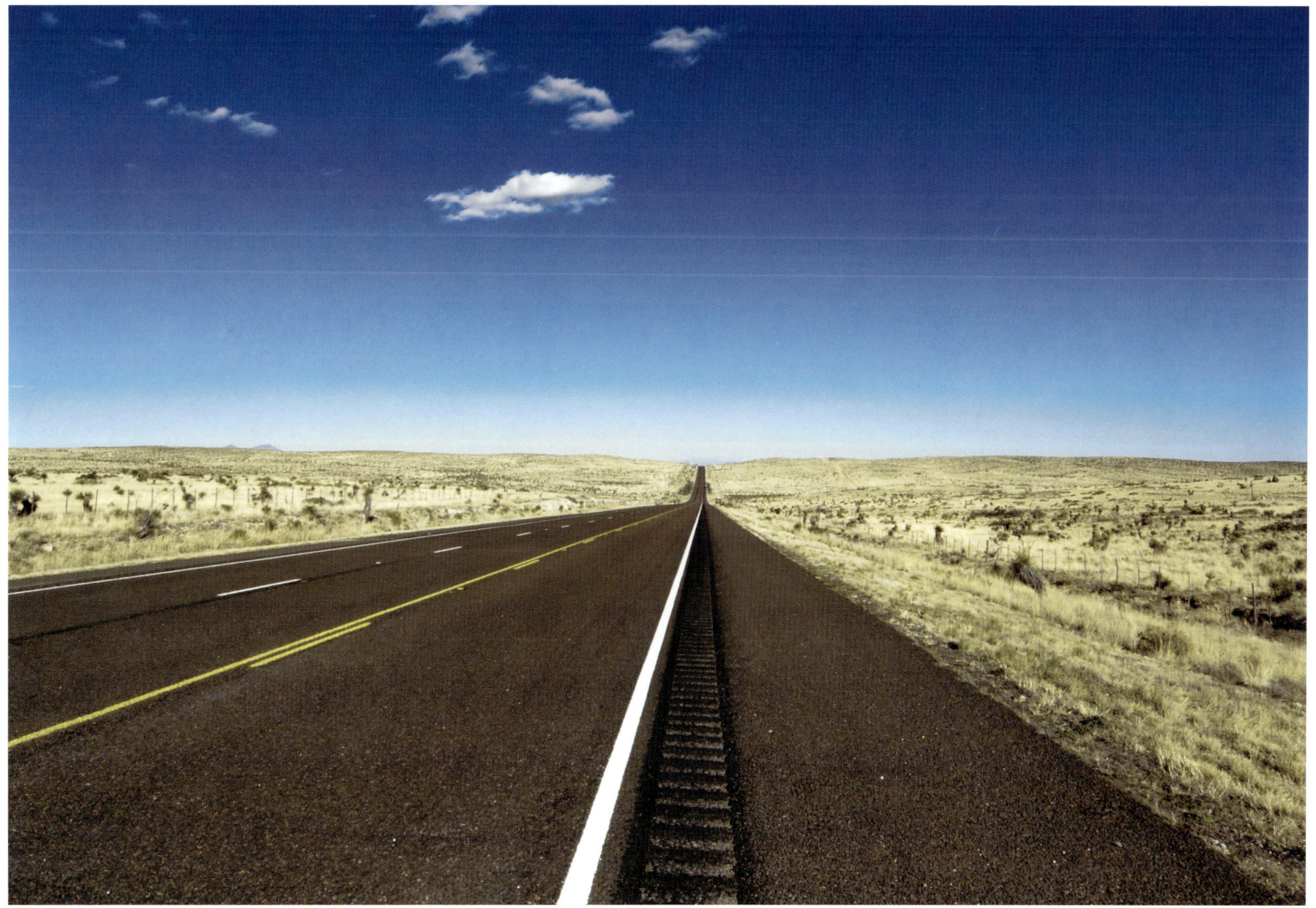

Long West Texas Road.
The American West and Southwest are well known for their wide-open spaces.

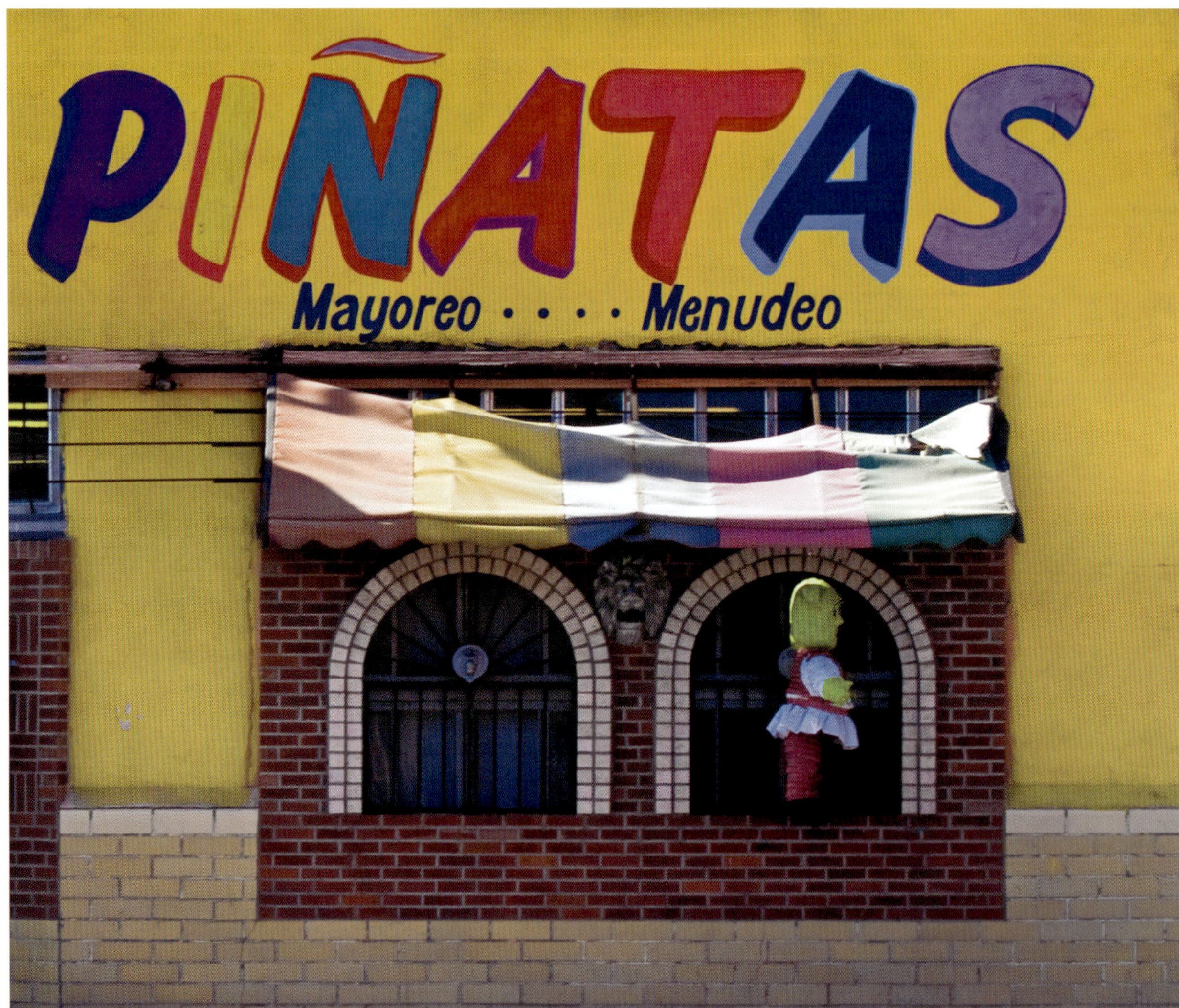

Combining Cultures.
The piñata is a brightly colored paper container filled with sweets and/or toys. It is generally suspended on a rope from a tree branch or ceiling and is used during celebrations. A succession of blindfolded, stick-wielding children try to break the *piñata* in order to collect the bounty inside of it. It has been used for hundreds of years to celebrate special occasions such as birthdays, Christmas, and Easter.

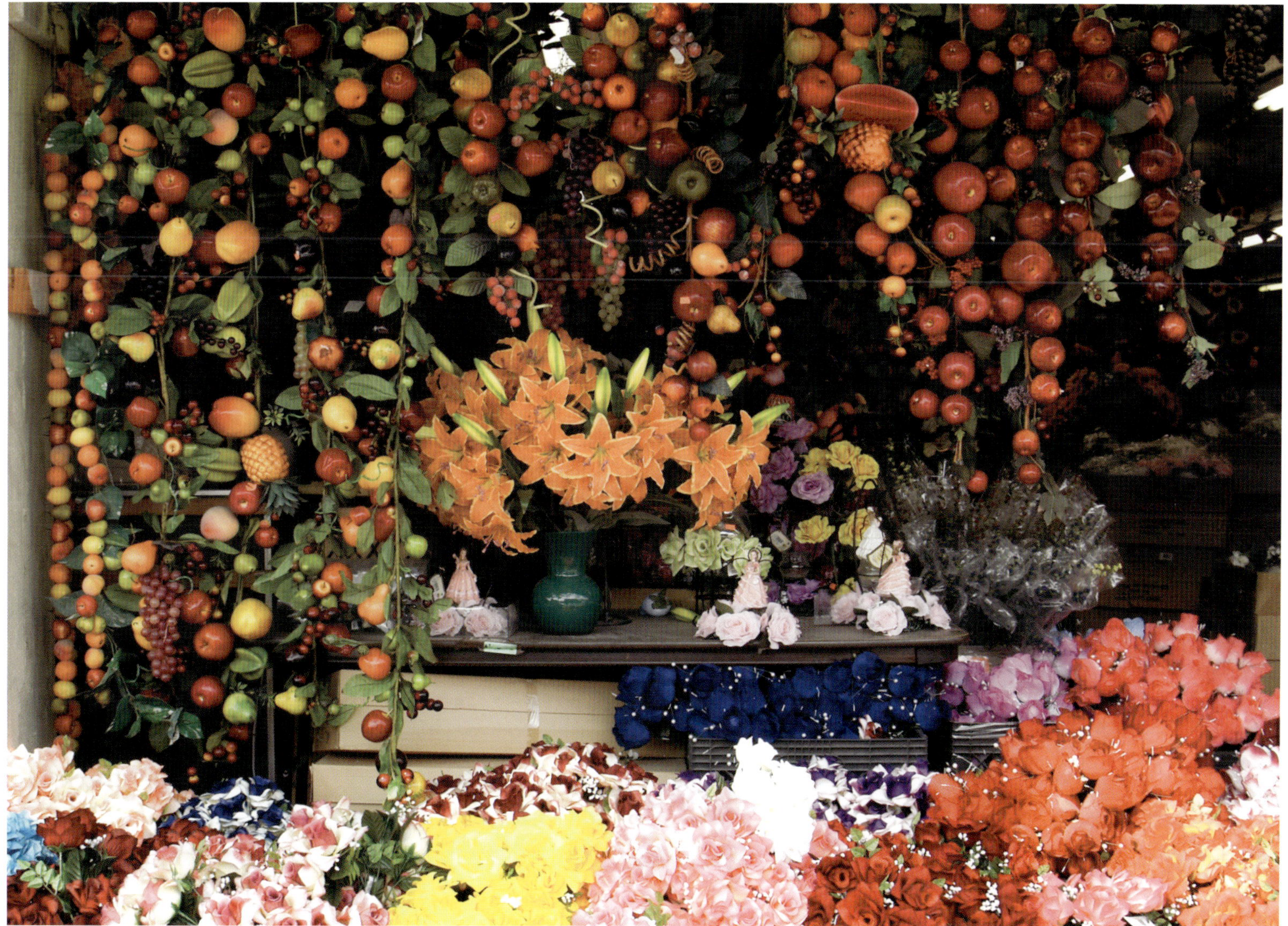

South El Paso Street.
Downtown El Paso shopping offers an eclectic mix for any shopper.

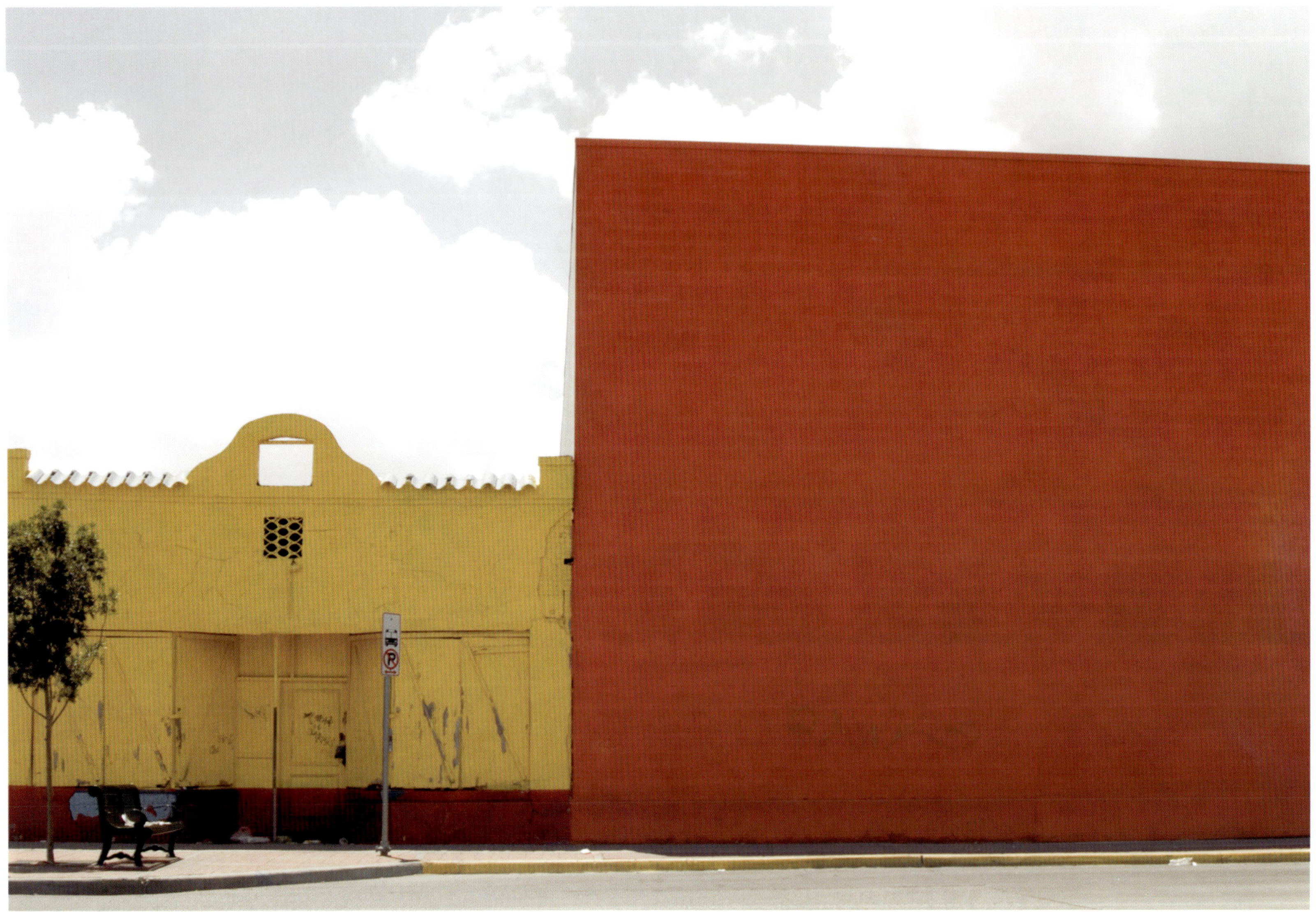

Alameda Avenue.
South El Paso.

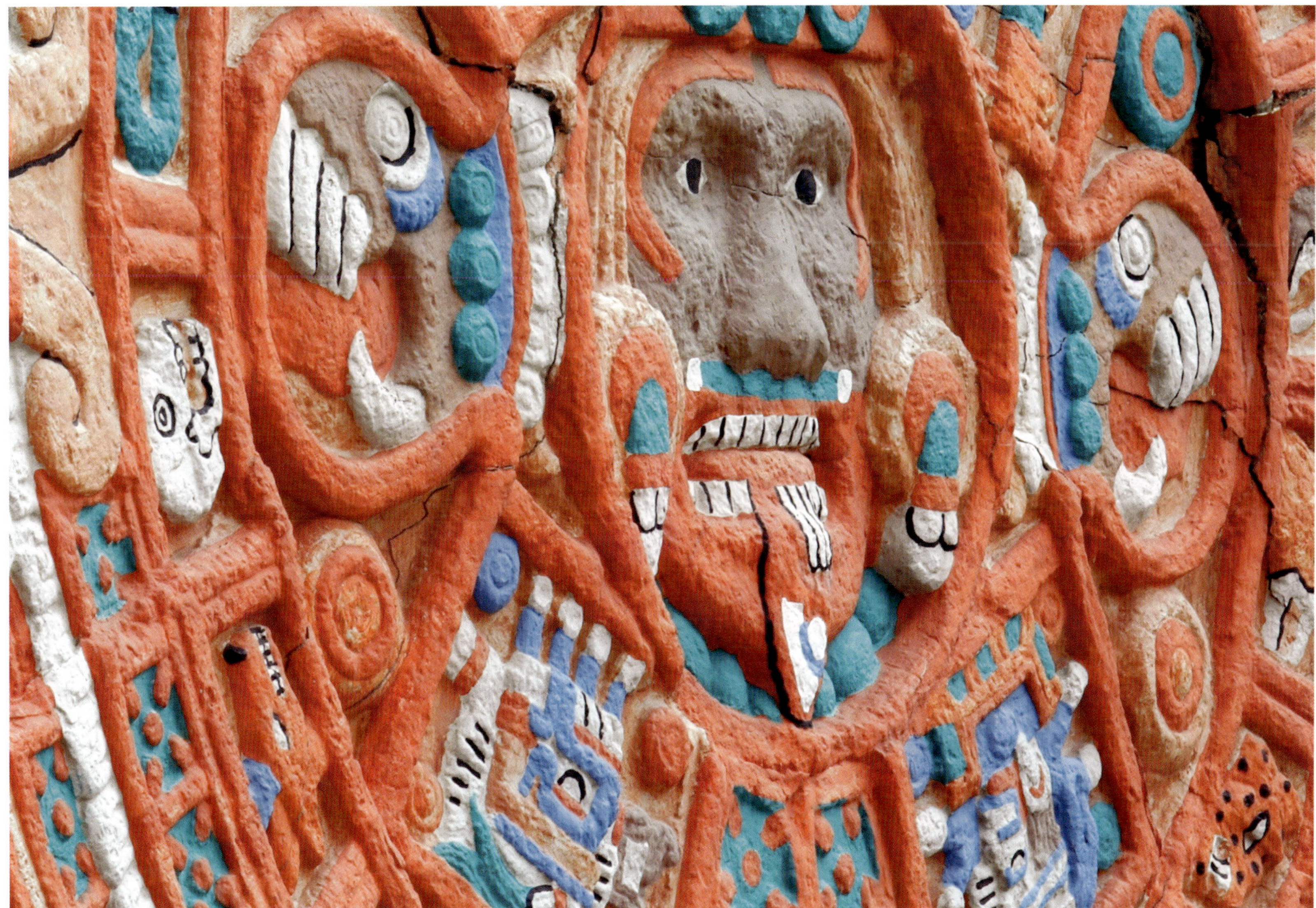

Aztec Calendar Replica.
A replica of the famous Aztec Calendar is located in a city park named for the same which is located next to the intersection of San Antonio and Kansas streets. This beautiful sculpture was a gift from the Mexican Consulate to the people of El Paso. This park contains several monuments dedicated to those El Pasoans and Juarenzes who gave their lives in defense of the United States.

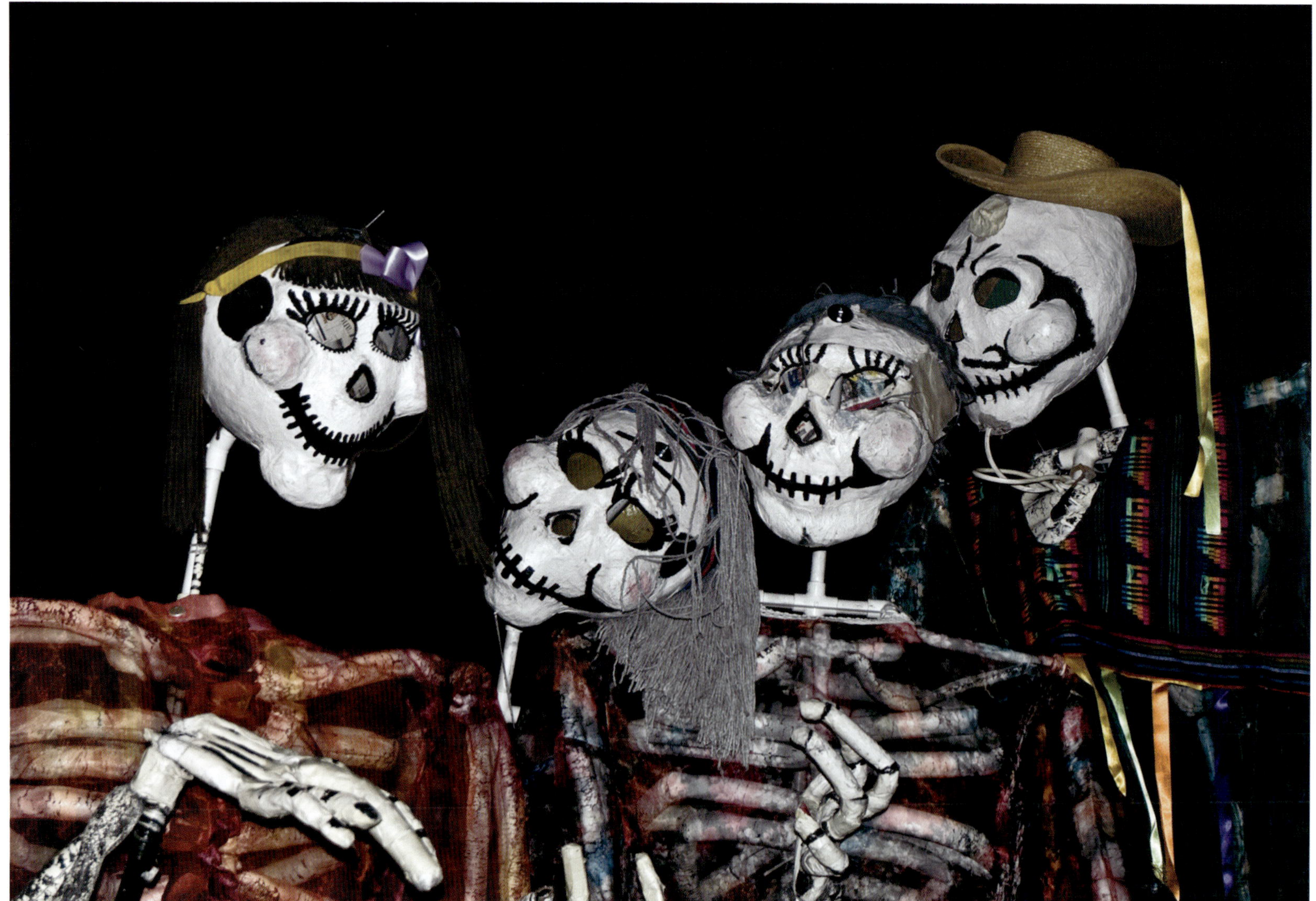

El Día de los Muertos.
This Mexican holiday focuses on gatherings of family and friends to pray for and remember friends and family members who have died.

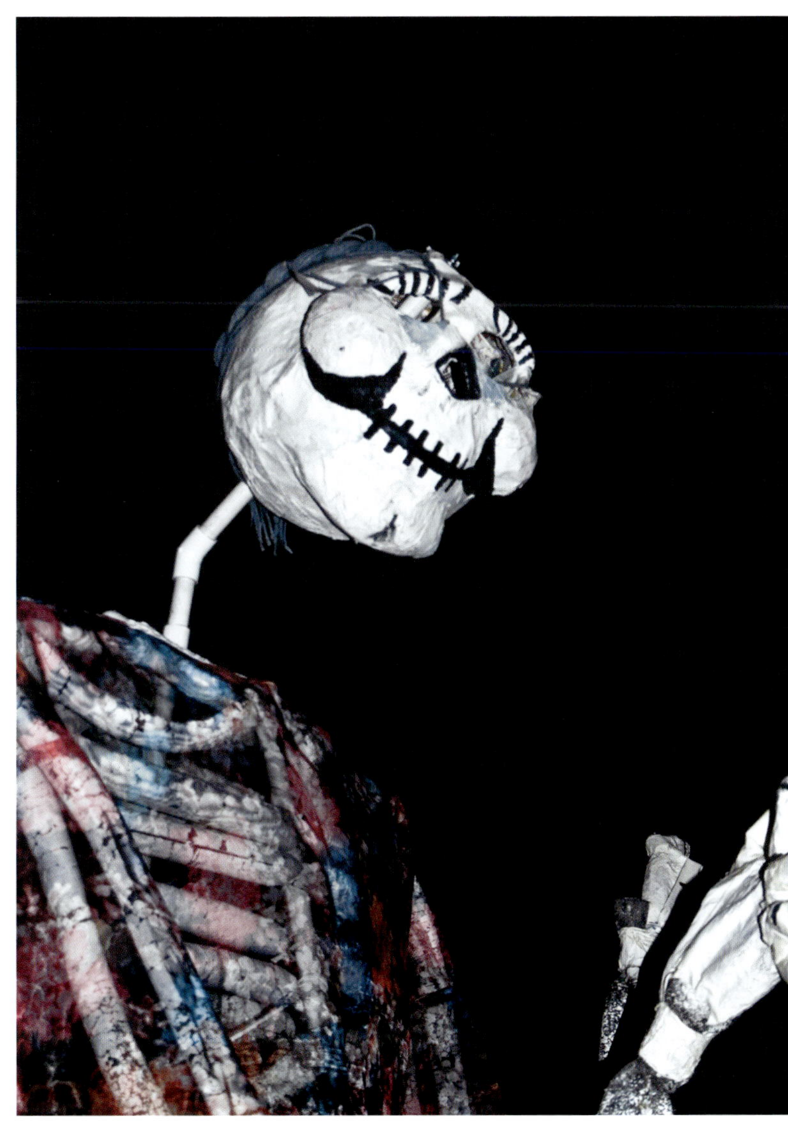

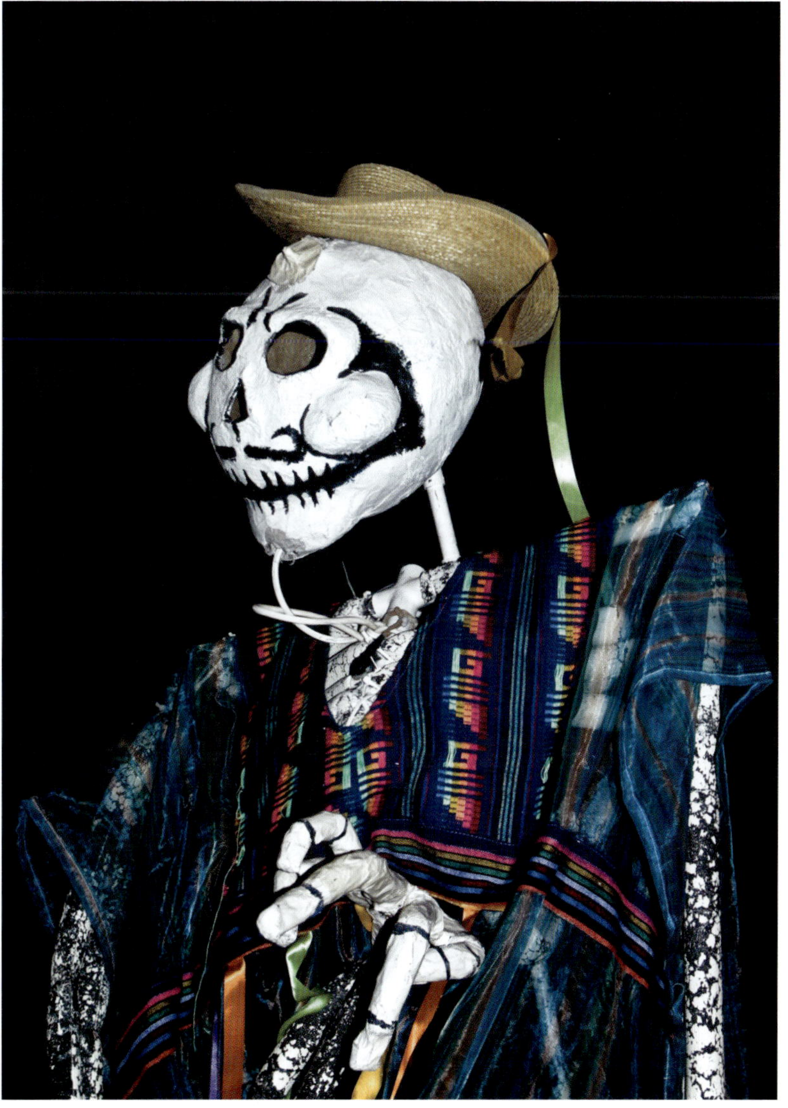

El Día de los Muertos.
The Day of the Dead (*El Día de los Muertos* in Spanish) is a holiday celebrated mainly in Mexico and by people of Mexican heritage living in the United States. The celebration occurs around the first and second of November, in connection with the Catholic holy days of All Saints' Day and All Souls' Day. Traditions include building private altars honoring the deceased and using sugar skulls, marigolds, and the favorite foods and beverages of the departed.

My El Paso is a place to discover with so many treasures waiting to be found and so much to offer.

— JOSEPH ODEH, BIG BUN

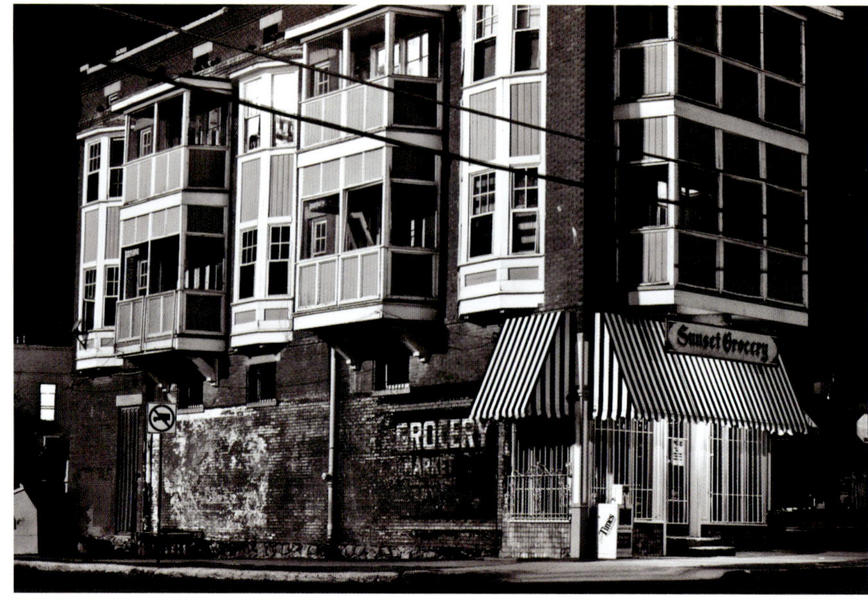

Historic Sunset Grocery.

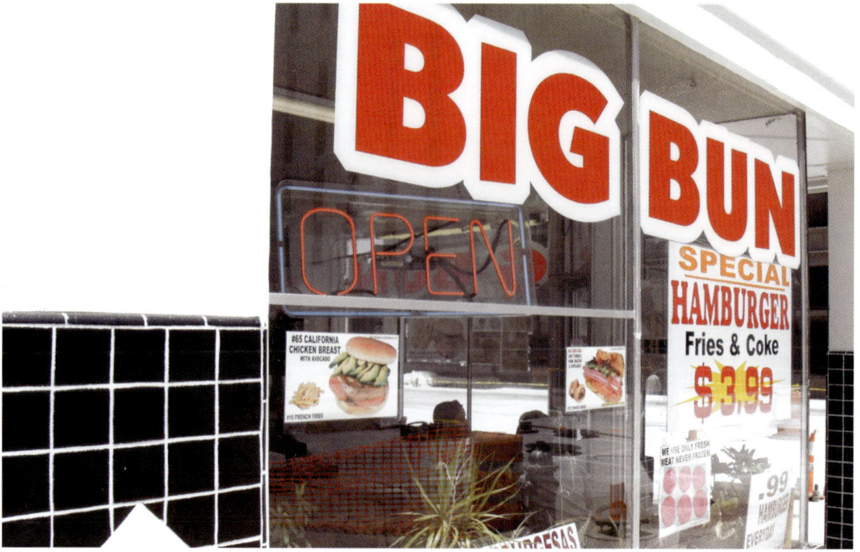

Big Bun Hamburgers.

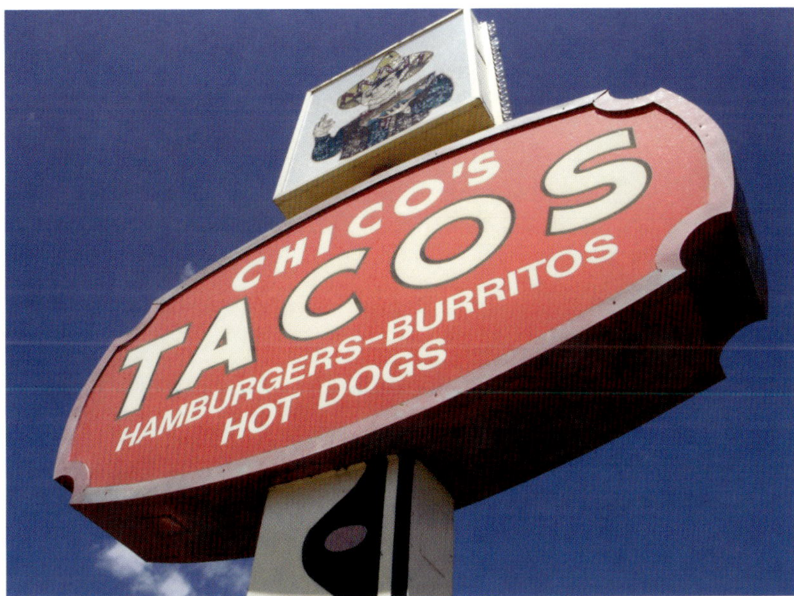

Chico's Tacos – An El Paso Institution.

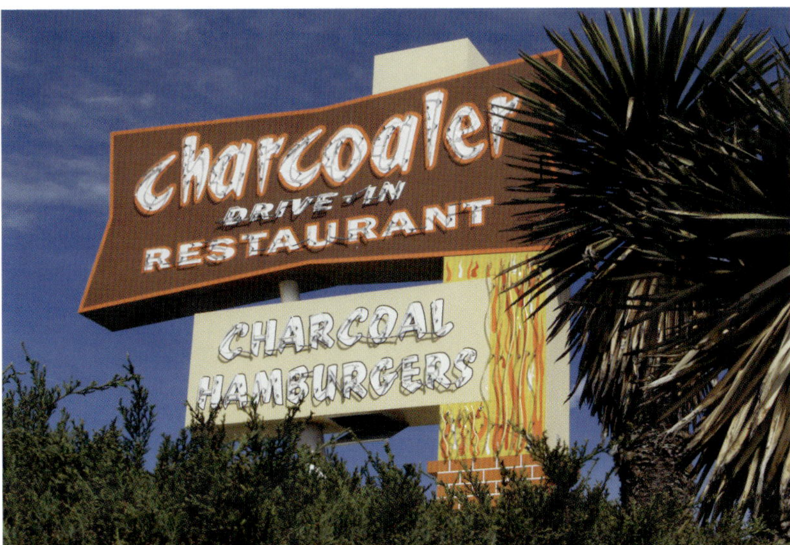

Charcoaler.

My El Paso is sleek and sophisticated con mucho cariño and big dose of down home charm.

—YOLANDA R. ALAMEDA, DIRECTOR, MUSEUMS AND CULTURAL AFFAIRS DEPARTMENT

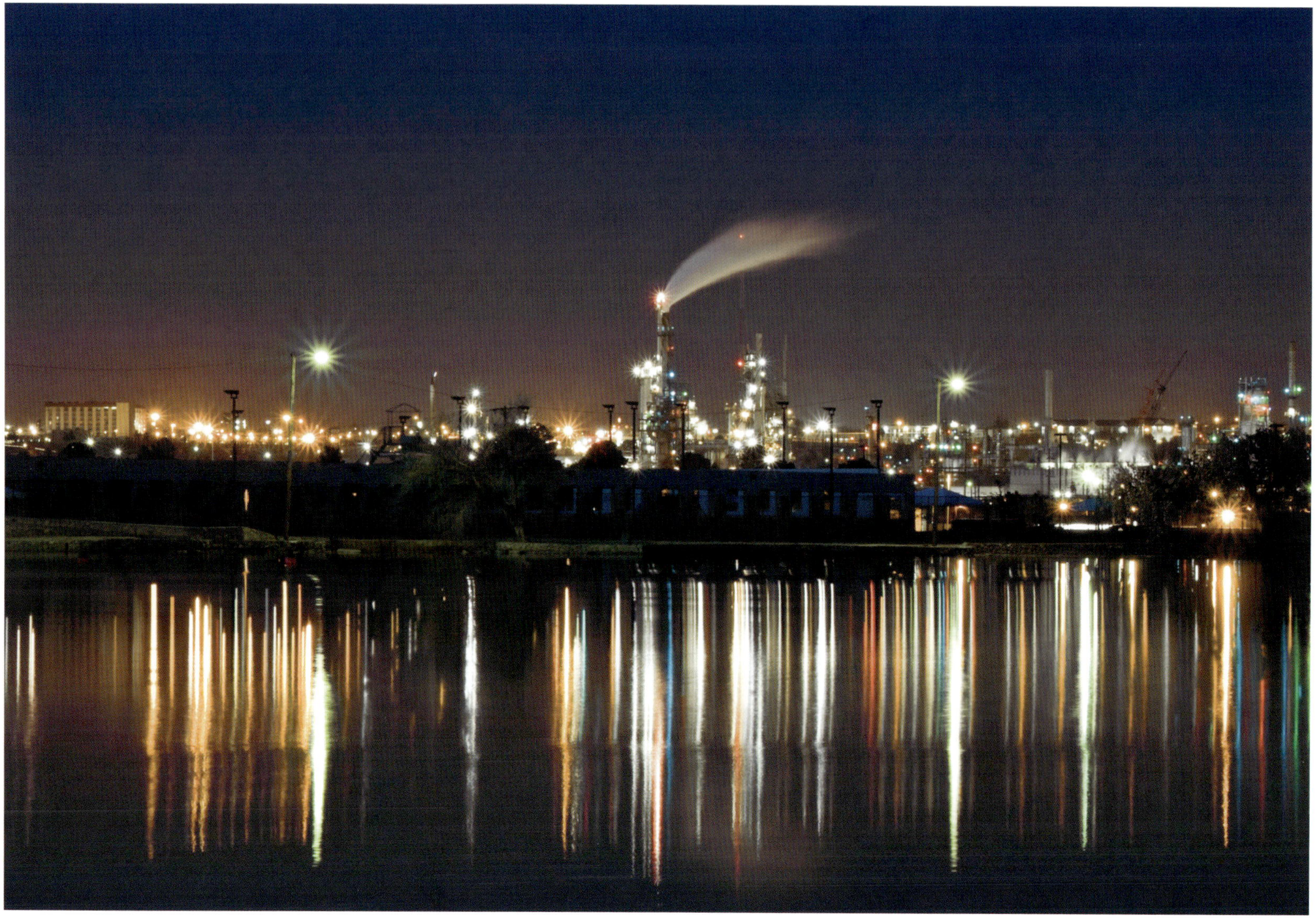

We've got the energy.
Western Refining, Inc., is the nation's fourth largest publicly traded independent oil refiner. With headquarters in El Paso, the company operates primarily in the Southwestern and Mid-Atlantic regions of the United States. Western has been publicly traded on the New York Stock Exchange since January 2006.

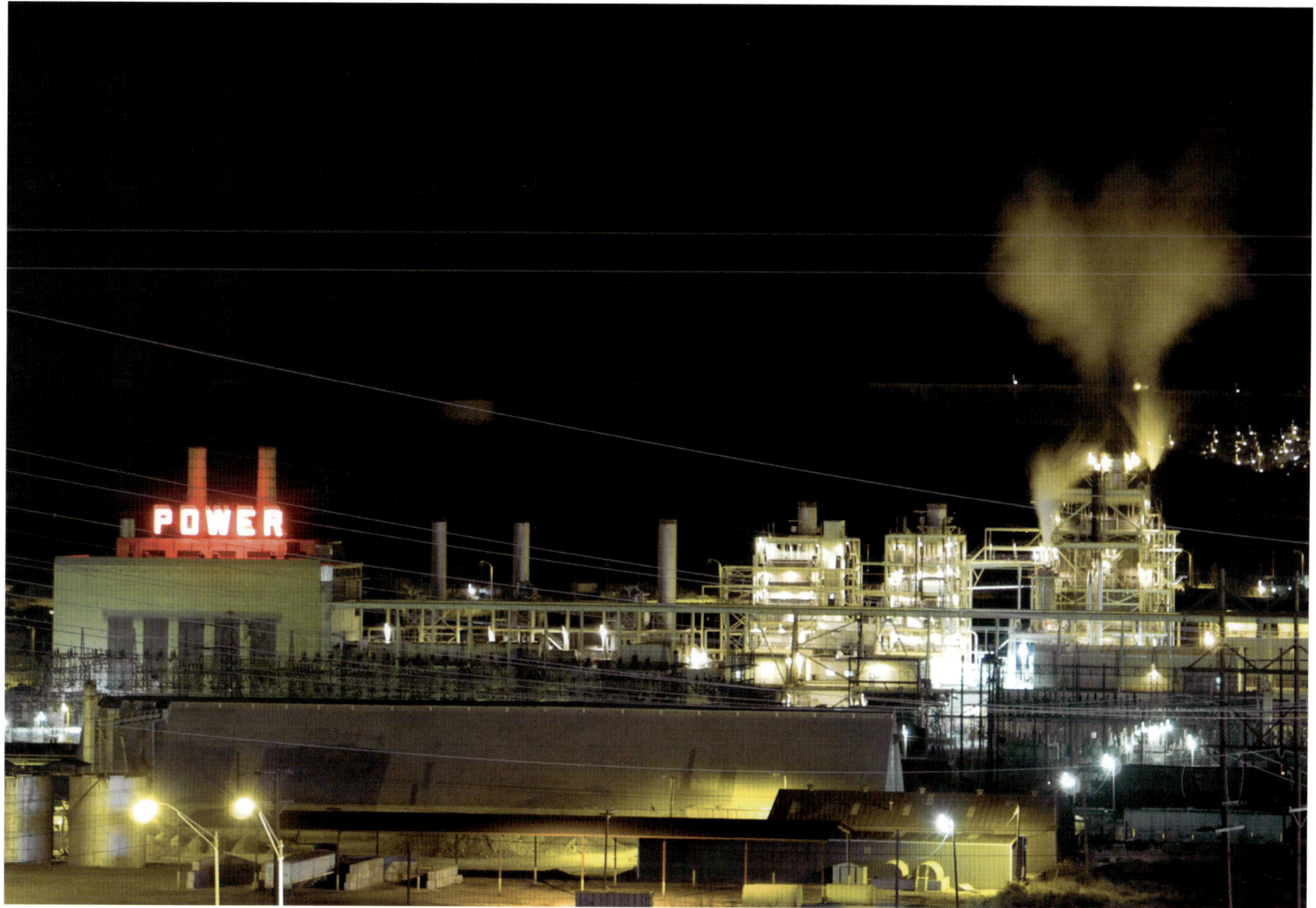

We've got the power.
In the 1920s the communities of West Texas and Southern New Mexico were expanding rapidly and with this expansion came the need for more electricity. El Paso Electric rose to the challenge and built a new power station to supplement the existing generating facility. The new power station, completed in November 1929, was named the Rio Grande Power Station.

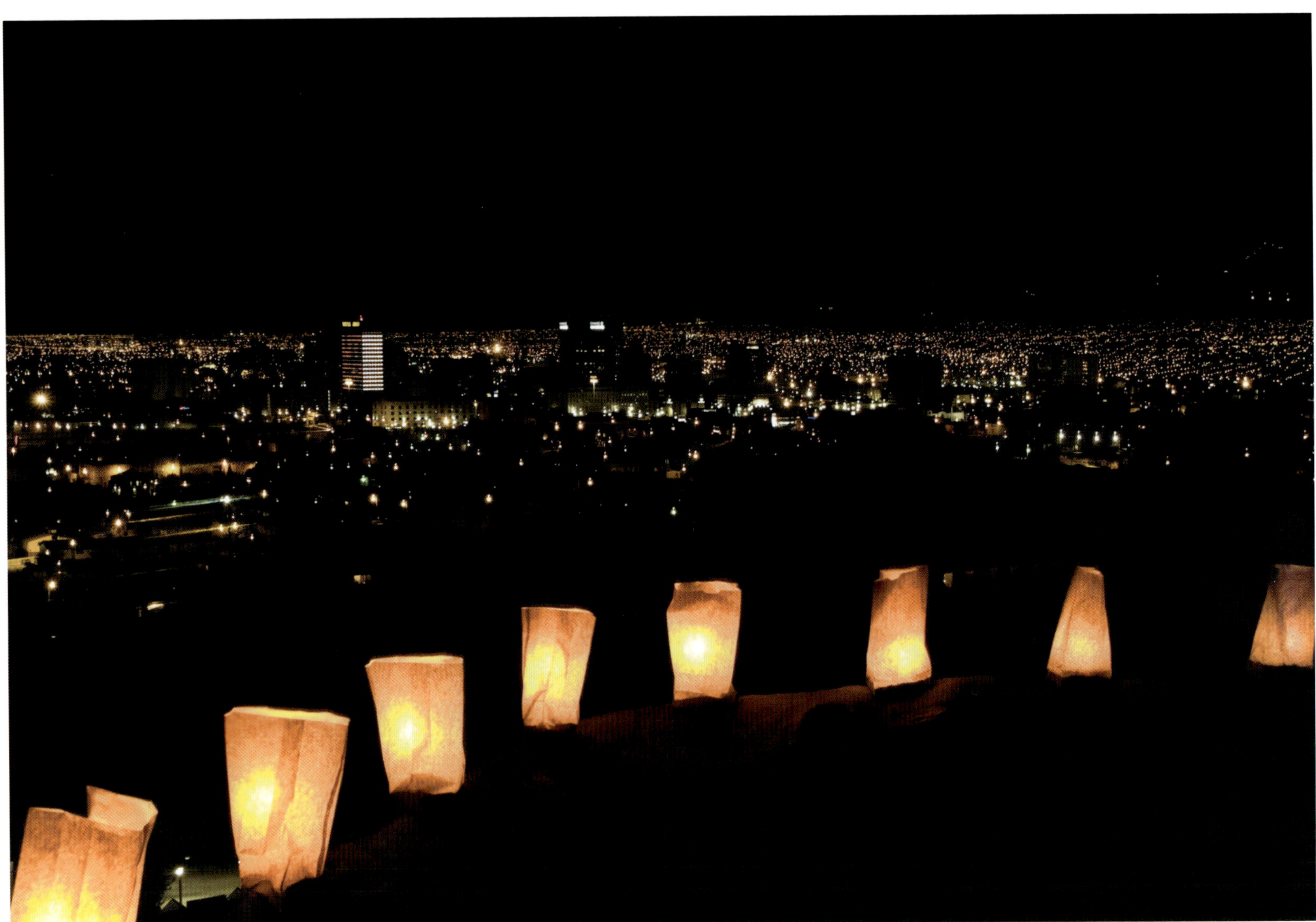

Luminaries over the city.
In the U.S. states of New Mexico, Arizona, and West Texas, luminaries are made from brown paper bags weighted down with sand and illuminated from within by a lit candle and traditionally displayed on Christmas Eve. These are typically arranged in rows to create large and elaborate displays. The hope among Christian believers is that the lights will guide the spirit of the Christ child to one's home. In recent times they are seen more as a secular decoration akin to holiday lights and have gained popularity in other parts of the country.

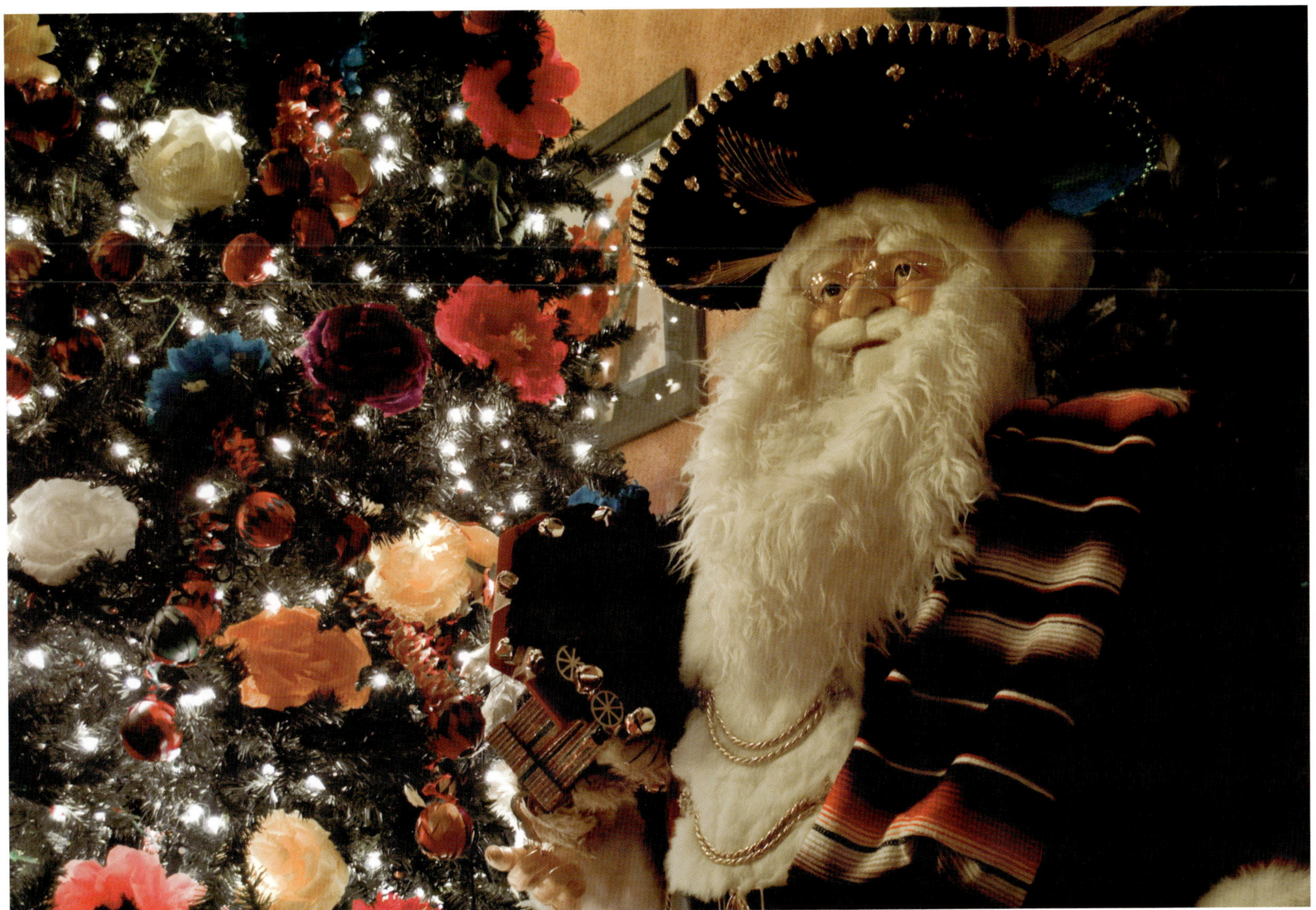

Bi-Cultural Christmas.
El Pasoans celebrate the city's rich and colorful cultural history by combining the influences of Mexico and the United States during the holiday season.

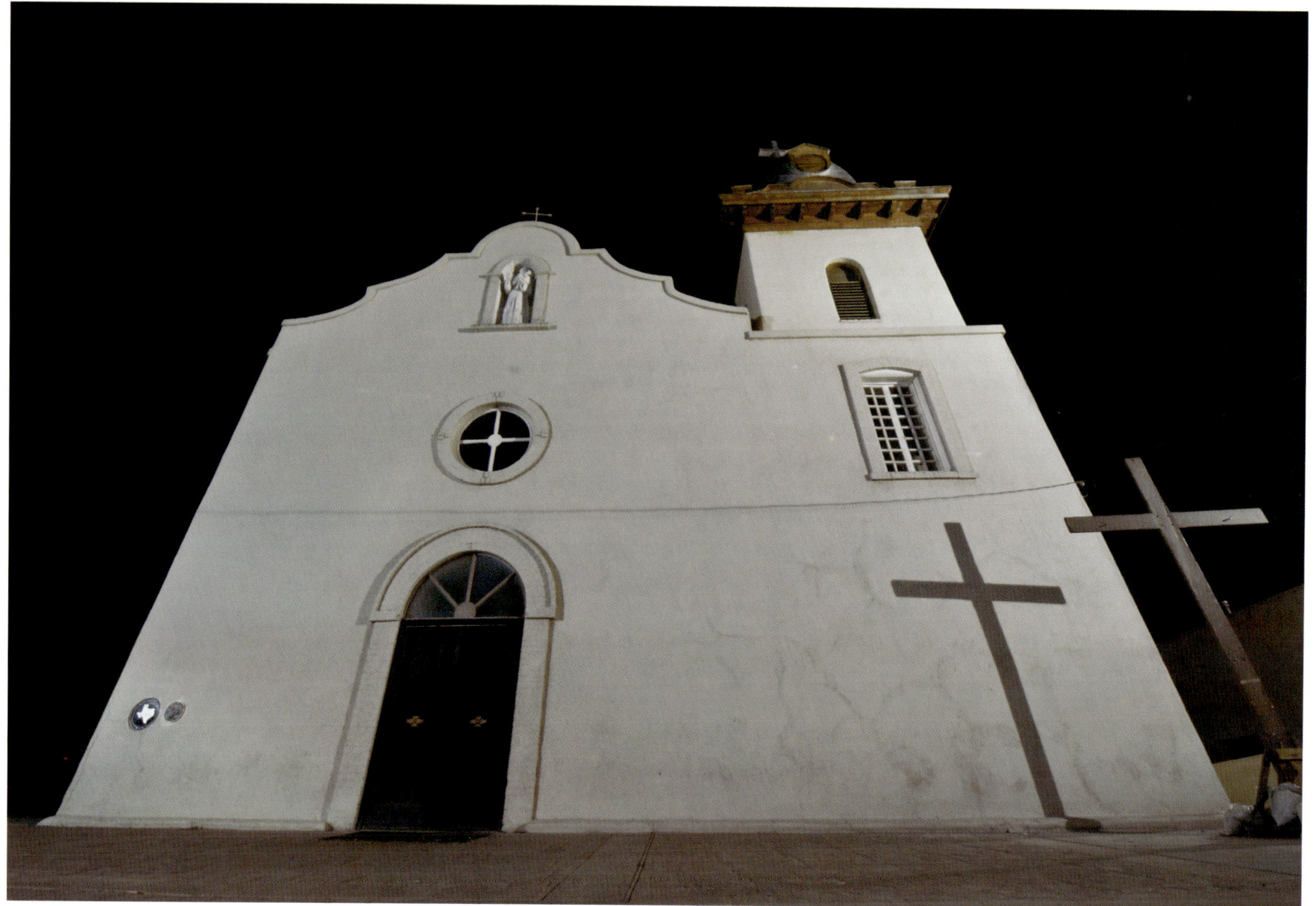

Ysleta Mission.
La Mision de Corpus Christi de San Antonio de la Ysleta del Sur was established by Spaniards Antonio de Otermin and Fray Francisco de Ayeta in 1680. It owes its heritage to Pueblo traditions, Franciscan missionaries, and Spanish colonial life in Northern New Mexico. This and the other two missions established here after the Pueblo Revolt of 1680 are children of the pain of intolerance between cultures and forced emigration.

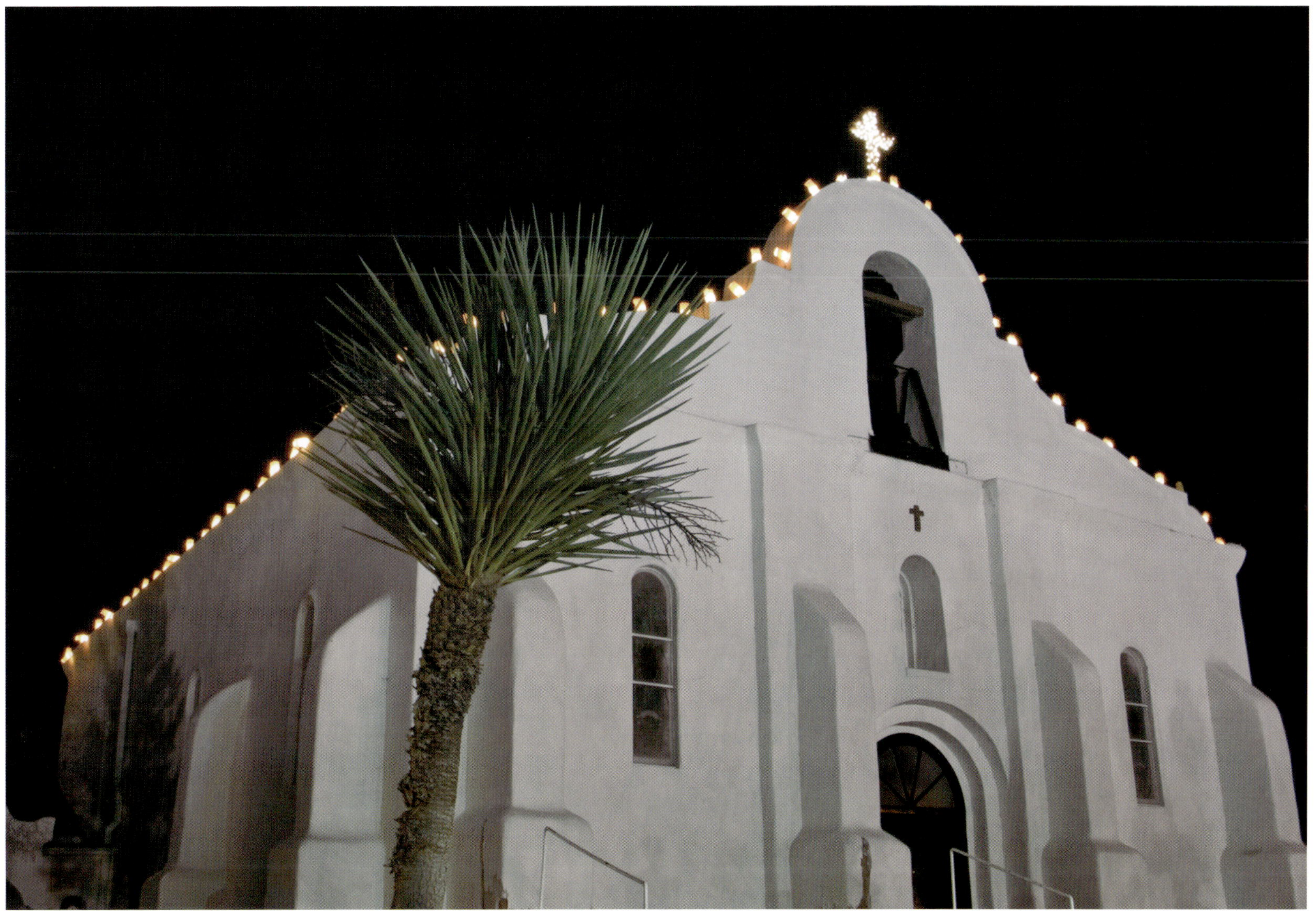

San Elizario Chapel.
San Elizario Chapel, known as La Capilla de San Elcear, functioned as a presidio chapel. It provided the religious needs of a presidio or an outpost of military personnel. The presidio was moved to the present site in 1789 to protect travelers and settlers along the Camino Real (Royal Highway), which ran through El Paso to Santa Fe, New Mexico. Its close proximity to the Ysleta and Socorro missions also provided protection for them.

My El Paso is positioned properly for progressive prosperity.

—WILLIAM THURMOND,
THIRD GENERATION EL PASOAN

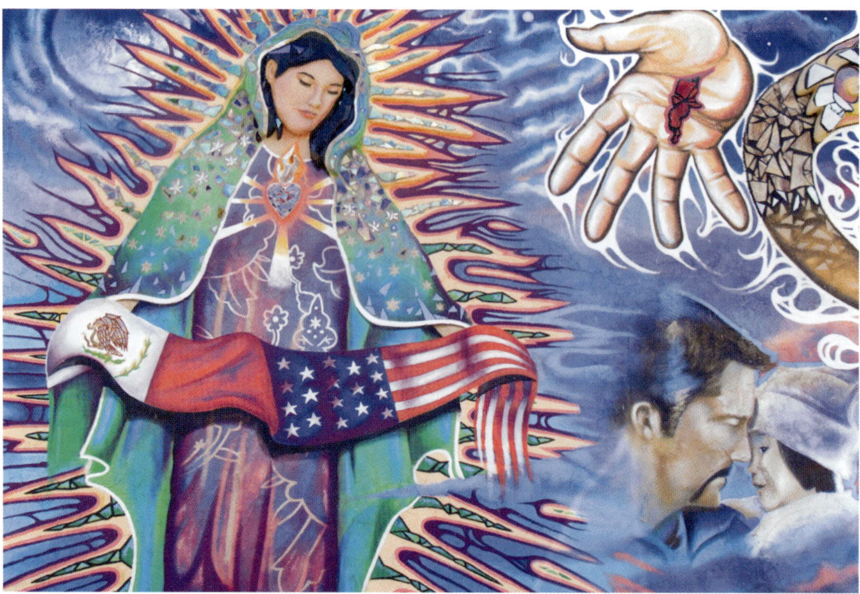

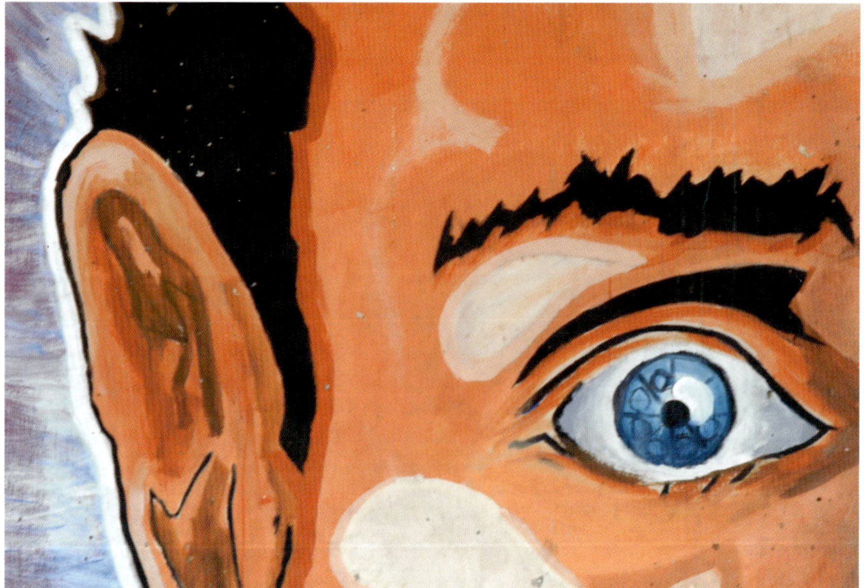

Murals have been painted on literally dozens of support structures of the interstate interchange reflecting an interesting blend of themes ranging from iconic Chicano images to religious images that depict the character of El Paso.

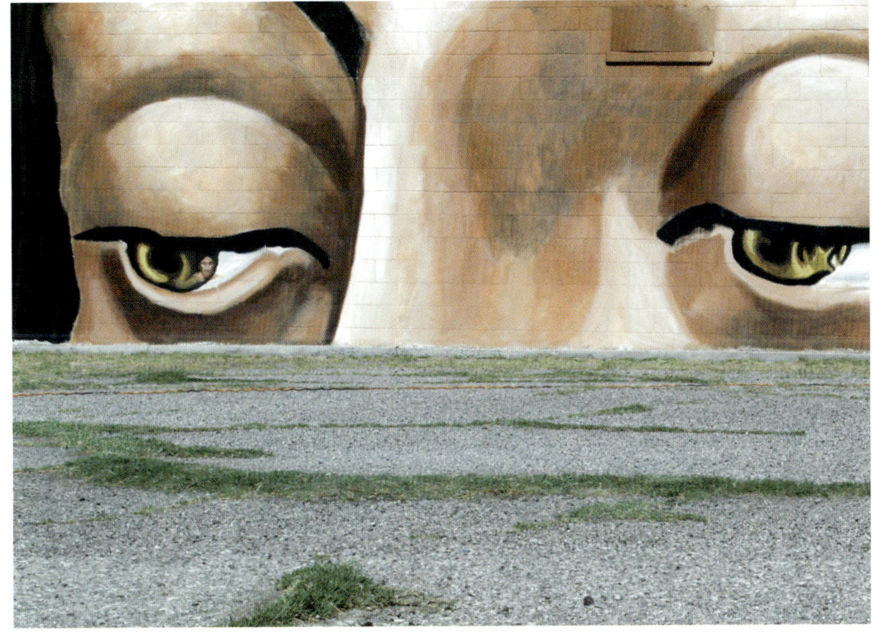

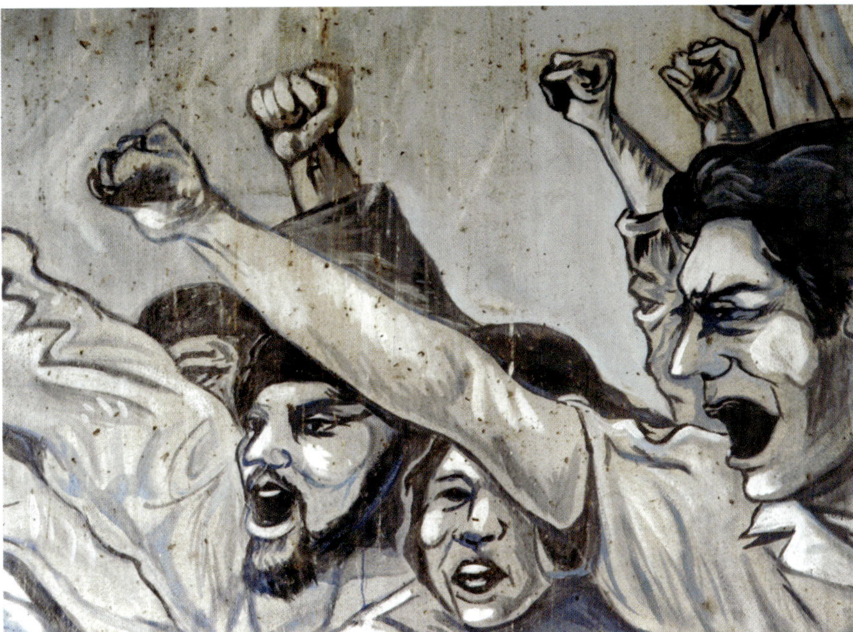

My El Paso is a place of color, excitement, and friendliness – an authentic borderland metropolis that I love above all others.

– JODY SCHWARTZ, EL PASO PHOTOGRAPHER

Rio Bosque Wetlands Park.

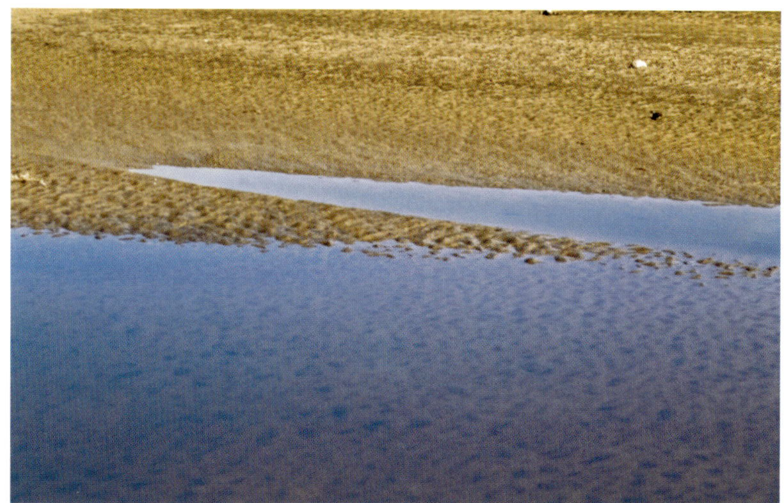

Rio Bosque Wetlands Park is a 372-acre City of El Paso Park.

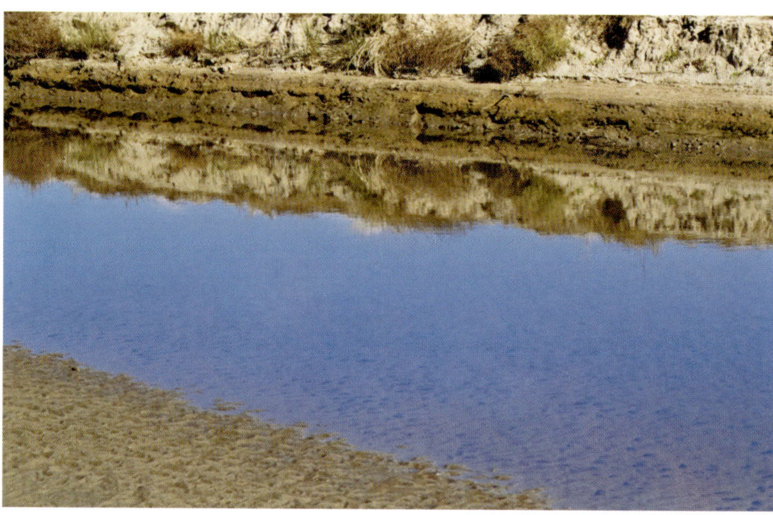

Wetlands and riverside forests once graced the banks of the Rio Grande.

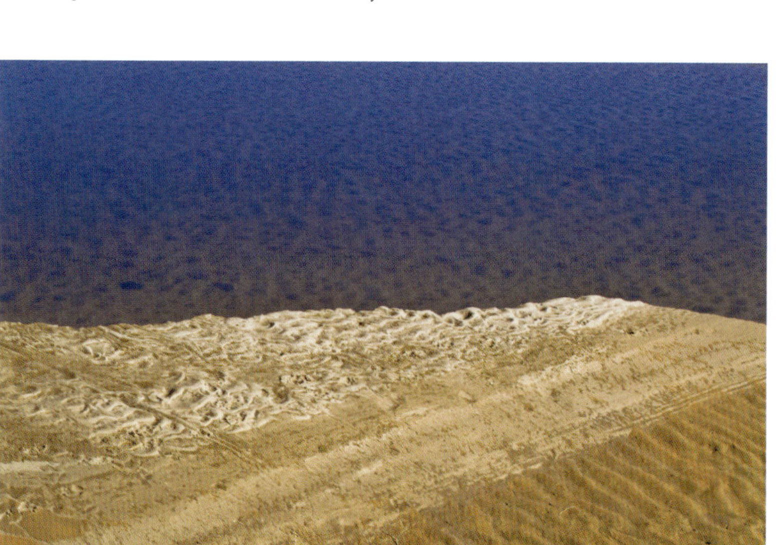

At Rio Bosque the environment is still changing, but in a new way.

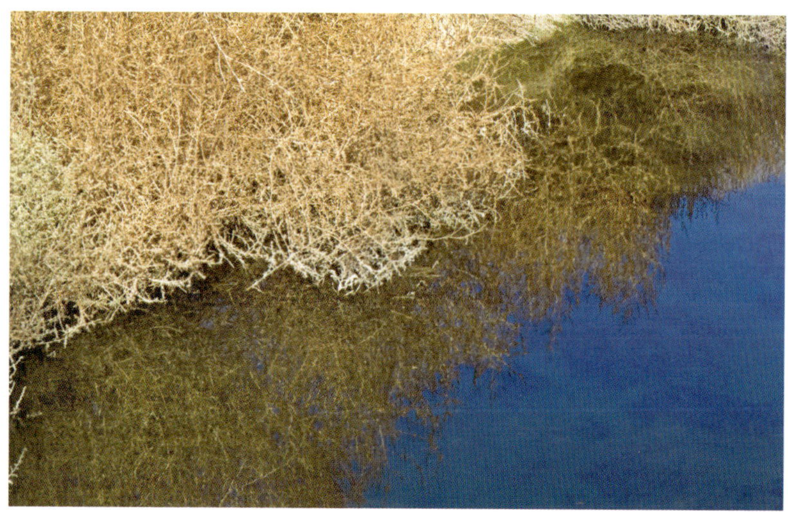

The park is enclosed by irrigation canals and drains on three sides.

Salt Flat Texas.

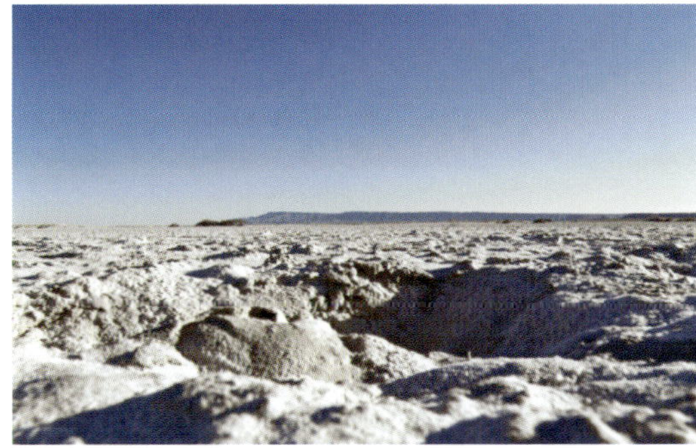

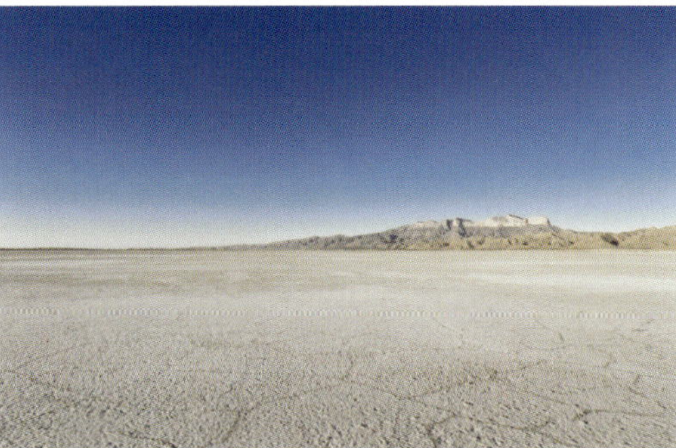

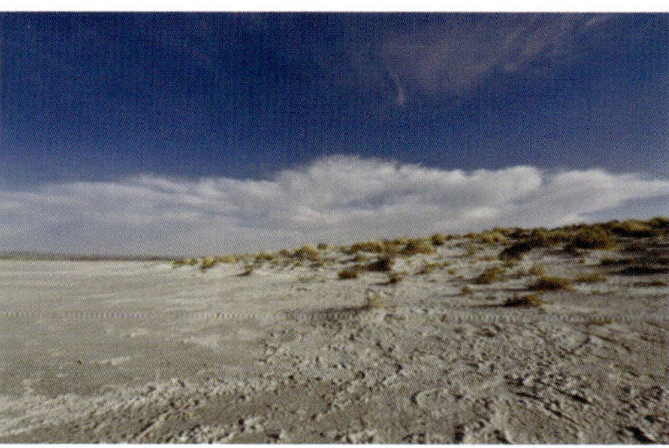

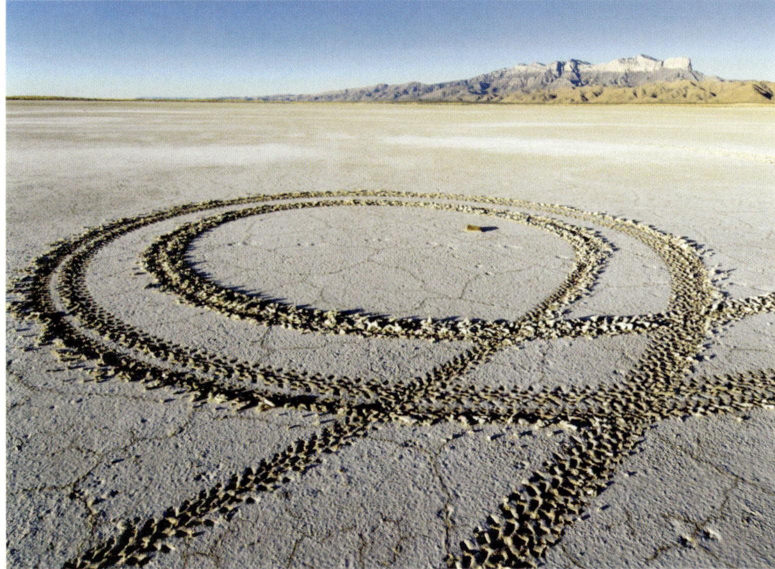

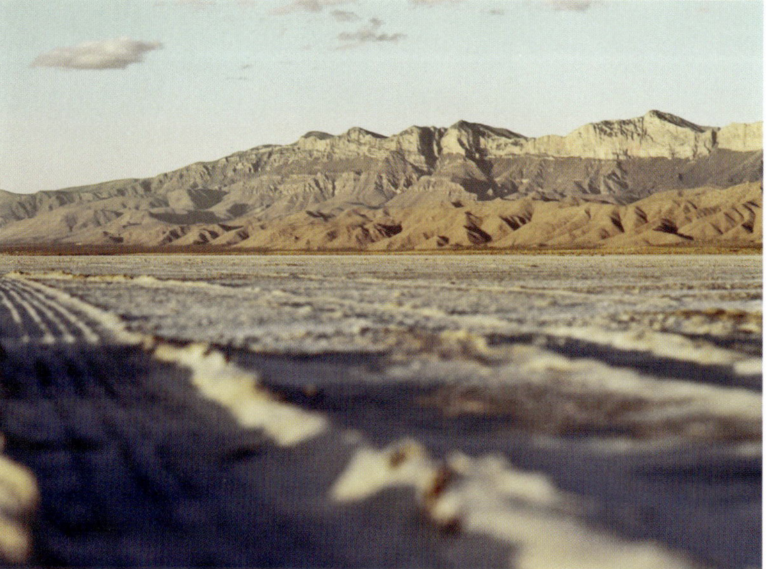

Salt Flat is a small community that grew near extensive surface salt deposits left by intermittent lakes in Hudspeth County just east of El Paso. The area became the focus of a bloody dispute known as the "Salt War" in the 1860s and 70s. Before the fighting reached a confused and tragic end, the dispute had involved both Mexican and U.S. citizens, political parties, judges, legislators, mob action, army troops, and the Texas Rangers. Murder, assassination and revenge killings took place on both sides. Some of the gray-white salt deposits may be seen today from U.S. 62/180.

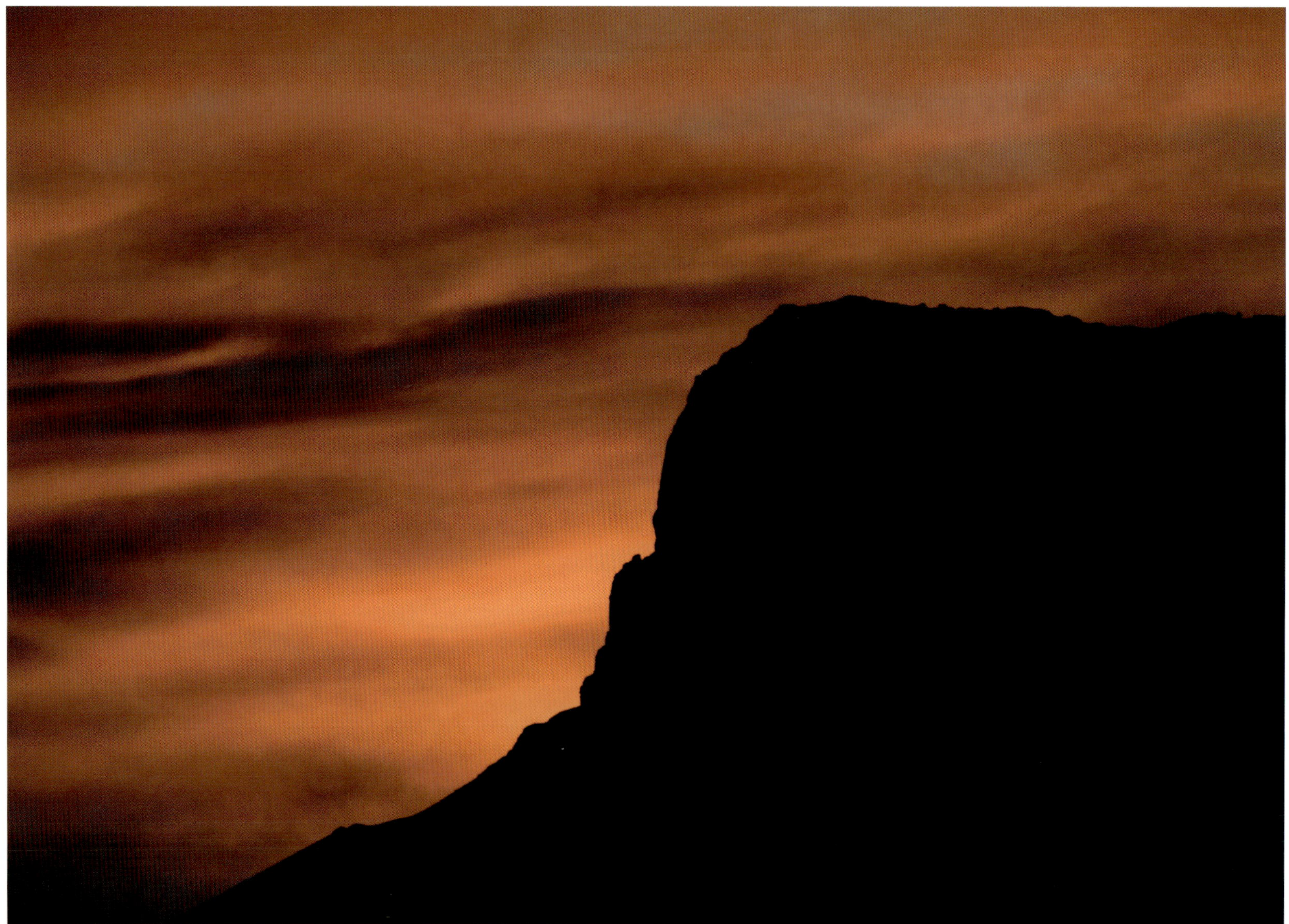

Guadalupe Peak.
Guadalupe Peak is the highest point in Texas, with an elevation of 8,751 feet. It is located in Guadalupe Mountains National Park, part of the Guadalupe Mountains range in southeastern New Mexico and West Texas. The mountain is about ninety miles east of El Paso.

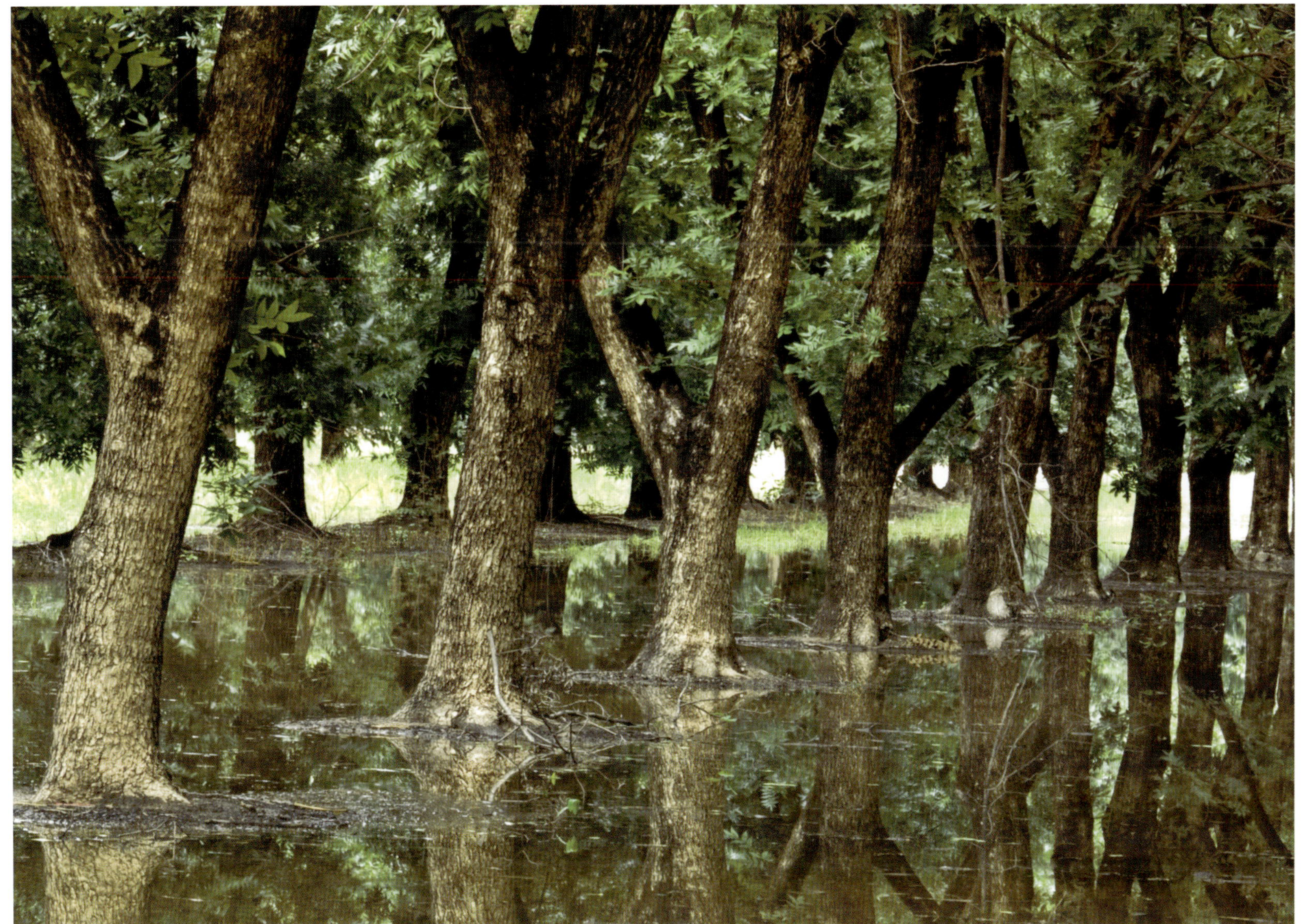

Stahmann Pecan Orchard.
Stahmann Farms owns the world's largest pecan orchard, located south of the city of Las Cruces, New Mexico, and north of El Paso.

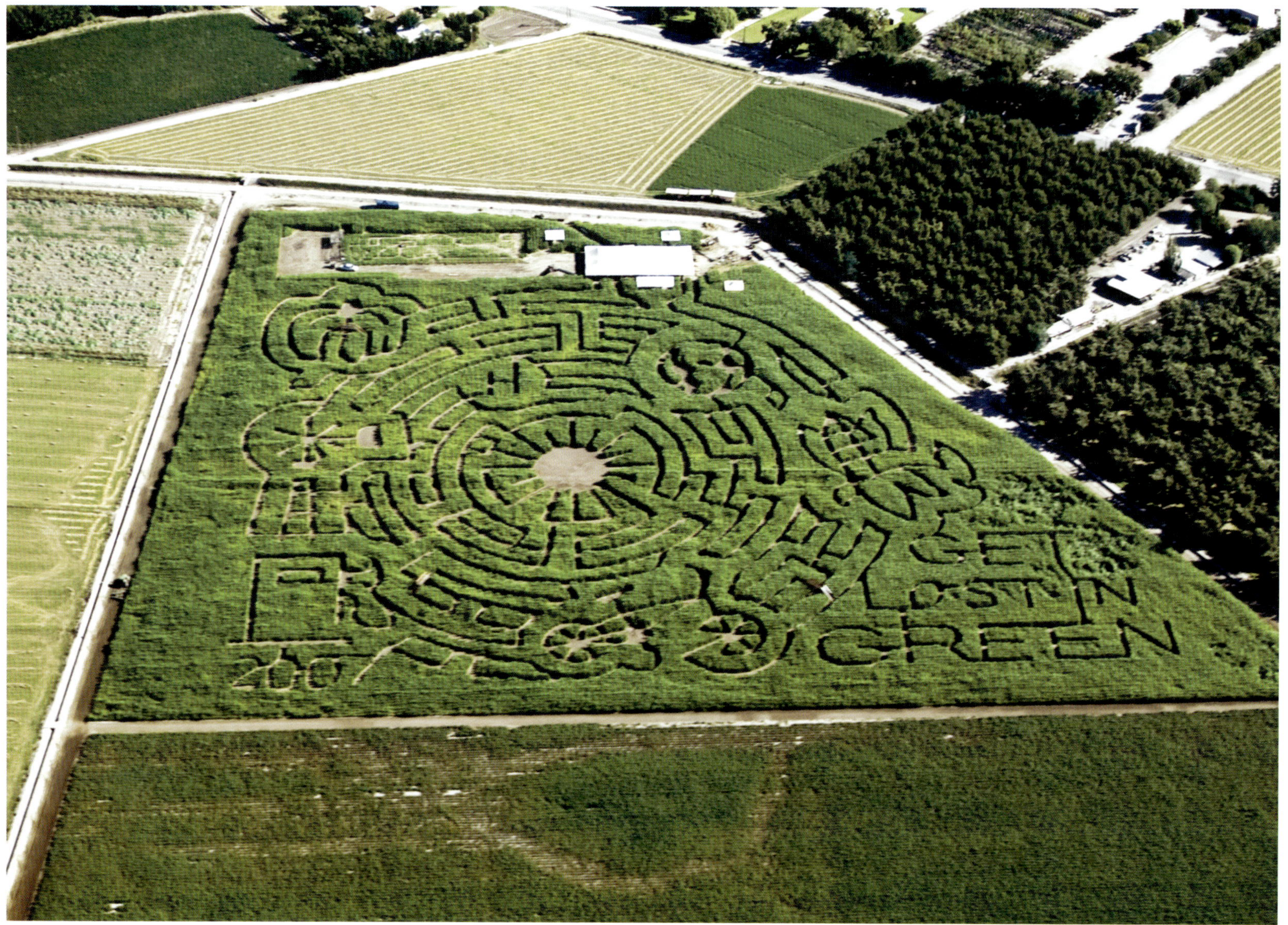

Get Lost in Green.
The maze, located in La Union, New Mexico, just north of El Paso, is made from sorghum, the fifth most important cereal crop, which can be made into several different products.

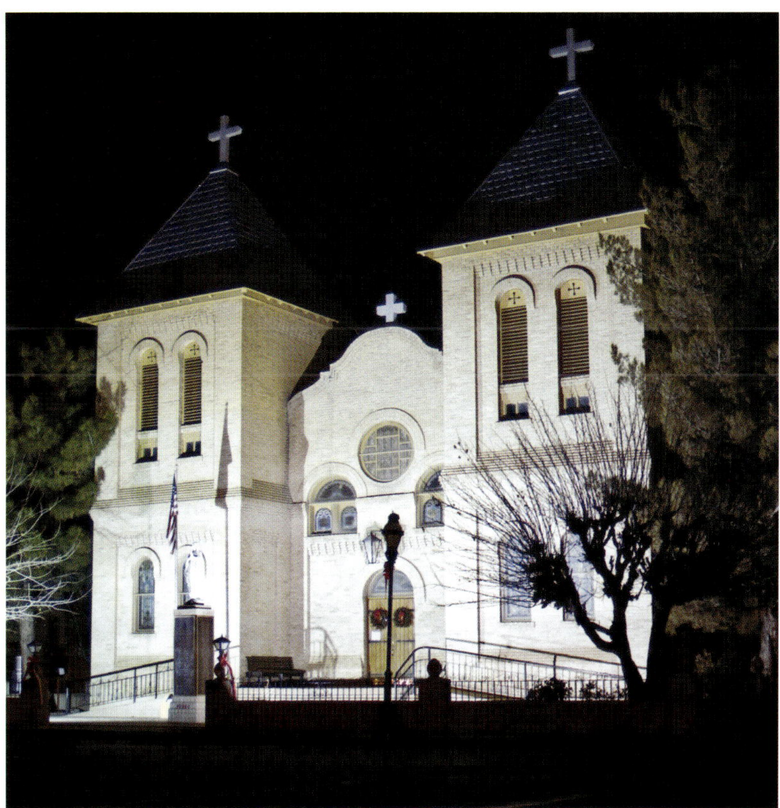

Old Mesilla.

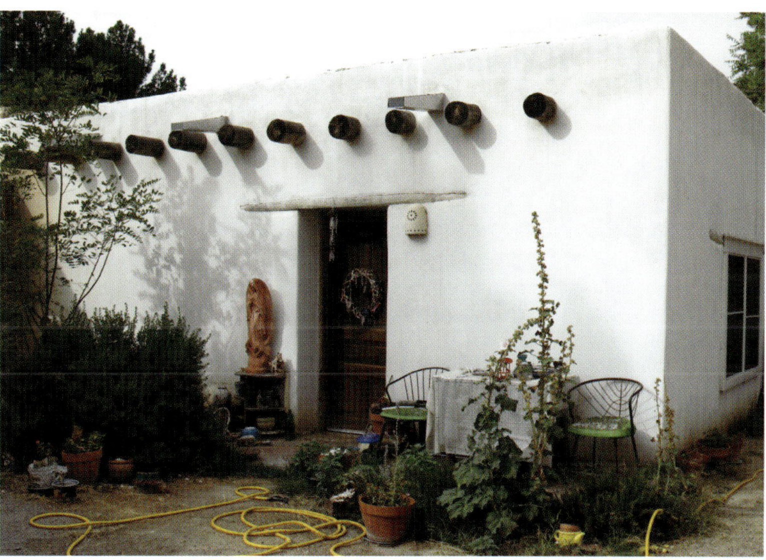

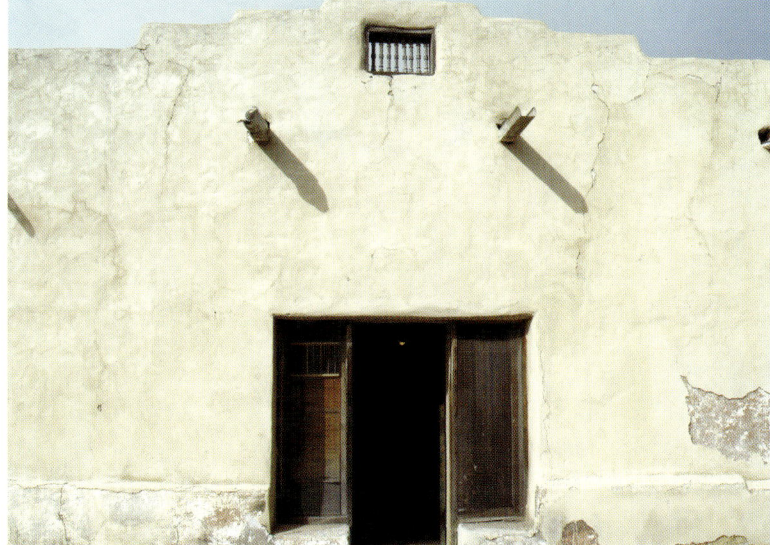

Old Mesilla.
From the Gadsden Purchase, to the Civil War, to the Butterfield Stage Coach Trail, to the trial of Billy the Kid, to being a lively social center in the 1880s, Mesilla has been a prominent part of the rich history of the Southwest.

White Sands National Monument, New Mexico.

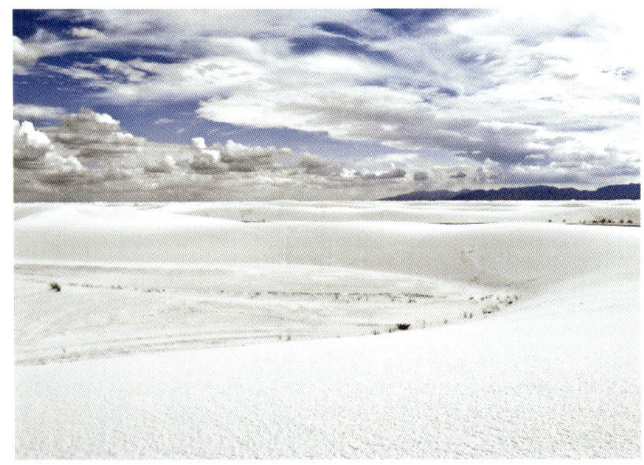

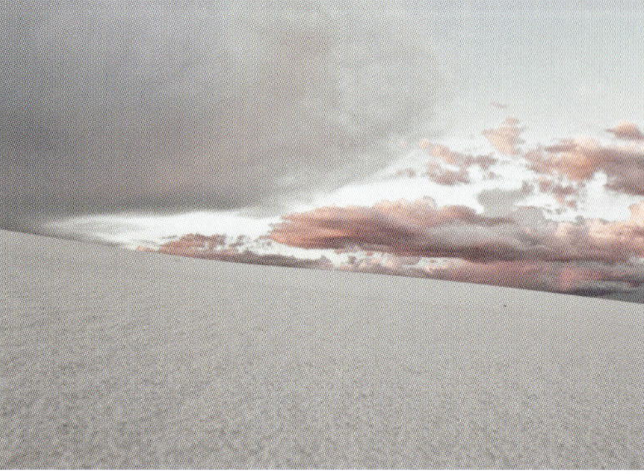

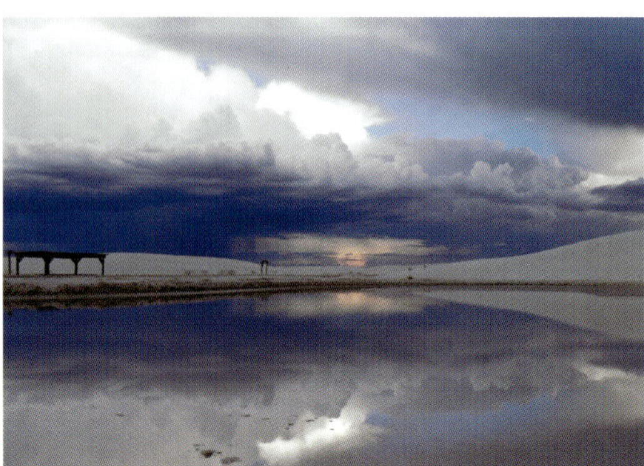

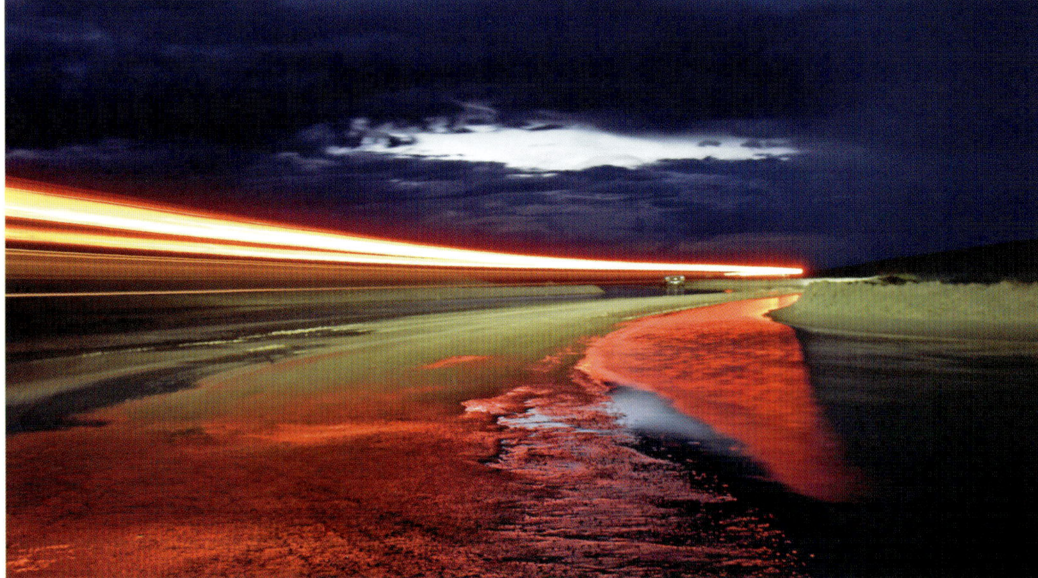

Rising from the heart of the Tularosa Basin north of El Paso is one of the world's great natural wonders—the glistening white sands of New Mexico. Here, great wave-like dunes of gypsum sand have engulfed 275 square miles of desert and created the world's largest gypsum dune field.

White Sands National Monument preserves a major portion of this unique dune field, along with the plants and animals that have successfully adapted to this constantly changing environment.

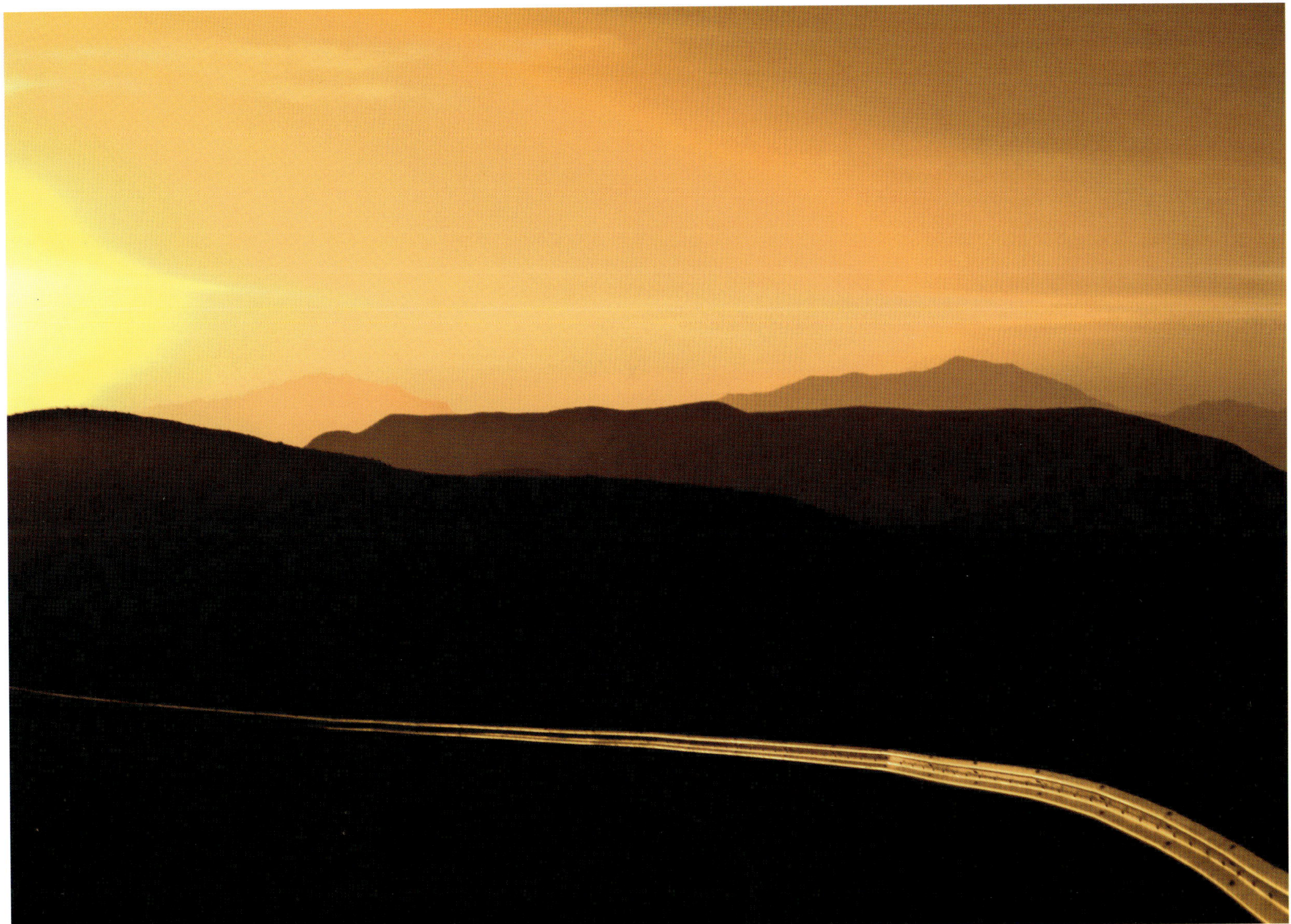

West Texas Sunset.
No matter the season, there's nothing quite like watching the blazing sun drop below El Paso's desert horizon. It's amazing to see the blue sky burn into radiant shades of yellow, red, orange, and purple before the light goes out. El Paso has countless places to watch this gorgeous scene before darkness fills the sky.

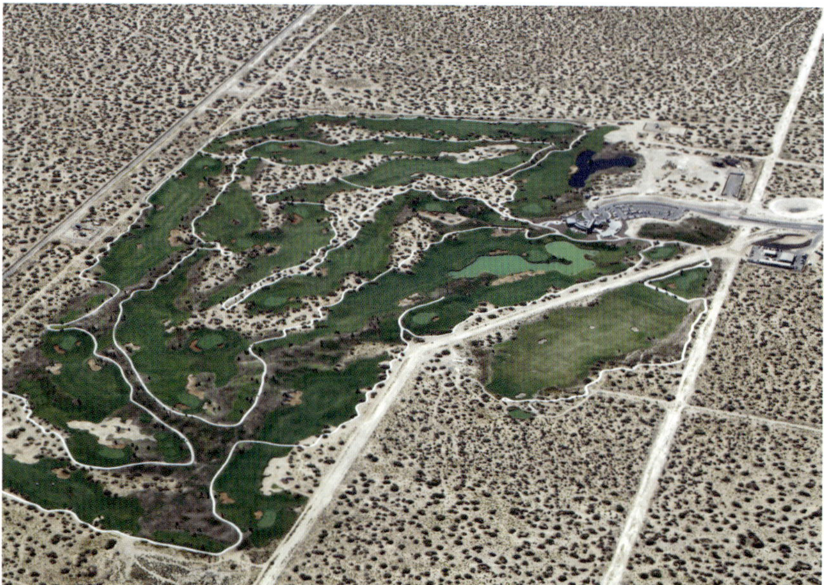

Butterfield Trail Golf Club.

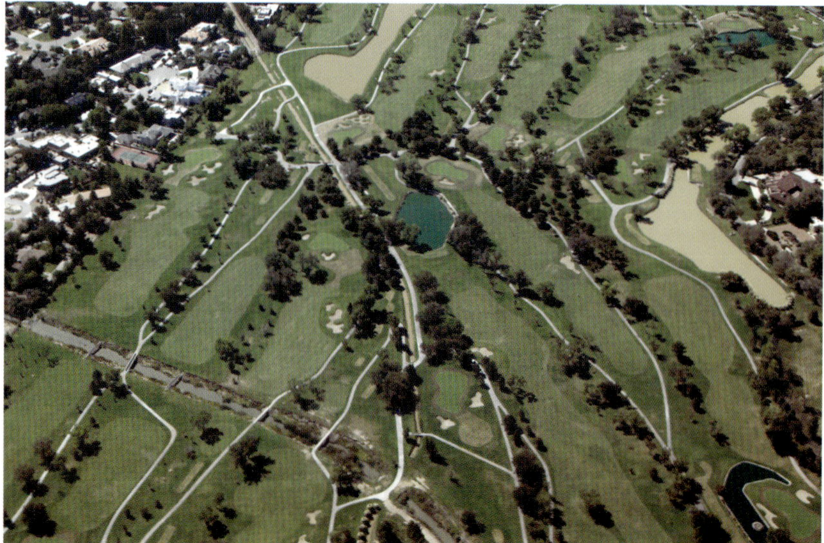

El Paso Country Club.

CELEBRATING EL PASO

This book would not have been possible without the assistance from friends old and new.

Special thanks to:

RICHARD G. SCHWARTZ

KAREN MARASCO

MAYOR JOHN COOK

SUZIE AZAR

ELIZABETH THURMOND-BENGTSON

CLARK MCCHESNEY

KOBI ISRAEL

RUPERT TRUMAN

JAMES BARTHOLOMEW

PRES DEHRKOOP

EDDIE AT PAT GOFF'S

HAL MARCUS GALLERY

AND, OF COURSE, MOM AND ROBERT